_DUCATION

Who Needs Parents?

The IEA Health and Welfare Unit

Choice in Welfare No. 31

Who Needs Parents?

The effects of childcare and early education on children in Britain and the USA

Patricia Morgan

IEA Health and Welfare Unit
London, 1996

First published October 1996

The IEA Health and Welfare Unit
2 Lord North St
London SW1P 3LB

ISBN 0-255 36368-0
ISSN 1362-9565

Front cover graphics from CorelDraw 6.

Typeset by the IEA Health and Welfare Unit
in New Century Schoolbook 10 on 11 point
Printed in Great Britain by
St Edmundsbury Press
Blenheim Industrial Park, Newmarket Road
Bury St Edmunds, Suffolk IP33 3TU

Contents

Foreword

It is always a good idea to be suspicious when we find a consensus view prevailing amongst the great and the good, whatever the subject. When politicians of all parties join forces with trades union leaders, industrialists, media pundits, welfare groups and feminists (establishment and radical) to promote the view that childcare is an unquestionable good, and that the more we have of it the better, we should at least ask ourselves if there might not be another side to the story which is not getting through.

In this remarkable book Patricia Morgan unearths the other side of this particular subject. She has examined a vast corpus of research data which reveals that, while the childcare bandwagon has been gathering speed, a considerable amount of evidence has been accumulating which calls into question the idea that third-party childcare is good for children.

Patricia Morgan criticises the relentless propagandising of 'show projects' in which lavish resources are allocated to severely deprived children, for whom almost anything would be an improvement on their home circumstances. She argues that we must look at the research into the sort of childcare which ordinary mothers actually use, and that this tells a very different story. It seems that childcare children may be disadvantaged in terms of their educational performance, their behaviour and their attachment to their mothers, compared with children cared for at home.

Childcare advocates defend themselves against the mounting evidence of adverse side-effects by claiming that, of course, they only want the best quality childcare, and that this must be made available to all. However, the mantra of 'affordable, high-quality, universally available childcare' serves no purpose, beyond, perhaps, providing peace of mind to those who chant it. High-quality childcare is so expensive that it could never be widely available, and those governments which have made ideological commitments to providing it have, in the end, largely given up—except on the rhetoric.

As Patricia Morgan demonstrates, childcare lobbyists draw their arguments from a vast arsenal of defence systems. The choice of argument to be deployed depends on the nature of the target group, be they Treasury officials, journalists, political candidates or teachers of 'gender studies'. Perhaps the least appealing of all the justifications which are being made for pushing public policy in the direction of providing childcare for working mothers (while doing nothing to support mothers who stay at home) is the claim that this is the way the world is going, and there is nothing anyone can do to stand in the way of such a trend.

This is an unsatisfactory response to any policy debate, but particularly where the welfare of children is concerned. It seems bizarre that policy makers should be contriving at the institutionalisation of large numbers of children at the very time when evidence of the abuse which seems, almost routinely, to take place in many such settings should be making us wary of separating children from those who are most highly motivated to care for them.

The childcare debate is charged with ideology, and some of the most passionately held beliefs are not based on a thorough knowledge of the academic research. However, we need to deal with childcare and its effects *as it is in the real world*, rather than as the gateway to the promised land. Patricia Morgan has provided a valuable service in giving us this exhaustive review of the evidence so far.

Robert Whelan

The Author

Patricia Morgan, Senior Research Fellow in the family at the IEA Health and Welfare Unit, is a sociologist specialising in criminology and family policy. She is the author or co-author of a number of books including: *Delinquent Phantasies*, 1978; *Facing Up to Family Income*, 1989; *The Hidden Costs of Childcare*, 1992; *Families in Dreamland*, 1992; *Farewell to the Family?*, 1995; and *Are Families Affordable?*, 1996. She has contributed chapters to *Full Circle, Family Portraits, The Loss of Virtue, Tried But Untested, Liberating Women from Modern Feminism* and *Just a Piece of Paper?*, as well as articles for periodicals and national newspapers. Patricia Morgan is a frequent contributor to television and radio programmes and is presently writing a full-length work on the relationship between capitalism and the family.

Acknowledgements

It gives me great pleasure to acknowledge the invaluable help and advice given to me by my colleague, Robert Whelan (Assistant Director, IEA Health and Welfare Unit).

I am also grateful to Professor Lynne Murray (Winnicott Research Unit) for her advice and comments.

Introduction

The Key to Utopia

Childcare: The Source Of Every Blessing

If anything is incessantly and authoritatively acclaimed as the key to economic success, the solution to the demographic crisis, the basis for social justice and equality, the answer to every woman's dream, a great business opportunity, the remedy for poverty, welfare dependency, crime, educational failure and the basis for children's success, it is childcare. For the last ten years or more this has been hammered home as the catch-all, miracle solution to a host of complex problems, which will transform the nation and open the gates of Utopia.

1. Childcare Is A Demographic Necessity

> *Childcare in Britain today is failing children, failing working parents, failing society. Most parents have no access to high-quality—or any quality—childcare or nursery education.*
>
> Childcare and Nursery Education: A TUC Charter

With birthrates below replacement since the mid 1970s, and numbers of school leavers dropping in the 1990s, employers are described as 'sitting on a demographic time bomb'. This has been likened to a wartime emergency, auguring some kind of return to halcyon days for women, who could once leave their babies for the munitions factories. The press reproduces patriotic posters from the Second World War exhorting women to work for Britain. Even Lord Kitchener reappears, although he is not summoning young men to the slaughter in the trenches, but pointing at women pushing buggies. Some local authorities have leafleted their boroughs with notices to mothers about workshops and facilities to 'get you back to work'.

Speculation has it that four-fifths of the teenage shortfall could be made up by mothers, who would also swell the tax-paying base of a society top-heavy with older dependants. If present trends continue, barely one in five Europeans will be under twenty by 2020, while the proportion of over 60s will be more than one in four. Increases in longevity have not been matched by a longer working life, but a falling retirement age and the growing expectation of 'golden decades' or a 'third age' of affluent leisure. This is doubly expensive, since older workers have not only ceased to make an economic contribution, they also have to be paid expensive retirement benefits.

Moreover, as female labour force participation rises steadily while economic activity rates for men fall, mothers are increasingly expected to replace men in the labour force. By the early 1990s there were 2.8 million fewer men at work and 2 million more women at work than there were 20 years ago. Predictions are that the number of women will soon outnumber men,[1] and Britain already has the second highest rate of women in the labour market in the European Community. Female employment suffered less in recent recessions, and it is the traditional male jobs in manufacturing, extractive and heavy industries which have been lost. For every 99 full-time male jobs lost in 1993, for example, 120 part-time female ones were gained. In 1971, 93 per cent of men under retirement age were employed but, by 1991, this had slumped to 75 per cent and is expected to fall further. Unemployment has been at a very high level for well over a decade. Since 1982 the number of 'official' unemployed (based on claimant counts) has never fallen below 1.5 million, and in most years it has exceeded 2.5 million. The overwhelming majority of the million unemployed for over a year are men, who are also increasingly dropping out of the workforce entirely.[2]

Only 47 per cent of women of working age without dependent children were in full-time work in the UK in 1994. However, like the men and the retired, neither the 29 per cent who are either inactive or unemployed, nor the 23 per cent who work part-time, have been the target of any campaign to 'get back to work'. This focuses exclusively on mothers, particularly mothers of under-fives.

The question arises of who provides a future generation if mothers' labour must be diverted from reproduction to production to make up for the missing children. This is rarely considered. When it is, the answer is that women will start to have children, or more children, so long as they do not have to look after them. Childcare is the antidote to the birth dearth, and once it becomes available 'those people who have been holding back from having babies feel free to make the choice'.[3]

2. Childcare Is An Economic Necessity

The job market in many parts of Britain, not just the South-east, is already uncomfortably tight; half the employers in East Anglia, for example, have recruitment problems. We need women at work if we are not to slide into inflationary competition for the shrinking numbers in the young workforce.

Edwina Currie, *The Times*[4]

Employers are calling for 'a national strategy for accessible, available, affordable, quality childcare',[5] on the grounds that this would help companies to be more competitive in world markets by increasing the labour supply, ensuring a flexible workforce, keeping down wage demands, and reducing inflationary pressures. Otherwise, according to the Adam Smith Institute: 'There is the prospect that lack of reserve employment will make industrial unrest more common and damage once again the country's ability to meet delivery dates'.[6] Bronwen Cohen and Neil Fraser, for the Institute for Public Policy Research, claim that childcare will galvanise the economy. Allowing this to run 'at a higher level' in one continuous boom time, they predict that: 'The extra labour force, much of it skilled, will relax the supply constraints, so demand can be kept up when it would otherwise be no longer deemed safe'.[7]

It is hardly new for employers to insist on access to the biggest labour pool possible, on the cheapest possible terms. As Allan Carlson points out, in the early decades of the century employers' organisations in the US like the National Association of Manufacturers 'waged a strong and consistent campaign to expand the labour pool through every category available: children, women—married and single—and immigrants'.[8]

Six million mothers, according to the Equal Opportunities Commission, represent a 'huge untapped resource' which could be 'drawn back into the labour force if the right measures are adopted'.[9] This talk is also reminiscent of the Stalin years in Russia, where the propaganda image of women was of a 'great army' or 'colossal reserve of labour power'. Childrearing was seen as needlessly holding women back from far more productive and serious work. Tremendous losses were represented by calculations that:

> ... 700 hours for every unit of population [was] used in cooking, laundry and childcare. This makes 86 billion hours for the whole USSR. If we divide this by 300 working days (the average working year) we have 30 million individuals giving their full time to unproductive household work, while our national economy is suffering from a great shortage of labour.[10]

Childcare is itself seen as 'a massive growth industry, solving social problems as it creates job opportunities'.[11] It increases both the labour supply and the *demand* for labour, since 'nursery schools would provide employment for teachers, nursery nurses, trainers and childminders, and breathe life into every sector of the building trade'.[12]

Under this scenario, the mother earns money, the caregiver earns money, the state makes money, the employer makes money. Where does all this money come from? Bronwen Cohen and Neil Fraser explain: 'Public childcare saves a lot of time in informal care provision, time which we are assuming will to a large extent be turned into productive and income earning work'. Compared with inefficient, unpaid, labour intensive caregiving: 'The economies of scale in public as opposed to informal childcare permit this considerable economic gain'.[13]

With home rearing of children seen in terms of 'a preference for the child rearing practices of a bygone age',[14] we have a resurgence of ideas associated with Friedrich Engels and Karl Marx. For them, industrialisation necessarily led to the dependence of all social life, and human interrelatedness, upon the market—or 'social production'—so that the population no longer relies upon organisations like family, kin or community.[15] Childcare is the most prominent way in which the personal services and functions performed by families are meant to enter the cash economy.

The present conjoining of Marxism and free market ideology in which society serves and is controlled by the market—instead of civil society being the ground of economy and citizenship—may be contrasted with more classical perspectives. Here the market is an instrumental device or arena in which people try to maximise their resources for satisfying goals which originate elsewhere in the private domain, and which are circumscribed by the ethical system.

3. Childcare Is A Necessity For Women

Unfortunately, politicians of all parties, faced with constructing a policy for women, live in fear of offending the non-earning wife and mother—and the Tories are more obsessed with her than most.

Maggie Drummond, *The Daily Telegraph*[16]

Women have to be 'seen as doing something more enterprising than amusing the children' says a journalist in a leading daily, with her quota of exemplars with immense salaries and 'efficient nannies'. One, a barrister and television presenter, feels that 'help must be available across the social scale ... to enable less well-off women to be functioning, productive and contributive'.[17]

This is not simply a matter of what is best for the individual mother's satisfaction. As embodied in European directives to achieve equality between men and women in the labour market, there is a top level drive to translate this into parity of outcomes. In recent years this has become the only identifiable labour market policy—replacing the post war concentration on full employment (not least to safeguard the economic foundations of family life). Opportunity 2000 was set up by John Major to encourage employers to set goals and put in place measurable programmes of action to increase women's participation at all levels in their organisations.

Mothers' participation in the labour market has certainly grown. Employment rates for those with a child under five have been rising: 43 per cent in Great Britain were in full- or part-time employment in 1991 (or 49 per cent if we include those seeking work) compared with 30 per cent in 1985. It is estimated that 48 per cent of women with children under five will be in employment by 2001.

However, the vast majority of working mothers of children under five work less than 30 hours a week. An estimated 1.93 million women work for 15 hours or less, and more than a half of these have children. Overall, only 20 per cent of women with dependent children were in full-time employment in 1992, and 39 per cent part-time (compared with 15 per cent and 34 per cent in 1979).[18] It is from graduate women that much of the growth in full-time maternal employment has come in recent years, especially where there are under-fives. The increasing polarisation of the female labour force[19] is shown by the way that, in 1990-92, 32 per cent of professional or managerial mothers with a child under five worked full-time, in contrast to only one per cent of mothers in unskilled manual occupations (47 per cent of whom worked part-time). The women who leave the labour market when they have a first child and work intermittently until all the children start school are described as having the 'biggest problems' or being 'the group that are most disadvantaged', in not occupying high paid, continuous full-time jobs.[20]

While there are still complaints that women are paid 'unequal wages' or discriminated against (both of which have long been illegal) the preoccupation with *maternal* employment reflects the realisation that it is mothers' generally lower level of paid work, compared to that of men and childless women, which is holding down women's overall wage levels. In 1992 women's hourly rate was 80 per cent of men's and their take home pay around 66 per cent. However, childless married women, single women and single men earn much the same.[21] Indeed, some figures suggest that full-time female employees earn, on average, more than single male, full-time employees.[22] Upon becoming parents, mothers reduce their efforts in paid employment, while men increase theirs. Fathers also do the overtime and bonus work which boosts the differential in take-home pay. Moreover, mothers taking part-time or temporary work have tended to be soaked up by the expanding service sector which pays less than the manufacturing sector which it has been replacing.

Clearly, children are the only remaining obstacle to equal opportunities, and they place women 'at a great disadvantage in competing with men in the labour market'.[23] The nearer the goal of parity looms, so the more intolerable the remaining gap appears and the more obtrusive the reason for it. Hence the rejoicing that 'mothers are returning to work sooner after childbirth' tends to be tempered by frustration that 'having a child still has a dampening effect on the quantity and level of paid work and the level of earnings.'[24] The claims of Heather Joshi are constantly reiterated about how the mother of two spends 15.9 less full-time equivalent years in employment and foregoes 57 per cent of her childless counterpart's gross earnings between the ages of 25 and 59.

If mothers are going to be put on an equal footing with childless women then, logically, there must be twenty-four hour, fifty-two week childcare. Does not 'life at the top' often involve an 18 hour day, three day conferences and evening meetings?[25] If children are older 'there's the question of who takes them to their swimming lessons, or who collects them from Brownies'.[26] Airport staff need 24 hour daycare centres, and shift workers need night care. Otherwise, as the headlines tell us, 'Children are blighting the careers of women'.[27]

Demands for daycare to facilitate female employment are inseparable from the assumption that occupational achievement alone determines the individual's status, sense of fulfilment and meaning in life. As observed, dual career couples have become a yardstick of achievement in the popular media, as much as in sociological literature.[28] Hailed as being among 'the key social innovators of emerging post-industrial society', the solutions to their highly pressurized existence are presented as ideals to be emulated, which must become 'accessible to the masses', now that they have been 'pioneered by an élite'.

A preoccupation with female marketability goes with the emphasis on putting child rearing out into the cash economy. Thus, childcare will not only preserve the earnings of women while they are using it, it will also enable the 'economy to utilise and conserve the stock of human capital embodied in women who become parents',[29] which would otherwise be wasted on caring. Mothers serve no intrinsic value or purpose by sustaining social relations, and transmitting cultural and civic resources, or the *social capital,* that furthers life chances in families and communities. This is demonstrably worthless and wasteful, since it does not issue in a wage packet.

> The expectation that women will depart from the labour force (especially the full-time labour force) ... on childbirth is likely to limit their acquisition of human capital ... even before maternity. Actual absence from the labour force will lead to depreciation of whatever human capital they have.[30]

4. *Childcare Will Fill The Exchequer*

> *Any cost-benefit analysis of daycare and education for under-fives shows that the public finances and the economy come out winners ... a study for the National Children's Bureau argued that a high proportion of non-working mothers would work, train or study if good childcare arrangements (and jobs) were available ... representing a considerable boost both to household income, the economy and the Government's tax revenues. With single mothers being enabled to work, the equation would be even more favourable for the government which would see not only a stream of tax and National Insurance contributions, but savings on a clutch of benefit payments.*
>
> Janet Bush, *The Times*[31]

As much as it is generally agreed that mothers need childcare, it is also accepted that few can afford to meet the costs themselves, particularly for babies. Places in local authority day nurseries are limited and cost an average of £5,958 per child (excluding capital charges) in Inner London in 1993/4, or £8,522 in Outer London (with an average of £7,228 for England). Even for the better off mother, childcare costs are a huge proportion of salary. With a private nursery costing at least £130 per week in 1994, according to the Working Mothers Association, she would have to earn £8,900 before having anything for herself. The total cost of a nanny would be £275 per week, so she would have to gross £20,300 to have anything over. As the Child Poverty Action Group complains: 'there is little incentive for mothers to take paid work if a high percentage of their earnings is then absorbed in meeting childcare cost to the point where they can be worse off working'.[32]

Tax relief for workplace nurseries in the 1990 budget met with an enthusiastic response. However, the dramatic expansion did not materialise, with take up by industry far less than expected. Having looked a little closer, employers decided that nurseries were a far too complicated, onerous and expensive undertaking for any but the largest enterprises to even contemplate. Moreover, the costs fall disproportionately on the consumers of particular products, the workers in particular industries and the firms that employ relatively more women of childbearing age. In 1992, the organisation Working for Childcare estimated that a 25 place workplace nursery cost £4,920 minimum per child per year in running costs alone.[33] It also costs at least £1,000 per child to minimally equip a nursery, with Network South East spending £500,000 on building and equipping two 50-place nurseries.[34] Moreover, for one to be practicable, there has to be a critical mass of children in one place and it would have to be close to where people live. (Amid all the hype about 'going to work with mother' nobody seemed to consider how a baby, plus perhaps a toddler, were to be conveyed, twice a day, through the rush-hour.)

This is where the state comes in. Here, almost any proposed expenditure which frees mothers to work promises to repay itself. Not least, there is the prospect of reducing the rising bill for means-tested benefits, particularly for lone parents, whose employment rates have decreased as those of married women have risen. In 1990, 39 per cent of lone mothers were in employment, compared to 60 per cent of married mothers. Among women with a youngest child under five, it was 22 per cent compared with 45 per cent of married women.

It is groups with the least employment who are supposedly the most desperate to work. Claims are that: 'Contrary to the myth of the "dependency culture", 90 per cent of single mothers want a job, but are unable to get one because of the dearth of good, affordable childcare'.[35] Indeed, it proves how lone parents are 'in general highly motivated in relation to training and work, [and] could form an essential part of a strategy to prepare the economy for the end of recession', or the 'skilled workforce ready to meet the upturn.' Particularly in the inner cities: 'job opportunities for lone parents... could contribute to economic and social regeneration'.[36]

At the same time as childcare promises to reduce the benefits bill, the state will scoop in the income tax, National Insurance and VAT. In their highly acclaimed *Childcare in a Modern Welfare System* Bronwen Cohen and Neil Fraser, for the Institute of Public Policy Research, predict that nearly 1,800,000 mothers will go out to work, overwhelmingly full-time, ceasing to claim benefit, gaining skills, and paying taxes. They present three childcare scenarios, whose cost is variously £8,136.8m, £10,986.0m and £3,693m per year (1989/90 figures) over existing public provision. With parents meeting 30 per cent of costs, they predict that the return to the Treasury would be between five per cent and 51 per cent on its expenditure.

Sally Holtermann's proposals for the National Children's Bureau (and now for Barnardos), have also been influential.[37] She envisages a four-fold

expansion of daycare and early education, where the total national
expenditure (in private and public sectors) at the end of the expansion
period would be running at £8 billion a year—an increase of £6 billion on
1990/1 levels. Additional expenditure on services to meet the desire of all
women who, it is purported, would like to work if childcare were 'available
and affordable' adds another £4.5 billion. Particularly after taking income-
related fees into account, it is estimated that the subsidies would be
reduced to £3.6 billion at the end of the expansion period, and that the
flowback to the Treasury from all the extra workers would be £5.5 billion.

5. Childcare: The Answer To Child Poverty

The worst option would be one designed to make sure there was no disincen-
tive to women who choose to stay at home with their children; a £10 allowance
could be given to all mothers, added to child benefit to spend as they choose.
Cost; £1,600m. Result: no more mothers back to work.

Polly Toynbee, *The Independent*[38]

Childcare is seen to be vital not simply because mothers want to work, but
because they *have* to work. There is no choice except to work, and mothers
cannot have a choice if young families are going to survive and keep the
roof over their heads.

As more maternal employment has become the only acceptable answer
to the downward drift of family incomes, the lack of it has also become the
explanation for family poverty. In turn, the reason why those most in need
have to forego opportunities to improve their circumstances is that they
cannot afford daycare.[39] Therefore, 'alleviation of family poverty' depends
on 'the wider availability of affordable childcare'.[40]

When Holtermann (for Barnardos) insists that 'Children are most at
risk of poverty when mothers do not participate in the labour market', her
'proof' is Heather Joshi's familiar estimate that a mother of two who takes
an eight year break, followed by twelve years of part-time work, foregoes
£224,00 in earnings over her working life (in 1990 prices).[41] The suggestion is that, if the woman could somehow realise the £224,000 she 'loses'
by having children, family poverty would be drastically reduced. What is
not taken into account is the extent to which one spouse may compensate
for a fall in the economic contribution of the other. The assumption is that
there are no joint resources—because no one *should* share within families.

Certainly, the number of people with children in low-income groups has
risen considerably, and children are in poverty disproportionate to their
numbers. The percentage of children at incomes below half the contemporary average rose from 10 per cent in 1979 to 32 per cent in 1991/2.
Couples with children occupying the bottom income decile rose from 39 per
cent in 1979 to 49 per cent in 1991/2.[42]

It is certainly a common response to economic insecurity to push more
labour onto the market, whether by increasing working hours or the
number of earners, or both. As well as the highest proportion of working

mothers in Europe, the UK also boasts the most fathers working over 50 hours per week (36 per cent). Even a third of men in dual-earner families in Britain usually work over 48 hours a week.[43] In 1979-81, eight per cent of families containing a woman of working age were poor. Had men not changed their working hours, and had women zero earnings, then 24 per cent of families would have been poor. Equivalent figures in 1989-91 are 18 per cent and 36 per cent respectively. However, with or without women's earnings, more families were poor. Moreover, only a quarter of the rise in poverty among two-parent families involved changes in employment status (from one to no earners or from two to one).[44]

Men's earnings are still the dominant component of family income, even if, on average, women (with and without children) provide a third of family income (up from a quarter in 1971). An unpalatable and little acknowledged fact is that men's incomes also keep families out of poverty and that children are very much at risk of poverty when men do not participate in the labour market. The decline of the male breadwinner is the principal factor behind the increase in family poverty since the 1970s. This increasing inability of men to provide for families is a significant factor behind the rise in both dual earners and lone parents.

Job competition has meant a sharp increase in both the proportion and numbers of men earning low pay. Full-time male employees with gross earnings below the Council of Europe's decency threshold (at 68 per cent of average earnings) rose from 14.6 per cent in 1979 to 29.9 per cent in 1994. The picture of destabilised, stagnating or declining male wages is more pronounced in the USA, where they fell by an average of 19 per cent between 1973 and 1987.

Since the 1960s families have also borne the bulk of the increasing tax burden, with income tax and National Insurance rising two and a half times as fast for families as for single people. Over the past 15 years taxes on single, childless people have fallen as those on families have continued to rise. At average earnings in 1995/6 a couple with two children had only £19.22 more left than a single man or woman after national insurance, income tax (minus child benefit) and council tax.

Added to rising taxation and the poorer economic prospects of men, women's higher wage rates and the elimination of gender differentiation from the labour market have pushed incentives in the direction of the two-income household. The average growth rate of real monthly earnings for women at work was nearly fourfold that of men in the 1980s. Wage and price adjustments (particularly for mortgages) have raised the importance of wives' employment to maintaining a living standard that earlier generations enjoyed on one income. What is certainly true is that, *the more that mothers enter the labour market, the less any can afford to stay out.*

As such, the two-income norm resting on sex equality in the workplace makes childrearing seem an expensive use of the woman's time in terms of the returns foregone from virtually any paid occupation. The higher her earnings at marriage, the older she is at the time of the first birth and the smaller her family—if she has any children at all.

Again, the process is exacerbated by the tax system. The removal of allowances disproportionately hurts one-income families, while lower tax bands and reductions in tax rates give double earners twice the opportunity to exploit cuts. On £30,000 per year in 1995/6 the one-earner family paid £387.50 extra income tax compared to a dual-earner couple with the same combined income (or £1,367.50 more if child benefit is excluded).

There are actually two basic ways of reducing the economic constraints on families. One may be to offer free or subsidised daycare, whether by financing state-operated daycare centres, aiding private daycare centres, or by providing a voucher to be redeemed at an approved facility. The other is to increase the disposable income of families by reducing taxes or offering cash benefits to help parents bear the cost of raising children—as examples of compensatory measures which help reduce both the standard of living penalty and the opportunity costs of children.

The ruling consensus dictates that Britain is, and must be, a society where it is economically necessary for both parents always to work.[45] The assumption that everybody is now self-supporting makes any allowance for domestic responsibilities 'an anomaly', in the words of one Tory Chancellor. Not least, there is the decisive shift of emphasis away from protecting the family's overall economic security and ability to meet the needs of a new generation, towards the attainment of economic power for women. The two things are often conflated, for example by the Save the Children Fund which speaks of the 'benefits for children of greater personal and economic independence of women.'[46]

6. Childcare Frees Women From Marriage And Men

Formal childcare is shown to play an important role in facilitating women's full-time employment. Full-time employment is the route by which women achieve financial independence from their partner.
                    Ward, C., Dale, A. and Joshi, H., *Journal of Social Policy*[47]

The drive for equal outcomes in the labour market has been accompanied by a concern for women's ability to support themselves and their children independently of men.[48]

Feminist researchers continually emphasize how the maternal role is a fundamental element in women's oppression because it underpins women's economic dependence on men. Male breadwinning undermines the capacity of women to compete and serves as 'justification for male control over women and children'.[49] The 'real barrier to change', as Save the Children see it, is the 'powerlessness many women experience within the family'.[50] The model now invariably used for analysing family relations is a Marxist one, concentrating on the distribution of power. The covenant of care, shaped by the rules of reciprocity that must operate within and between generations, has come to be seen as the basis of servitude. Insofar

as there are exchanges of income or services, or allocation of tasks, power
is not possessed by women, but keeps them subordinate. Depending on
other family members for assistance subjects someone to the arbitrary will
of another. When someone transfers income, the recipient may feel 'a
sense of obligation towards the provider', so that they end up supplying
'unpaid domestic work or childcare'.[51]

Therefore, mutual support, interdependence, or any division of
household labour, have become the real problems. Starting from the
assumption that 'pooled income is wrong' and 'what is needed is better
access to independent income for women', Heather Joshi and colleagues
have been foremost in establishing 'income dependency within couples' as
a chronic problem, particularly with their analyses for the Rowntree
Foundation and the Family Policy Studies Centre.[52]

With a wife defined as dependent if she does not match or exceed her
husband's net earnings, three-quarters are characterised as dependent,
or 'receive income flows from their partner'. Just under a half (46 per cent)
exist in 'hidden poverty', in that their own income from the market or the
state falls below the Income Support line. Childless women are most likely
to be 'independent' (54 per cent) in terms of 'the balance of economic
power', compared to only 17 per cent of those with children. However,
while 'the best way for women to achieve financial independence within
a partnership [sic] is to work full-time',[53] mothers face the prospect of
having their independent income eaten away by household costs and
childcare. If this is not provided by the state 'a large group of women are
left dependent on financial support from their spouses in the short- and
long-term'.[54]

The demise of the 'complementary' family, in favour of the 'symmetrical'
family, where each spouse supports themselves separately and does the
same tasks, invariably goes with an insistence on the viability of single-
parent homes. Divorce law reform has transformed marriage into an
association terminable at will by either party. Under such circumstances
it becomes less rational to 'try hard to build a good marriage—or, in
economic terms, to invest heavily in marriage-specific capital,' and 'more
rational ... to withhold such efforts, and instead to take a look-out-for-
number-one approach', and accumulate personal resources.[55] Every
mother is a potential lone parent and, as one person cannot look after
children and earn a living at the same time, one or the other of these
functions must be taken over by outside agencies.

7. Childcare is Better for Children.

*Decent childcare is as fundamental to the quality of life of the nation's
children as decent shelter, sustenance, and schooling.*
                 Transport and General Workers Union, *Mothers in Employment*[56]

Not only is childcare supposed to deliver the cornucopia of benefits listed
above, it also, by a happy co-incidence, happens to be good for children. A
Times leader claims that a universal system of childcare integrated with

nursery lessons would not only 'release thousands of mothers' but, at the
same time, would produce children who would be 'more likely to perform
well at school—and beyond—and less likely to slide into disaffection'. It
would help both 'parents and their children to become self-reliant and to
improve their chances in life'.[57]

As daycare has been piggy-backed on early education, or treated as
synonymous with it, so educational and social failure have been laid at the
door of a lack of pre-schooling. Findings from the 1970 British cohort
study are said to have 'blamed poor pre-schooling for the fact that about
six million adults struggle with reading and simple calculation'.[58] Actually
they did not, but the assumption has by now become such a part of
received wisdom as to render evidence superfluous. Sally Holtermann's
grandiose plans for Barnardos, with universal daycare, nursery education
and care outside school hours in integrated centres, parade as the panacea
for all childhood disadvantage. As a result of this truly wondrous package:

> ... pre-school age children would have enhanced social and educational
> opportunities; their parents would be more relaxed at home; school age children
> would have opportunities for play with other children in secure and familiar
> surroundings outside school hours; incomes of the least well-off families would
> improve. There would be far reaching social gains and the possibility of savings
> in other services (such as special education and crime prevention) at a later
> date and the economy would gain the working experience and skills of women.[59]

Easily available childcare would even, it has been claimed, reduce the
rate of childhood accidents and deaths. Ian Roberts, and Barry Pless
(writing in the *British Medical Journal*) point out that children of lone
mothers have twice the injury rates of children from two parent homes
and the highest death rates of children from all social groups.[60] Indeed, the
children of lone parents on Income Support have a death rate 42 per cent
higher than that of children in social class V, the poorest socio-economic
group. Lone parenthood is the strongest socio-demographic predictor of
childhood injury at home and the hospital admission rate is twice that for
children in two-parent families, while the risk of pedestrian injury is over
50 per cent higher. Roberts and Pless conclude that: 'Probably the most
important reason for the comparative disadvantage of British lone
mothers is the lack of affordable daycare'. Not only would this 'put the
mothers into paid work', it 'would provide a safe environment for their
children', counter environmental hazards in their homes and on the
streets and even 'transform the social position of these families'[61] along
with the health and welfare of the children.

Just in case there might be any lingering doubts, it is also claimed that,
whether married or single, working mothers make better parents. The
mother at home is not much use to her children since she spends her time
doing chores. Lacking the childcare that will preserve their sanity:

> Full-time housewives were more likely to be vulnerable to anxiety, depression,
> minor illnesses, insomnia and general stress. Depression often robbed them of
> the ability to think clearly, as well as causing general sadness and apathy. The

most blithe and fulfilled were those who worked most hours away from home or had big families.[62]

Redundant Parents

Using some or all of the above arguments, childcare advocates give the impression that the care of children by their parents is moribund and must be superseded, in everyone's best interests, by specialised child-rearing institutions. In the words of the Equal Opportunities Commission, it is 'unreasonable to assume that all parents will by some magic be endowed with the capacity to make the best possible job of caring for young children'.[63]

Save the Children Fund, Barnardos, the Child Poverty Action Group and the National Children's Bureau agree. Plans for reforming or reconstructing the welfare state, like those from the Labour Party's Commission on Social Justice,[64] insist that 'childcare must be one of the top priorities of a new Beveridge'.[65] A typical rendering of the case for childcare is given by Malcolm Wicks, when Director of the publicly funded Family Policy Studies Centre. 'Current and future work and family patterns demand it; the changing role—and expectations—of women require it.' Those who stand in the way are just 'the ideologues of hearth and home'.[66] (Another commentator sees them as 'overwhelmed by Neanderthal sentiments about family values'.)[67] Without two earners there is 'family poverty, economic insecurity—and unpaid mortgages.' But, most fortuitously: '... the purpose of childcare is the care of the *child*... Consequently *every* child should be entitled to good provision, not just those whose mothers have economic clout'.[68]

Childcare services have grown apace in recent years, while allowances for childcare have been developing at numerous points in the system, whether it is tax relief for workplace nurseries, vouchers for government staff[69] or vouchers which can be redeemed at pre-school provisions for all parents of four-year-olds. While the means-tested benefits system provides no help to enable couples to bring up their own children, an income disregard of up to £60 is available to lone parents to pay for their childcare when they are on Family Credit (the means-tested benefit for low

To the National Childcare Campaign this is a drop in the ocean of unmet need. It wants the provision of a statutory service for all 0-5 year-olds, with before- and after-school care, and holiday schemes for children up to 12. So does the TUC Charter for Under-Fives, but with facilities for all up to 14, and special emergency cover when a child is sick, or has an appointment.

This is an area where bosses are in complete agreement with trades unionists. Employers for Childcare, supported by the CBI, wants a Minister responsible for co-ordinating a childcare strategy, monitoring progress and reporting to Parliament. With the government setting national objectives, coverage with 'available, affordable, accessible, quality childcare' is meant to come within the life of the next Parliament. According to John Monks, general secretary of the TUC, a mixture of public and non-taxable private provision must deliver this 'universally available, good-quality, easily accessible childcare' as the 'most dramatic way we could capitalise on women's skills and maximise their contribution to the economy'.[70] Barnardos sees parents paying a third of the costs of daycare administered by local authorities (although they do not necessarily provide the services) which also need to support the growth of facilities though grants and other help. The Under-Fives Unit of the National Children's Bureau wants to induce employers to provide workplace crèches by only allowing planning permission to firms over a certain size if they provide nurseries.

From both sides of the political spectrum there are the calls to abolish Child Benefit, the last vestige of recognition in the fiscal system of the costs of parenthood, and to spend the money on crèches or nursery schools. Business and media women have waged a high profile campaign for the right to offset their nanny costs against their tax. Even if the government does not provide a nationally organised system, 'at the very least', as the Employment Department agrees, 'there should be a guarantee that high-quality, affordable childcare is readily available everywhere in Britain'.[71] While the government may not have come up with the money, or the minister, in August 1996, it had responded with a consultative document asking how best the state can help parents and employers by providing a national framework for childcare.[72]

The 'lack of affordable, accessible childcare' apparently 'affects almost all parents', although 'some groups like lone parents are affected to a greater extent'.[73] The reason that any woman does not return to work after childbirth is taken to be not 'choice but rather the result of the absence and/or cost of childcare'.[74] In turn, part-time work is held to be 'not often desired and has negative consequences for a possible career'.[75] The fact that only 14 per cent of British women with children under ten work full-time does not show that they 'are home-bodies who want to devote themselves whole-heartedly to raising their children' but that 'our system is simply not geared to women who want to combine a career with having a family'.[76] While under a quarter of care arrangements are paid for by parents—in spite of the fact that the proportion of women using professional childcare has doubled between 1980 and 1991[77]—it is insisted that mothers do not use relatives out of preference, but because of a dearth of public or commercial facilities. Hence, childcare must be the key to the woman's vote, and wish fulfilment has a habit of jumping into headlines like TAX CUTS TO HELP MOTHERS WORK.[78]

It would seem, then, that we have here a subject on which there is an unusually complete consensus, embracing right and left, capital and labour, childcare experts, mothers, feminists, economists and media pundits. Surely there could be no serious case to be made in the face of such an harmonious chorus. Or could there?

Structure Of The Book

In this book we will be examining the claims which are made for childcare and early education to see if they stand up to scrutiny.

Section A asks what good caregiving consists of, as well as what constitutes a healthy environment, physically, emotionally and intellectually, and where it is most likely to be found. We will review the research which has been carried out into the effects of childcare on children, and the extent to which childcare can be said to be as good as, or better than, home-care.

Section B examines the reality of the sort of childcare and after-school care which mothers actually use, rather than the idealistic and unrealistic models of the university-based 'show-projects'.

Section C looks at the way in which childcare and early education have been conflated in 'educare', and asks what benefits small children can derive from long periods in formal school situations at very young ages. The chapter on the famous Perry Pre-School Project shows how this lavishly-funded and quite unrepresentative programme has become the principal mortar in the propaganda arsenal of childcare lobbyists.

Section D looks at the impact on the whole family of a policy which seeks to put both parents to work while their children are placed in third party care. It covers the repeated findings of poor parent/child attachment for infants who spend long periods in non-parental care. It also considers the pressures to which dual-earner couples are exposed, the feelings of maternal 'guilt' to which working mothers are prone and the question of whether going out to work can save mothers from depression. This leads on to the role of fathers in dual-earner compared to one-earner families. A special chapter is reserved for evidence relating to what we know about the long-term effects of different levels of maternal employment on children's development.

Section E considers the public policy implications of the above. In a sense this section of the book can stand independently of the earlier sections dealing with research, because it asks whether, even if all of the fantastic claims which are made regarding childcare were true, we could ever afford the childcare Utopia. The book concludes by asking if the present policy of supporting only childcare out of the home is either fair or in the best interests of families, children and society.

SECTION A

THE RESEARCH FINDINGS

The claims which are being made for childcare are so extravagant that they make parental care look like a poor substitute, or a form of neglect. Infants require intensive care from regular caregivers in order to thrive. They need to be cared for in small groups. It is unlikely that group care could meet their needs. Research shows that only the very best childcare can hope to equal the outcomes for children cared for at home, and most childcare is not of this very high standard. Small children are often placed in large groups with limited space. They receive little attention or stimulation and may fall behind with language skills.

Childcare centres can spread infectious and parasitic diseases, as large numbers of children are kept for long periods in confined areas. Physicians in America refer to the childcare cloaca, or sewer.

Research findings on the effects of childcare on children have been distorted as the issue has become politicised. However a careful examination of research which has been carried out, mainly in the USA and Britain, reveals an increased risk of low levels of language and social skills, poor academic performance, and behavioural problems, in childcare children.

Certain 'show' projects are used for propaganda value by childcare advocates. Sweden is often cited as a country which has had good results from childcare, but the resources allocated are large, and parents are given leave-of-absence from work for the first 18 months, with short days thereafter.

Children from bad home backgrounds may do better in childcare in some respects than they would if left at home, but children from good homes will probably do worse.

Aggression in children is one of the most serious negative correlations with childcare. Daycare is sold to parents as a means of teaching their children social skills, but it may have the reverse effect. Children do not learn to socialise from contact with other children but from contact with adults. Childcare staff are often less motivated to set standards of behaviour than parents would be, and the children are in an environment in which they have to compete for toys and attention. They do not learn the social skills necessary to resolve conflicts from exposure to large groups of other children. The effects are more serious for boys.

What the Research Tells Us

There is now a considerable body of research to show that, far from having their physical and emotional growth stunted, children with good early-years experiences outside the home are if anything more creative, confident and assertive than those without such experiences.

Equal Opportunities Commission[1]

A campaign for the mass institutionalisation of children, virtually from birth, raises complex issues which need to be critically analysed before being adopted. Wherever there is any cause for concern, there is an obligation to act with due caution until more is known.

Whether or not childcare is actually better or, at least, harmless, for children, compared to parental care, is an unpopular question to ask. It tends to invoke furious reflex accusations about 'putting women back in the kitchen', or of a political 'backlash against women'. It is also depressingly usual for those who express any doubts to find themselves righteously attacked for personally insulting childcare staff, childcare businesses or working mothers. All this is bound to make the effects of childcare and maternal employment 'among the most controversial and emotion laden issues that developmentalists study'.[2] The result is that 'Some findings, and the methods and analyses that discern them, are simply more 'politically correct' than others. For science, this is a major problem.'[3]

The Suppression of Dissent

There is the suspicion that daycare advocates and professionals have both avoided or retarded research on the effects of childcare, and kept quiet about evidence that might not show this in the best light. Others who may not take an entirely positive view are frightened of incurring the wrath of its partisans.[4] As one American professor who voiced his doubts and suffered for it, exclaims: 'There are a lot of people out there who don't open their mouths because they know how vehement the reaction can be'.[5] In Britain Paddy Holmes, Chairman of the Independent Schools Association, expressed alarm at the 27 per cent rise in the number of two-year-olds in prep schools in 1995. The furious response to her concerns over their emotional and moral development meant that she soon resigned.

Elsewhere, academic timidity or cowardice shade easily into disdain for the vulgarities and difficulties of public discourse —to which we might add more practical concerns over tenure, promotion and limited research funds.

The public and those in a position to influence policy tend to hear about research results in this area from highly partisan sources. Moreover, childcare lobbyists have long benefited from heavy public funding; with access to the finances and facilities of the Commission of the European Communities, as well as British government-funded bodies like the Equal Opportunities Commission, the National Children's Bureau and the Family Policies Studies Centre.

It is not as if the evidence on the outcome of childcare presents an unanimously rosy picture. There is much that is very disquieting and this is not going away as studies accumulate.

A survey of available research by Jay Belsky and Laurence Steinberg appeared in 1978 and become something like a consensus statement.[6] They concluded that there was insufficient data to give daycare a clean bill of health and that such a view would be 'premature and naïvely optimistic'. Indeed, the state of knowledge was grossly inadequate. They noted observations of increased aggression towards peers and adults. While daycare did not seem disruptive of children's bonds with their parents, they also noted that the sparse data was contradictory and could be interpreted 'as evidence in favor of home-reared children'. They complained about the lack of work on the long-term effects, or any consideration of the impact of alternative care arrangements on the family, marriage, parental behaviour and cultural patterns. Only evidence from high-quality daycare centres appeared to show 'neither salutary nor deleterious effects on the intellectual development of the child'. This observation was the one which was pounced upon, and Belsky and Steinberg's paper was taken as an emphatic endorsement of daycare, despite all their misgivings.

Moreover, partisans like to present childcare as something which gives children 'a head-start which benefits them right into adulthood'.[7] The public get fed partial or misleading findings from very unrepresentative early intervention or other 'showpiece' projects, usually for highly disadvantaged children. Such results are promulgated as if they were normal, but they have little or no relevance to non-parental care as it is routinely experienced in the UK or the US.[8]

Model projects certainly provide no reason to assume that negative consequences of daycare will not emerge, or do not exist. By 1986 Jay Belsky was expressing serious concern over a slow, steady trickle of evidence that contradicted the view that childcare was not harmful to development.[9] Research was now coming in which related to ordinary children and focussed on the sort of daycare which working mothers actually use, rather than university-based and experimental studies, and was looking at the amount of time spent away from parents. A number had found extensive non-maternal care in the first year of life associated with increased incidence of disturbed parent/child relations, as well as greater aggression and non-compliance. It was unclear exactly why these outcomes were emerging, and what they meant, as they were not picked up in each and every study. Because of this clouded state of affairs, Belsky could be no more precise than to conclude, upon reviewing a growing body of evidence highlighting such disconcerting associations, that extensive infant daycare 'as we know it and have it' was a risk factor in infant development.[10]

By drawing attention to evidence which was, after all, only in line with what attachment theory might predict we would find, Belsky 'stimulated a "firestorm" of controversy', although there was 'little hesitation' in embracing other findings 'as evidence in favour of legislative action on behalf of daycare and working mothers'.[11] As even specialists who did not question his findings criticised him for publishing them, we can imagine how different the reaction would have been if 'the results were just the opposite; that is, early and extensive employment [of mothers] was related to *higher* adjustment and *greater* cooperation with adults'.[12]

We have not heard about the large run of American studies upon which Belsky's reservations concerning the effects of childcare on parent/child attachment were based. The same goes for the Bermuda studies and other work revealing greater anti-social behaviour. There is silence on, for example, the amount of retardation found in an English sample of children going to childminders. Instead, it is the results of Perry Pre-school which have crossed the Atlantic to become childcare folk law in the UK (see pp. 76-79).

At very least, the way that the childcare propaganda jars with the experience of many people at the grass roots should alert us to the possibility that all is not as it is made out to be. There is the mother who told me that, as she approached the nursery gates, her 22-month-old son would throw his hands over his eyes and scream. He did not sleep at night, and his speech had not developed. Both parents had to work to keep their home. There was a temporary respite from the dilemma as the mother embarked on another course of maternity leave. The boy rapidly began to speak, and his sleep disturbances and other behavioural problems improved dramatically. Another case, which reached the press, was described by the father:

> Our little boy, aged 15 months, seemed happy enough the first day we took him to visit his prospective nursery ... We booked him in from 8.30 am to 5.30 pm, five days a week.
> Within three days he was in a miserable state. It was as if all the joy in his life had been extinguished. He lost interest in his toys, stopped smiling, whimpered piteously, and had to be held for hours on end.
> His mother could hardly take a step without him running after her in a panic ... we put his behaviour down to a bout of flu ...
> Each morning, as we dropped him off, he would clutch our knees and cry harrowing sobs of despair. In the afternoon we would find him sitting in a row

of high chairs, like an orphan, waiting to be fed, or lying in his cot, awake but silent, dazed, and almost catatonic.

It was not the nursery's fault. The staff are highly trained and, by all accounts, most parents are enthusiastic about the place.[13]

A community medical officer for children under five recounts how she:

... saw many disturbed, unhappy children, among them one sad, small boy in particular. ... In the morning he was taken straight to a child-minder, who gave him breakfast. She then took him to a pre-school unit, where he spent the morning. She picked him up and looked after him until his mother fetched him and took him home to bed. Small wonder that he woke in the night wanting his mother's love and care.[14]

One investigator described, in unsettling detail:

... the struggles between center workers trying to maintain order and the unhappy children wailing 'I want my mommy.' ... As former operators of a high-quality daycare center, William and Wendy Dreskin have likewise concluded that children fare poorly when they lose maternal care prematurely. After three years of watching 'how children in daycare suffer from separation anxiety and depression despite competent staff', the Dreskins closed their center.[15]

Evidence and Outcomes

The difficulty of predicting outcomes for *individuals* is a characteristic argument of those who are desperate to deny that there might be any harm in childcare. Even if poorer outcomes occur at a significantly higher rate in the exposed group, the results are often repudiated on the grounds that it is not present in 100 per cent of the sample. We hear how: 'The view that non-parental care is *necessarily* harmful for children under the age of three is not supported by research in any country' (emphasis added).[16] On these terms, it is impossible to demonstrate that non-parental care could ever be harmful. By the same reasoning, smoking is not *necessarily* harmful.

In the behavioural sciences we do not look for strict, exceptionless laws, as in physics, but for probabilities. This means something which occurs at a significantly higher rate in one group compared to another, and whose distribution is not due to accident or chance. Thus, if the evidence suggests risk factors with regard to daycare, this means a probabilistic, not inevitable, association between non-parental care and patterns of development that could be regarded as troubling.[17]

In social science there is no problem in finding ambiguous studies or studies contrary to all the rest. Childcare is no exception, given the number and complexity of the factors involved. We are doomed to frustration if we demand complete consistency across different studies. What should concern us are the clusters of findings, and the convergence of results.

Unfortunately, while any 'positive' findings are eagerly publicised as a direct effect of daycare experience, negative findings are invariably held to prove that there is 'nothing to show that non-parental care is, *per se,* damaging'[18] or that there is nothing inherently harmful in daycare. This staple move of those who wish to exonerate something in the face of adverse associations involves dispersing or dismembering its components. There is an exact parallel with the way that the effects on children of family structure are denied through an alternative emphasis on 'parenting processes' (supervision or affection, for example) in such a way that one ceases to be a function of the other.

Applied to childcare, we often hear that it is the *quality and stability* of care a child receives which is important, as if these are quite independent of context. Yet, what are we to make of the admission that: 'the greater number of staff and high staff turnover [in nurseries] may well produce considerable instability of caregivers'[19]—other than that instability of care is a hazard of nurseries? It is in the nature of things that the effects of a childrearing environment, like family structure, are indirect. They make their impact on child development by influencing those intervening variables that directly affect child well-being.

We are often faced with a *fait accompli,* and told that it is too late anyway, or pointless, to consider childcare effects, because the realities of economic and demographic life tell us that infant care is inevitable. But none of this alters the facts about its effects on infant and child development. Moreover, it is nonsense to say we could not halt developments in this direction, when we are engineering more maternal employment and out-of-home-care through employment, benefit and tax policies.

At the very least, parents need more access to information that would allow them to evaluate the quality of the childcare their children are receiving, or might receive. Reassured by the childcare lobby, and bombarded with all the talk about educational and social gains for children raised in groups:

> Many parents are not aware of any of the ambivalences and caveats of some experts. Perhaps because they have neither the time nor the energy, many daycare parents do not concern themselves about issues like leashes, cage-like cribs, or health risks. And, parents are reassured when daycare professionals talk in jargon and claim educational and social gains for children raised in groups.
>
> It is no wonder that they overlook many of the negative aspects of institutionalisation, especially if they feel that they are helping their child get 'reciprocal and stimulating interactions'. Because they might wish to hasten their child's development and consequent independence, they might be impressed with the idea of infants playing at higher developmental levels.[20]

Confusion is also sown by the lip-service given to the idea that childcare is better than maternal care or, at least, as acceptable, so long as it is 'quality care'.[21] Since this implies that there must also be 'non-quality care', how do parents, policy-makers or practitioners distinguish one from the other?

Because we have all been so ill-informed on this issue and exposed to a very selective presentation of the material available, it is necessary to correct the balance. But, if we expect great certainty, it will not be there.

Childcare is not only a very emotionally, politically and ideologically charged subject, it is also notoriously difficult to investigate—not least because of the large number of factors involved. When it does seem possible to draw some tentative conclusions, it is necessary to qualify these to explain to whom they apply and under what circumstances. Experimental programmes may be able to randomly assign children to different groups. Others may use sophisticated 'matching' techniques to create a control group comparable to programme children. However, usually it is impossible to randomly allocate children to different arrangements, and so have a proper experiment. Instead, the 'self-selection' of children to home or daycare can distort the results, to the point at which any differences could be as much or more due to genetic or environmental differences.[22] Children who get sent to nurseries may be more developmentally advanced, healthier and resilient than those who stay at home, while parents may be more likely to withdraw children who cannot cope. This can bias samples in favour of childcare. Elementary controls for socio-economic status of parents, sex and age of children, etc., may not remove effects due to uncontrolled, individual variations.[23] An awareness of such problems and where and how they might affect any particular study, or whether they have been satisfactorily controlled for or resolved, is often important to any understanding of the research.

Fortunately, since the 1970s far more studies of childcare, including childcare as ordinary parents experience it, rather than that developed by specialists in model projects, have become available. The downside is that comparatively little research has been carried out in the UK: most is from the USA. Nevertheless, enough evidence is now available on which to base tentative, but long overdue and more realistic assessments of the effects, and implications, of childcare for children and society.

A Rare British Study

A rare but contemporaneous British study of childcare comes from the Thomas Coram Research Unit (TCRU).[24] Beginning in 1982, it focussed on children of full-time working mothers in 33 private nurseries, many of which were workplace nurseries attached to hospitals, schools and colleges. While three-quarters of the mothers returned to work by the time the child was nine months old, the attempt to create a balanced sample with which to compare the effect of childcare with rearing children at home was undermined by the very large number of employed mothers who had given up full-time work by the time their child was three: 77 out of 184.

The childcare children went to nurseries before nine months for more than 20 hours per week. While distress and negativism was evident at 18 months, and the results were generally poor, much emphasis has been put on the finding that, at three years, daycare children tended to be less timid and more sociable with unfamiliar adults than non-daycare children. However, they performed less well on language tests. This is particularly striking considering how the nursery group parents had higher status jobs, more qualifications and higher salaries than average. (And, we must presume, children who had coped badly in childcare would more likely to have been among the ones to have dropped out.) Such an 'advantaged' and selected group would be expected to show *better* development than other groups, not worse.[25] Moreover, while any social differences between the nursery and non-nursery groups evaporated once all children had settled in school, the language problem remained at six. However, as a glass which is half empty is also half full, it is possible to maintain that there is 'no question that the nursery children were ... delayed in their language ability' but rather 'in comparison to other groups in the study, they did not do as well'.[26]

Even more worrying is the way that children who had experienced frequent changes of care setting were significantly slower in both cognitive and linguistic development. In the unpublished and unpublicised part of the research, this was, again, present when the children were six.[27] The proportion of children who had at least three moves in their first 36 months of life was 24 per cent: 20 per cent had at least four moves, and 14 per cent had more than five moves. As the figures for moves include children who were looked after at home, it shows both how changes of placement are ubiquitous for children in alternative care, and how much better children fared with maternal care. However, since cognitive development has been related to moves, rather than to nursery placement *vis-à-vis* maternal care, it is possible to maintain in published sources that there 'is no overall daycare effect on intellectual development [at six], as there was not at any other age'.[28]

The Thomas Coram findings on children in daycare have an uncanny similarity to those for children reared in residential institutions and it is surprising that the comparison is not made. Back in the 1970s, Barbara Tizard described how two-year-olds living at home were far more willing to approach a stranger than children who were living in institutional nurseries, and fewer of them ran away or showed signs of distress when left alone with her.[29] In contrast, children in the nurseries were much more clingy, crying when nurses left the room and running to be picked up when they entered, as well as being highly aggressive and competitive. At four the nursery children were indiscriminately friendlier and much more attention seeking than home-reared children. This behaviour could be considered adaptive where large numbers of adults come, go, and disappear, at irregular and unpredictable intervals. The institutionalised children were also slightly intellectually retarded, while children who were adopted in the interim showed large intellectual gains. However, when children were adopted after the age of four, there was no intellectual acceleration. Nor were there improvements, at any age, when children were taken back, often by neglectful parents. Unlike adoptive parents, these did not try to compensate for earlier deficiencies, but expected restored children to automatically fit in with the existing family. In parallel, the daycare children in the Thomas Coram study had not made up their intellectual losses at six, and it is unlikely that two full-time working parents would have recognised the need, or had the time, to give them the necessary attention in the early years.

Clearly, the Thomas Coram findings have been uncomfortable, and attempts to explain away the obvious associations can lead to absurd claims that, for example, the results are: 'most easily interpreted not as the effects of daycare but as the effects of type of care in that the effects are strongest for nursery care'. If nursery care is not daycare, what is it?[30] Attempts to 'lose' the associations by disaggregating the components abound, as we have already seen. We are told that: 'if communication (received by the child) and responsiveness (to the child's communications) are controlled for, the [adverse] nursery effect on language disappears'[31] —when what we have here is evidence that nurseries can be comparatively unresponsive and uncommunicative to children. Again, while aggression was greater in nurseries and least in the home for 18 month old children, and this is 'consequence of the greater number of children in nurseries', it is difficult to see how you can have nurseries with less children than homes.[32]

121 American Children

A similar study to Thomas Coram's is Anne Robertson's investigation of the impact of full-time attendance (at least 20 hours per week for at least two pre-school years) at 30 American centres on 121 children at five to six years and eight to nine years.[33] Most had attended for 30 hours or more, often beginning at age three. The centres served from 15 to 60 children, in groups averaging 15, with child/adult ratios from 5:1 to 8:1. Many incorporated traditional nursery school programmes. Control groups of home-care subjects had all been cared for primarily by their mothers (just under two-thirds had some form of play-group or nursery school experience of between five and seven-and-a-half hours a week by four-years-old).

Daycare boys generally turned out to be more troublesome in school. Home-care middle-class subjects had higher school achievement, scoring higher for reading and arithmetic than daycare subjects, although the achievement of children from low socio-economic groups was unaffected.

Trouble in Texas

Robertson's findings are amplified in Deborah Lowe Vandell and Mary Ann Corasaniti's work on 236 eight-year-old school children in Texas.[34] Children who had received the most extensive (over 30 hours a week) and earliest childcare (begun during first year of life) received the poorest teacher and parental ratings for peer relationships, compliance, work habits, and emotional health, as well as the most negative peer reports. Intelligence scores were also negatively associated with extensive care experience, as were academic and conduct grades and ratings on standardized tests of social adjustment.

Children who began extensive care after infancy also performed badly. They also had poorer academic, interpersonal, and work habits grades than children in part-time or exclusive maternal care, and rated themselves more negatively in social, intellectual and general abilities than children with less extensive childcare histories.

Is Childcare to Blame?

None of this means, of course, that childcare was the strongest, or the only predictor of child outcomes in the Texas research. However, the children's academic and conduct grades were still best predicted by their childcare history, even after tests to see how much of any differences in the outcomes could be accounted for by other circumstances. The self assessments of social, intellectual, and general characteristics, and interpersonal reports, were predicted most by family type and marital status. As expected, IQ and basic skills were best predicted by the parents' socio-economic status and the child's birth order.

Obviously, variables also effect each other in a child's development. In the Vandell and Corasaniti study a combination of childcare history and the parents' marital status were related to children's self assessments, grades for academic work, work habits and interpersonal skills, peer evaluations and compliance. Children received the poorest work habit ratings by parents when there had been both extensive infant care and divorce, and the same goes for reduced IQ. The children from lower class families who were also rated by teachers as the most difficult to discipline were the ones who had also been in extensive childcare as infants. This subset of low-income children had the worse peer evaluations, and conduct was particularly poor for boys who had been in daycare from infancy.

Looking for reasons, the researchers pointed to the low standards set for childcare providers in the community from which the Texan children were draw. There are no educational requirements for childminders, and centre-based caregivers are only required to have 15 hours of in-service training each year. Up to 12 children (including four infants) may be cared for by a minder and, in centre-based care, ratios of 1:6 for infants and 1:18 for four-year-olds were permitted. However, many children had better ratios.

The Message of Meta-analysis

It is findings from studies like those of Anne Robertson, Vandell and Corasaniti and the TCRU study in Britain that are really relevant to assessments of the effects of daycare. Instead of simply focussing on 'showpiece' programmes, often serving deprived children, they deal with the impact of childcare of varying quality on ordinary children who typically attend for 30 to 40 hours per week, often for years at a time. Moreover, since the subjects represent attendance at many different childcare centres, not one particular nursery with a certain régime, this greatly increases the general validity of the findings. Any care effects found would have to be attributed to those 'variables common to nearly all daycare centers (daily parent/child separations, multiple caretakers, the presence of large numbers of peers, and the increase in structure and routine that this usually necessitates)',[35] instead of the characteristics of particular centres.

The same applies to C. Violato's and C. Russell's large-scale synthesis of information from 88 studies (involving 22,000 children) published since 1957. Given the apparent disparity of results within the complex field of non-parental care, they conducted this meta-analysis in order to clarify the current state of knowledge.[36] The results were that regular non-parental care for more than 20 hours per week had an unmistakably negative effect on social-emotional development, behaviour and attachment. A lesser negative effect was found for cognitive or intellectual development. None of the important variables that might mediate the effects of non-parental care, such as the quality of care, family structure and socio-economic status, infant versus older care (after three years), made much difference to the overall outcomes.

Is Sweden Different?

If we are going to find good outcomes for childcare anywhere, it would be in Sweden, where standards are vigorously enforced. Child nurses have two years of special training and pre-school teachers an extra two-and-a-half years of training after leaving college. There tend to be 12 children in the younger centre age groups (up to two and a half years) and 15—16 in the older age groups of three to seven years, with four staff. Where problems with childcare have been suggested, there has been a rapid tactical retreat. In the early 1970s the move was towards uninterrupted full-time maternal employment and early, full-day crèches. Information on babies suggested not only depression and distress, but lower ratings on personal/social aspects of development compared with home-reared infants.[37] This partly accounts for the way in which the time that parents can stay at home without losing pay or risking their jobs has been progressively extended (up to 18 months per child by the late 1980s). While daycare refers to at least five to six hours a day, the right of parents to work a short day until the child is at least seven years of age means that this length is rarely exceeded. (Only 14 per cent of both parents of under-threes worked over 15 hours a week in the mid-1980s.)

Brngt-Erik Andersson's study from Sweden ranks second only to Perry Pre-school in the canon of childcare propaganda.[38] The claims made for this are that children who go to daycare, starting in the second half of the first year, perform better on intelligence tests and in terms of school achievement and social/personal development than children in home-care or those entering at later ages.

Even British childcare enthusiasts from the research field warn that: 'because childcare in Sweden is of such high quality the results may not apply to other countries'. Moreover: 'because the children were not

recruited to the project until they had been attending daycare for some
time it was not possible to say whether there were differences between the
two groups when they first started'.[39] Only 16 of the study's 128 families
had used centre-care in the first year of life, compared to the 66 providing
care at home and another 16 using private or public minding arrangements.

Where not enough is known about the characteristics of children when
they first go to different forms of care, this makes it increasingly difficult
to relate later outcomes to events in early life with the passing years.[40]
Certainly, what is known from Andersson's study is that it was children
from upper middle-class families and with highly educated mothers who
tended to be the ones entering centre-care at an earlier age. Socio-
economic status had significant effects on children's school performance
at eight and 13, and it is this which Andersson claims is partly indirect,
or mediated, through early entry into daycare. (Meaning that high status
and educated parents advanced their children's school performance not
only though the home background and inheritance, but because they
choose early daycare.)

Even so, there was a decrease in the amount of school performance
attributed to age of entry into daycare at 13, with an increase in the direct
impact of the family's socio-economic status. With school adjustment, the
home background played a direct and more important role at this later
age. The most socially competent were also children from middle-class
families, girls and more verbally talented children. Indeed—despite the
way in which this study is reported—there was *no connection* between
early entry and social competence at the age of eight, and only a slight (or
not statistically significant), one at 13—which might well be a function of
the different way that social competence is measured at the two ages.

Other observations from Sweden throw doubt on any suggestion that
even its high-quality care *typically* has the effects reported by Andersson.
One previous study showed that Swedish children of highly educated
parents were more intellectually competent when they stayed at home;
only children of less educated parents showed any benefit from daycare.[41]
Another, in the mid 1970s, showed home-reared infants to be generally
more explorative and communicative with adults at 18 months.[42] (As the
daycare group had entered between six and twelve months, it provides a
good comparison with the Andersson study, with the advantage that the
home-reared controls were selected from the waiting lists.)

Other Swedish work has failed to pick up differences between children
from home-care and daycare, or not, anyway, when daycare is entered
after the first year. One main investigation involved 140 first-born
Swedish children from two-parent families obtained from waiting lists for
childcare centres.[43] They were tested just after 53 obtained centre-care,
and a year afterwards. (All had exclusive parental care at home for an
average of 16 months.) Personal maturity was related to background
variables, like high family socio-economic status, high quality of home-

care, affectionate and involved parents and easy temperament in the child, all of which existed prior to the daycare experience. Availability of support from maternal grandparents had a smaller, but still significant effect. As Sweden generally provides closely controlled care of a similar type, this may have diminished its importance for child development, so that it has little impact over and above that of social class and family background. This contrasts with the Bermudan and many American findings, where widely varying quality of care has a pronounced effect on children over and above the family background.

Compared with What?

Clearly, the impact of daycare on child development is dependent upon the quality of non-parental care compared with the standard that the home can provide. Even mediocre childcare may not adversely affect (and might sometimes even enhance) the intellectual development of children from the worst homes, while leading to poorer outcomes for other children, and perhaps a general detrimental effect on the behaviour of all. However, reflecting what we know about the quality of care generally available in the home compared to that available, on average, in childcare centres, the advantage is likely to lie with the parents. Certainly, educated or higher status parents are likely to provide better learning environments at home than any provided by non-parental care.

This is seen in data from the National Longitudinal Survey of Youth,[44] on the achievement of 867 white, Hispanic and Afro-American children at five and six. Only children from unresponsive and impoverished homes did better in terms of higher reading recognition and maths scores if they had routine non-maternal care starting in the first year of life. Children from better homes did significantly worse on both counts.

Overall, while many children in poor facilities may lag behind those in higher quality care, this does not mean that even 'quality care' provides an extra boost to development, or an advantage to any but those from relatively unstimulating homes. Certainly, 'quality care' is important if children are not to be put at risk, but, as Penelope Leach says, it 'seldom gives them anything they positively need'.[45]

Better Than Home?

Like thousands of other women, [Joanne Weinrich] ... has discovered that working on after having a family makes her a better, more relaxed mother. Her children reap benefits they would not have if she stayed at home. What's more, going to a daycare centre does the children good, helping them to relate well to each other and to their parents. There are enormous benefits in terms of getting children as young as possible used to an educational environment. But, most important, every child would have the advantage of individual attention, early learning of social skills and the joy of mixing with other children.

The Sunday Express[1]

Some very big claims are made for daycare. It purports to give children 'individual attention'—an 'advantage' that, by implication, they do not get at home. It not only means they learn social skills 'early', it even helps them relate to their own parents! Any delays in getting children into this 'educational environment' amounts to a loss of such 'enormous benefits' as to suggest that parental care is a form of child neglect.

To assess the appropriateness of any care, whether at home, at the centre or at the childminder's, we have to ask questions about the developmental needs of babies and small children. The next step is to see the likelihood of these being served in different environments. Moreover, as differences in the ways in which these are met affect outcomes, how far is it possible for one environment to compensate for another? The American National Center for Clinical Infant Programs[2] maintains that the basic requirement of appropriate and beneficial care *anywhere* is that it should provide:

1. Physical protection and attention to health and nutrition.
2. Awareness of and respect for individual differences in infants and toddlers.
3. Sensitivity to the infant's cues and communication.
4. A capacity to shift caregiving practices as the infant develops and changes.
5. Warm, loving human relationships based on constancy of care.

Stimulation matches the infant's level of understanding. Tasks are repeated frequently and carefully paced so that the infant is not over-whelmed. The infant is rewarded and re-enforced for efforts so that he or she will be motivated to continue and will gain pleasure from small accomplishments. A caregiver is sensitive to signals that indicate limitations, fatigue and tolerance levels. At the same time, slightly more is expected than children are capable of accomplishing, so that they are subtly stretched.

The stability of caregivers is important because early communication tends to be idiosyncratic, and pre-verbal children need time to develop patterns of behaviour based on mutually understood signals. Familiar caregivers know a particular infant's style of communication and can 'decode', while unfamiliar caregivers are more likely to misunderstand, or not comprehend at all.[3] The reciprocity created in a secure relationship generates a momentum of its own. Through this process their young children come to co-ordinate their activities with those of others, acquire inter- personal skills and the interdependence important to intellectual and social development. The child not only builds up more and more complex patterns of behaviour with the caregiver; these also get carried over to other times, places and people.[4]

There is a sense in which the distinction between education and care is artificial for babies and very young children. But this is 'education' in a very wide sense, in which the 'genesis of the self' proceeds in the context of intimate personal ties, where children are provided with the concepts and values which shape self-identity and help root them in a particular language, culture and history. It is through relationships with others that individuals learn to interpret their experience, act intentionally and provoke appropriate responses from others.

As such, young children not only need to be with an affectionate adult, but one who is also very familiar with both the child *and the child's world*. While two commentators assert that 'there is no reason why this should not be someone other than the mother'[5] it is difficult to avoid thinking of parents when we read this job description. In fact, those interested in assessing child/adult relations in daycare have gone to the work on mother/child interaction for guides to 'optimal caregiver behaviours'.

Impressed by their reciprocity, developmental psychologists involved in infancy research have derived notions of sensitive, contingent and responsive care from parent and child relations. Strategies used by parents with their infants are very similar to what are known to be best for successful childrearing.[6] Parents who are adapting well to the birth of a baby behave in ways which are subtly and well attuned to the intellectual, social and emotional needs of infants.

A basic, almost insurmountable, difference between hired caregiver and parent is that it is the adults who know, have known and will go on knowing an individual child who also have the greatest motivation to serve his welfare and invest in his development. To this we add the morally binding commitment which commands a parent to suspend self-interest and to care *for this particular child*. In contrast, an:

> ... outside caregiver has less reason than a mother to celebrate an infant and therefore needs less cause to be indifferent to him. A nursery worker has less

reason still to celebrate this infant because she has others to care for who may overload her or whom she may prefer. How well an infant thrives ... depends on how much time he also spends with someone who cares not just *for* but *about* him.[7]

Moreover, as John and Elizabeth Newson have pointed out, a function of parents is not simply to relate to the child as a person with known characteristics, but to act as a memory store which plays back and compares his present experiences to the past.[8] Children in residential institutions, who have no adult to develop this scaffolding, have difficulty in interpreting their experiences as they get older, so that events bewilder them or they ignore or exclude experiences they cannot interpret.[9]

This information makes it difficult to maintain that, as a matter of course, daycare is going to be equal, or superior, to parental care. Instead, it seems that only those toddlers cared for in very small groups and with favourable adult/child ratios have experiences in any way comparable to those at home.[10] Reporting on the characteristics of young children's care, from the 1985 'sweep' of the US National Longitudinal Survey of Youth, Linda J. Waite and colleagues[11] show how care in children's own homes best provides the features linked to high quality, and conforms closest to government guidelines for standards in care arrangements. As infants under two benefit from one-to-one care provided in very small groups, the Federal Interagency Daycare Requirements recommend no more than three children per caregiver and no more than six children per group. On these criteria:

> ... at all ages, pre-school children cared for in their own home or in the home of a relative almost always received care in groups no larger than the recommended size, with at least the recommended number of adults.

Compared with home:

> ... nursery schools and organised childcare centres often failed to meet the requirements for group size and numbers of children per adult; only one-third of the infants and toddlers in centres and at nursery schools had adequate numbers of adult caregivers. And only one infant in five in a centre and half of them in a nursery school received care in groups of the recommended size of six children per group. About one-quarter of toddlers and about half of pre-schoolers received care in too-large groups—i.e., over 12 children per group for those age two, and over 16 per group for ages three and four.

Speaking of how the results 'challenge the conventional wisdom', the researchers observe that, while:

> Arrangements where a child is cared for at home or in a relative's home generally fall outside the purview of these childcare licensing agencies [yet]. Ironically, these private arrangements are more likely to satisfy the criteria than are childcare centers and nursery schools.[12]

In the most extensive study of relationships in American daycare, it was observed how caregivers are often quite narrow in their dealings with infants: their level of stimulation was low and lacking in variety, with little play with their charges.[13] Given the infrequency of affectionate one-to-one contact, concern was expressed at the lack of attention given to the development of the individual child. There are plenty of similar observations, such as the finding that home-care children experience more than twice as much verbal interaction with adults than centre children.[14] Talk between caregivers and *individual* children in centres often tends to be of a simple 'control' variety, so that 'few *valuable* experiences between an individual child and a caregiver appear to take place in average centers, no doubt due to the many demands on caregivers'.[15] Even with Swedish 'quality care', adults at home converse more with children than those in daycare centres.[16]

These findings about the responsiveness of parents and caregivers are duplicated for Britain. At three years old, in the Thomas Coram Research Unit (TCRU) study:

> ... there were significant differences between the childcare groups, with mothers and relatives showing higher levels of affection toward the study child than childminders who were in turn more affectionate than nursery workers.

Moreover:

> ... children in the home, relative and childminder groups received significantly more vocal communication than children in the nursery group and ... the home group received significantly more than the childminder group.[17]

This replicates results from the 1984 study of childrearing in Stoke on Trent, where the time a child spent with an adult at home on a one-to-one basis far exceeded all other pre-school contexts.[18] There were a small group of children who received very little verbal stimulation and encouragement from their parents, but this was not true for the majority of children from all social classes. Of course, there were more joint, organised activities in nursery schools, playgroups and educationally oriented nurseries, and more educational toys, typical of middle-class homes, which develop skills like colour and shape discrimination. However, adult/child conversations at home were more frequent, more complex, more wide-ranging, longer and more evenly balanced, as others have found when 'childwatching' at nursery schools and playgroups.[19] A typical conversation ranged over food, jewellery, kangaroos, animals in the zoo, animals in the park, reindeer, Santa's home, the whereabouts of toyland and its colours.[20] Such free flowing conversation in nursery school has been found to be a rare event. In turn, parents do not make just the relatively superficial comments typical of pre-school staff: 'that's nice', 'lovely', 'make him fatter' etc.

Clearly, extended conversation requires lengthy attention to the individual child, where the adult draws on a fund of shared experiences. Neither is available to staff who have to cope with a large group of competing children. Hence, the 'widely held view' that a 'more enabling verbal climate' is provided even in the nursery school, as 'compared with *most* working-class children's experiences at home, seems open to doubt'.[21] Moreover, these elaborate exchanges often go on while parents are preparing food, ironing, sewing, etc. These are precisely the circumstances which are often used to epitomise the 'wastefulness' and 'uselessness' of maternal care—'you won't be doing anything for your child at home, just doing the housework'.

Much the same picture emerges from all research on childminding. One prominent American study[22] compared employed mothers, substitute care-givers, and non-employed mothers of five- to six-month-old infants. They had similar social and economic backgrounds and attitudes towards child-rearing, although the daycare women were responsible for twice as many children as the mothers. Both groups of mothers exceeded the minders in responsiveness, affection, and the overall level and variety of stimulation. The big differences were not due to the behaviour or nature of the infants, many of whom were observed with both their employed mothers and their childminders.

Many of the children in B. Mayall and P. Petrie's study of British childminders in the 1970s spent unstimulated days in cramped surround-ings, without love or attention and sometimes with unsettling changes. The consequences are indicated by the fact that the language development of 85 per cent of the two- and three-year-old minded children was below average—with a quarter functioning at a level which gave serious cause for concern.[23]

The first Thomas Coram Research Unit study of childminding in the 1970s considered that 18 per cent of children were in grossly overcrowded conditions, and playspace in the minders' homes was unsafe in nearly half the cases. In the later 1980s study, their figures were 36 per cent and 71 per cent.[24] For many children, being minded was not like being at home with their mother and perhaps a brother and sister. Children's days were governed by the minder's domestic routine and few set aside time to do anything with them, but mostly left them to occupy themselves somehow. Often 'the minder's day has just *too many commitments*—so that she has to rush in and out dragging the minded children with her'.[25] Around a third 'had too much to do ... looking after 6.7 children compared to the rest who had 3.9'. Nearly a fifth of the minders 'did not report even minimal play with the child, during a day which lasted on average eight and a half hours'.[26]

There are the 'typical' childminders,[27] who demonstrate the wide variation in the quality of care provided. Peter is lucky enough to be looked after by Mandy for 40 hours a week. Mandy regarded childminding as a proper job, and was a trained nursery nurse, who spent time providing children with an enjoyable day with a wide variety of activities. At the other end of the spectrum, Kevin had been looked after by Mary since he was two months old. Since a divorce, she had been unable to get work. When it was suggested that she could get work as a childminder she was 'delighted' and registered with her local authority.

The two children that Mary looked after were restricted to the two upstairs rooms. The larger was Mary's bedroom and most of the space was taken up with a large double bed, wardrobe, a hard chair and a large television squeezed into the room. ... During the day the television was always on and the children were frequently told to sit quietly and watch it regardless of which programme was on.

She knew about the drop-in centre and had been once but she found taking the children out anywhere difficult as they were 'too naughty'. As a result the two children ... spent over forty hours a week in an extremely confined space with almost no stimulation, toys or conversation ... When she spoke to the children it was usually to tell them off (Kevin in particular tried to get rid of some of his energy by jumping on the bed, the girl seemed too passive to do even this) ...

... Kevin, who had not had any exercise apart from bouncing on the bed or any outings apart from the car journeys to and from Mary's house, was often not asleep until 11.00. Jane [Kevin's mother], not unsurprisingly, described herself as permanently exhausted.[28]

It is not uncommon to find childminders who refuse to go on taking a child once he has become mobile, starts to explore and becomes defined as a 'nuisance' or 'naughty'. The milestones which parents take pride in may be frowned upon, since the 'good' child is a quiet, passive child. One speech therapist, who worked on courses for childminders run by a local authority, confided to me her misgivings about the numbers who seemed only to want 'deaf and dumb paraplegics who slept most of the time'.

It is commonly observed how the relationships which minders and mothers have with children are quite different. Not only do minders often not initiate much contact with a child, but, apart from their physical needs, minded children make few demands.[29] The relationship is usually a distant one and, it is frequently the case that the same child:

... who is lively, affectionate and naughty with his parents sit[s] quiet, sad and strangely good at the minder's. Such a child makes few demands on the minder and indeed minders often comment that children are easy, no trouble, never naughty.[30]

If childminders do not usually provide care equivalent to a parent's and, sometimes, nothing remotely like it:

This is not because minders are cruel and neglectful, but rather because the nature of minding means that the conditions under which minders work, and the attitudes they have to their work, provide major obstacles to achieving good childcare, although there are of course notable exceptions.[31]

Thus: 'it is particularly striking how few women take up minding because they are *interested in working with children* (emphasis in original).[32] (The same is likely to be true for *au pair* girls.) In the B. Mayall and P. Petrie study, only five out of 39 gave this as a reason for minding.[33] Nor is it a 'proper job'. It is more likely to be undertaken because the woman wants to earn extra money in ways that do not interfere with her other commitments or she is not well enough to go out to work. The researchers found minders who had a long-term disability, like a heart condition or a bad back, and even some who had been advised by their doctor to mind children as an antidote to depression! Many will mind only for a short time while their children are very small, or between other jobs. This often accounts for the frequency of moves experienced by minded children. The reliance on play equipment from their own children's younger days is an indication of a 'fill-in' occupation that does not merit any special provision or investment: 'A common sight at minders is children extracting odd bits of different toys from a large cardboard box—a piece of a puzzle, a few bits of Lego or Sticklebricks, a car that has lost a wheel—and sitting fiddling with them'.[34] In the second Thomas Coram study over a third of childminders were rated as 'inadequate' for baby equipment, with seven per cent so 'ill-equipped' as to raise serious concern about the child's well-being.

Competing Influences

If variations in parental care affect child development, it stands to reason that variations in childcare may also have implications for the social and emotional development of children. Even with family characteristics controlled, the quality of the childcare setting, usually exerts a consistent influence[35] and is significantly predictive of progress, skills, and behaviour problems, well into the school years.[36] For example:

1. Deborah Lowe Vandell and colleagues found that middle-class children in better quality daycare had more friendly relations with their peers, were more socially competent, co-operative, happier and less withdrawn. Those from poor centres were less sociable, less considerate, and low in empathy for others. There was significant continuity between these four-year-olds' behaviour at the daycare centres and the children's functioning at eight years. While the differences were 'a cause for concern', they could not be put down to the way in which parents who choose different types of childcare also behave differently towards their children.[37]

2. In the Bermuda studies, Deborah Phillips and colleagues looked at 166 children aged three to five who had attended nine representative childcare centres that varied widely in quality. The average age of entry was 19 months. With family background, the children's ages and childcare experience taken into consideration, childcare quality was significantly related to later differences in considerateness, sociability, intelligence and task orientation; showing, for example, 30 per cent variations in some cases.[38] The variation in the quality of care was greater than with parental care, with poor quality care more likely outside the home. This was reflected in the way that family background accounted for a smaller amount of the differences between children's social development.[39]

Childcare and family contexts both have a role in deciding outcomes, and they also have mutual influences on each other.[40] Good home conditions might go some way towards counteracting the threats from mediocre childcare. However, it is worrying that the children who lose out at home are more likely to be losers outside as well, so that they are less likely to get the compensatory care they need.[41]

The effect which childcare centres have on child behaviour may have knock-on effects at home, given findings that children in poor quality daycare do not converse much at home, even when their mothers were fully attentive to them. [42] Thus, children may be less, not better, able to relate to their parents, if they get little in the way of compensation when in daycare for the time that home-care children spend communicating with their mothers.

Whose Influence?

Very few studies have examined age of entry into childcare, childcare quality, and family background in combination, while following the children over time. One exception compared the adjustment of four groups of middle-class children entering a variety of high- and low-quality childcare centres before first birthday and between first and fourth birthdays.[43] The children who went into low-quality care in their first year had the most problems when seen at ages two, four and five—whether with peers, self-regulation, distractibility, task orientation, considerateness, hostility and non-compliance. The best outcomes were for older children entering high-quality childcare.

For older children, those who were enrolled in poor childcare were also more hostile and less competent in a number of ways. As we might expect, differences in the family backgrounds and in families' choices of care, as well as the quality of the care itself, were related to their later behaviour. However, when children were enrolled in daycare before their first birthday, *the family made much less difference*, compared to childcare quality. Here, the 'influence parents would otherwise exert on their children is "lost" to, or at least assumed by, non-parental caregivers.' This was something also detected in the Bermuda studies. *Early, extensive daycare may mean that parents have little power to shape their children's development*; including the ability to compensate for damaging experiences of daycare.

The 'Childcare Sewer'

It is often claimed that childcare represents a 'healthier' physical as well as mental environment for small children. The reference is usually to accidents in the home and on the street, which disproportionately affect children of lone parents. What is ignored is the age-old capacity of institutions to spread infectious disease. Arrangements where small children play, eat, sleep, and excrete in a confined space, with a lot of unrelated children, are no exception. Parents cannot keep taking time off work, so they may minimise children's illnesses and send them to daycare to infect others. It is also difficult to maintain standards of hygiene if children are in nappies—particularly considering how toddlers instinctively mouth objects or suck their hands.

Daycare infections have become an important public health problem in modern America, and a growing number of children also suffer from parasitic infestations. Physicians refer to the childcare cloaca, or sewer. The *Journal of the American Medical Association* remarked in 1983 that the epidemics of enteritic illnesses they were seeing were 'reminiscent of the pre-sanitation days of the 17th century',[44] and the first national symposium on infectious disease in childcare centres was held in 1994.[45]

In general, American children in centres run risks of infection two to three times higher than those for children cared for at home. This also means a greater chance of experiencing complications that can affect development as well as lead to complex medical or surgical treatments. Many infectious diseases go in cycles, with peaks and troughs, that do not greatly change over long time spans. However, a study for the Center for Disease Control found rates of infection for giardiasis 15 to 20 times higher among daycare children than among children cared for at home.[46]

Since many of the diseases spread in childcare centres are highly contagious, even when the child carriers are free of symptoms themselves, they can be a source of transmission to daycare providers, parents and siblings, unborn children and the community as a whole.[47]

Other societies which have used daycare on a large scale have had problems with infectious disease. At the turn of the century the maternal and child welfare movement to promote child health and reduce mortality rates concentrated heavily on reducing infant diarrhoea. As there were massive outbreaks of gastro-intestinal disease in the North West, often starting in the nurseries of the mill towns, this increased the emphasis on looking after babies at home. In 1980 the 25th Congress of the Communist Party of the Soviet Union provided pay for a new mother to take leave for a year (extended to 18 months in 1986) as a way of 'improving the country's system of protection for maternity and infancy'.[48] Particularly alarming was the way in which socio-hygienic studies of infant health demonstrated how the early return of the mother to work was associated with respiratory disease, especially pneumonia.

Aggression

... daycare ... can teach your infant or toddler lessons about co-operation, independence, self-sufficiency and even friendship he wouldn't learn were he at home with you.

Sirgay Sanger and John Kelly[1]

Children in Groups

Nursery advertisements tempt parents with the promise that their child will have the 'stimulating company of his peers'. It is widely believed that simply putting small children together is good for their social development. This assumption is wildly at odds with a truism of criminology, which is that there is nothing like a child's peer group for encouraging aggression and delinquency, while its capacities as a humanising and socialising agency are small.

If a child in a daycare center sees her peers as her major role models, she sees behaviour that parents might want to discourage. She sees aggression. She sees anger. She sees fear. She sees disruptive conduct. She sees passivity. Children do learn from each other. They learn from adults. They learn from their own experience. What they see they tend to incorporate into their own behaviours. In daycare they see mostly other children.[2]

On the one hand there is the idea that children, however small, are missing out if they are not in some kind of school room, with professional educators. At the same time, notions about the beneficial influence of group care are haunted by notions of adults as simply enablers who provide the circumstances for the unfolding of spontaneous processes of development. This received input during the 1960s from observations that monkeys are able to acquire all the skills they need in adult life in peer group play. However, the human process of cultural transmission, basic to our process of social reproduction, is not found among the other primates and depends upon children either receiving instruction, or learning the skills they need, from constant association with adults.

The much misinterpreted overview of 1978 by Jay Belsky and Laurence Steinberg[3] (see pp. 19-20) described how claims about daycare-reared children being less timid and more sociable with peers had to be offset against reports of aggressive behaviour towards other children, and more defiance of adults. (The two are not incompatible: many aggressive people are very outgoing and confident—*too* confident.) One group of researchers concluded in 1974 that their study should provide 'a caution light', after they found that three-and-a-half year-old children who had been in daycare since about nine or ten months were more physically and verbally aggressive with grown-ups and less tolerant of frustration, compared with those reared at home.[4]

Accounts of daycare children being more sociable and more inclined to join in group activities also have to be handled with caution. A case in point is the report by Tiffany Field and colleagues[5] in which teachers found two- to five-year-old children who had spent the longest time in special learning centres to be more positive towards their peers and interact generally with them at a higher rate than children who had not been there for so long, or who were only there on a part-time basis. However, despite the way that this 'model' educational project emphasized the development of language, imagination, problem solving and social skills, the same children were also seen as the most aggressive. In turn, very 'positive' approaches to strangers sometimes have to be treated with some caution, since this can be a sign of loneliness or neglect. It is a typical observation made of children in orphanages. There is independent evidence that extreme expressions of pro-social behaviour are predictive of later problems, including depression, reflecting a basic insecurity and search for attention.

In 1985 Ron Haskins took up the aggression question.[6] While they had received little or no publicity, a total of ten studies from four different countries now related the extended use of daycare to negative and aggressive behaviour, and decreased co-operation with both peers and adults, in both large and small samples. The age at which these negative traits appeared varied between two and fifteen years. Backgrounds ranged from low-income to professional, and the pattern appeared in children who started full-time daycare as toddlers as well as during infancy. They emerged from the assessments of psychologists, behavioural counts, and the ratings of teachers, parents and peers. These negative aspects of substitute and group care applied particularly to boys.[7]

Behavioural problems have been evident in the batch of childcare studies which have been carried out on the island of Bermuda, where non-maternal care is commonplace. At the age of two group-care infants were more apathetic, less attentive, less socially responsive, less verbally expressive, and more maladjusted generally. Those children who spent the longest hours in care were the least well adjusted.[8] The differences were unaffected by the parents' education or socio-economic status, but were stronger for black children and varied with the quality of daycare. The same research group also reported on a large number of three- to five-year-olds, and found that the children who began group care in infancy were rated as more maladjusted—or more anxious, aggressive or hyperactive—than those cared for by a minder at home, or who began centre-care at a later age.[9]

A similar story emerged from the New York Infant Daycare Study following assessment of the psychological adjustment of over four hundred low-income children in minder, group, and home-care. Tested when they entered care and again at 18 and 36 months, it was the group-care children who were the most disadvantaged linguistically, emotionally and socially with adults.[10] Much the same was later reported for a small sample of middle-class children who had been enrolled in five infant/ toddler centres toward the end of the first year. Compared with a group who had been continuously reared at home, at three-and-a-half years they had more fears, were more active, were less compliant with their mothers and far more inclined to intense tempers. This 'reflected a more anxious and angry child ... non-compliance and temper tantrums are more charact-eristic of two-year-old than three-year-old behaviour.'[11]

Attempting to clarify the situation, Haskins compared children who had attended full-time day centres between about three months of age and the time they entered school at five, with three other groups of similar background who had less extensive periods of group care. Assessed before they went to school and followed over three years of schooling, the former were more likely to hit, kick and push; bully, threaten, swear and argue; not to use strategies like discussion or walking away to deal with difficulties and to be rated by teachers as having aggressiveness as a serious deficit of social behaviour. Moreover, the children had not been in poor quality daycare, but involved in one of the more well-known intellectually orientated intervention programmes—designed to help disadvantaged children do better at school. The excessive aggressiveness of the experimental children diminished over time, although significant differences still remained on several measures at eight years.

Raised aggressiveness which is independent of the quality of care in the centres or at home has since been recorded in other studies, as in the work of Margaret R. Burchinal and colleagues on the overall effects of high to average quality childcare or pre-schools on a Seattle sample of middle-class children.[12] Similarly, analysis of data from the National Longitudinal Survey of Youth showed how four- to six-year-old white and black American children were less compliant if their mothers were employed for over 30 hours per week during the child's first two years,[13] compared to children whose mothers were not employed during their first three years. It is noteworthy that early and extensive maternal employment exerted a stronger influence than factors like poverty or mother's education.

Whether insecurely or securely attached to their mothers, daycare children have been shown to be generally and significantly more aggres-sive, more non-compliant and more prone to behavioural problems on starting school. In one disadvantaged sample, only the home-reared children who had insecure relationships with their mothers showed similar difficulties.[14] The differences faded out after a couple of years at school where, presumably, the daycare children became socialised into school norms and learnt to control their impulses. While schooling itself may be a great 'levelling' experience, this also means that daycare, rather than being a preparation, can be a net contributor to the problems with which schools must contend.

Lasting Problems?

It is not clear whether the aggression associated with infant care actually *disappears* with enough time. That big study of the after effects of childcare 'as we know and have it' on the general child population in Texas, by Deborah A. Vandell and Mary A. Corasaniti, showed discipline problems among the many negative findings for eight-years-olds who had spent their early years in non-parental care.[15] In particular, the children from lower-class families who were the most difficult to discipline at school were the ones who had also been in extensive childcare as infants. The level of interpersonal conduct was especially poor for boys who had been in daycare from infancy.

Similarly, Anne Robertson's study of a population sample who had attended childcare or nursery school centres for long hours and long periods in their pre-school years showed how the younger boys, aged five to six, were 'substantially and significantly more troublesome than younger boys reared at home'.[16] A less detailed analysis of the behaviour of older, or eight- to nine-year-old boys, suggested that, while there was some diminution, enhanced disruptiveness persisted. This is reminiscent of another retrospective investigation of 191 middle-class nine- and ten-year-olds from the Bermuda series. Children who had entered daycare before 18 months were rated by their peers as badly behaved, more likely to be loners and 'most likely to be labelled troublemakers'.[17]

A similar picture has emerged in Britain from the longitudinal Child Health and Education Study.[18] As we shall see, pre-school provision had no beneficial effect on children's adjustment or behaviour, and more than a couple of sessions a week at a playschool or nursery school did not increase any educational benefit. However, while the most favourable *behavioural* outcomes at age ten were associated with children who had no pre-school experience, the least favourable outcomes were associated with local authority day nursery attendance, involving hyperactivity, conduct disorders and extreme extroversion, particularly for boys. Conduct disorders and extreme extroversion were also a feature of children who attended independent day nurseries and nursery schools.

Children in public day nurseries are, of course, often disadvantaged and in adverse home circumstances. However, the adverse results were *after* adjustment had been made for social and family variables, and many of the children who had no pre-school experience were also disadvantaged, yet they did not show the same high rates of deviance. Full-time attendance and long hours over a long period in day nurseries seemed to be the reasons—or over five (half-day) sessions a week.

The results are a sharper version of the previous large scale study of the effects of pre-school education carried out in Britain by Douglas and Ross in the 1960s.[19] They found a small increase in deviant behaviour among older children who had attended nursery schools and classes.

Just Being Independent?

It is argued that increased aggressiveness is nothing to worry about, and even something to celebrate. Children 'raised in groups are highly individualistic' because parental values are not 'imposed' on the develop-ing child.[20] As Alison Clarke Stewart put it:

> What this pattern of behaviour may suggest ... is ... that children who have been in daycare beginning in infancy or later ... think for themselves and that they want their own way. They are not willing to comply with adults' arbitrary rules... Children who have spent time in daycare, then, may be more demanding and independent, more disobedient and aggressive, more bossy and bratty than children who stay at home.[21]

But are aggressiveness and disobedience virtues in children? How are children in a position to judge rules as 'arbitrary'? By what standards and with what knowledge could they possibly assess and dismiss these rules? Is it a good thing for children to be 'peer-oriented'? Are they more 'free' than 'adult-oriented' children, or more dominated by group pressure in what are often unfruitful, fearful, and destructive ways? Moreover, how helpful is it to be 'independent' as early as possible? After all, studies of the life course suggest that it is the people who were the most 'dependent' in early life who often turned out to be the best balanced and assured adults.[22] In turn, there are many accounts of disturbed and violent people who, for various reasons, failed to have their dependency needs met in childhood.

Studies of pre-school children's relations and their later school success suggest that peer orientation, like aimless wandering in childcare, may be problematic.[23] Peer orientation is not peer competence, or even peer popularity. Children's sociability is related to their communication during the day with adults, and their social comprehension is developed by how much adults are prepared to teach. Children who are more susceptible to peer pressure are often the least liked, and both peer orientation and peer rejection are powerful predictors of later negative outcomes, whether school failure, school drop out or delinquency.

Managing Groups

Of course, heightened aggressiveness, like other problems connected with groups, is not *unique* to children who have been in pre-school facilities. We know that behaviour problems tend to emerge where children receive little adult attention and associate closely with peers, just as language development is held back where peer conversation replaces more important adult/child talk.

Such drawbacks are likely to characterise facilities which bring together large numbers of young children of the same age. It is unsurprising that we find research showing daycare children to be more peer-oriented and disinclined to seek the help of adults than home-reared children.[24] Moreover, the amount of time which children spend in centres makes it all too likely that they will lapse into bickering relationships with each other. They vie for adult attention, compete for equipment and get on each other's nerves.

Certainly, children will not learn to follow social rules, resolve social conflicts, or become competent with peers simply from extended contact and experience, but through the special efforts of adults who give them direct training in social skills.[25] A particular onus is placed on adults dealing with groups of children to monitor and regulate their behaviour. As well as encouraging the children to be better behaved, it is necessary to pay careful attention to the physical environment, since a lot of aggression occurs over limited equipment and in a confined space. As the number of children per square foot increases, so does aggressiveness, destructiveness and unoccupied behaviour.

On the whole, if caregivers provide interesting and developmentally appropriate activities, children are both less likely to wander alone and more likely to involve themselves co-operatively with both peers and adults. Close involvement of skilled adults with small children's groups can also provide opportunities to teach socially appropriate and competent behaviour. Where staff, trained in managing problem behaviour, plan activities so that aggression is reduced, and childrens' social understanding is increased, the result is a significant decrease in difficult behaviour in the care setting and at starting school.[26]

Generally it has been found that, where group size is low and adult/child ratios are low (particularly for infants) caregivers tend to be more stimulating, responsive and affectionate, and the children more co-operative, as well as intellectually capable and emotionally secure.[27] In turn, there are significant teacher as well as class-size effects. Preschoolers who have better trained teachers are more co-operative with adults, as well as more persistent, and perform better on pre-school ability and readiness for school tests.[28] But toddlers are less compliant and more impulsive when they attend daycare centres with poorer adult/child ratios, less training, high staff turnover and/ or permissive attitudes. Increasing group size and a falling adult/child ratio signal an increasingly uphill struggle. More distress is evident as the number of children per caregiver increases and, understandably, staff spend more time in management and control, and less in informal teaching and with the individual child.[29]

The Problem of Uninvolved Adults

The picture is also compounded by home factors, since parents as well as the caregivers of children in low-quality centres may be less involved when it comes to behaviour than parents who put their children in higher quality care, and they lead more complex lives.[30]

Unfortunately, there seem to be a large number of children in daycare centres with poor or barely existent relations with the caregivers. This is seen in a detailed assessment of the quality of relationships with adults and peers for 414 children aged 14 to 54 months in a large cross section of centres in California and Georgia. Certainly, children whose caregiving was good or very good were more likely to be emotionally secure with teachers, while those whose caregiving was inadequate or barely adequate were more likely to be avoidant or ambivalent with staff, and less competent with peers. However, there was a large and 'disturbing' percentage of staff-avoidant children in spite of the fact that many were enrolled in subsidised centres that met the most stringent of state licensing requirements.[31]

While centre-based variables play a role in moderating any potentially negative daycare effects, age at entry also seems to matter, as does the amount of time spent in the centre, since levels of hyperactive, aggressive, hostile and anxious behaviour in children up to five have been related to early entry into group care at centres, independently of quality.[32] Similarly, another study of four-year-old children who had been attending high-quality nurseries attached to universities found that those who had attended full-time daycare were more aggressive and assertive than those who only attended part-time.[33]

Trouble With Boys—and Girls?

Much of what has been documented about the heightened aggressiveness and disobedience of children raised in groups obviously refers to boys. It seems that home-reared infant males are more adult-oriented, whether to their parents or to strangers, than daycare males or even home-care females. Indeed, the behaviour of daycare females is similar to home-reared males in their tendency to seek proximity to, and maintain contact with, their mother or other adults.[34] Daycare may increase imitation, and perhaps conformity, in female children, while decreasing these in males.[35] Males are clearly more vulnerable than girls to inadequate childcare quality, as borne out by the rates of non-compliance among children in childcare of different quality.[36]

Research on early parent/child relations and later outcomes helps us to understand these gender differences. For boys, early maternal responsiveness is closely linked with future child compliance, decreased child coerciveness, more independent exploration and increases in overtures to unfamiliar people. However, girls are more likely to explore and to approach strangers when mothers are less responsive.[37] There is a general tendency for boys to be more vulnerable to the ill effects of all manner of family stress and bond disruptions. Boys tend to be more obviously and adversely affected by maternal depression, family conflict and family breakdown than girls, and to react in more anti-social ways. The same seems to hold for unresponsive and inconsistent caregiving in early life.

Inherent sex differences may mean that girls are better able to maintain continuity by conserving and building on existing personality and cognitive structures, where they experience the instability, or loss, of secure, sensitive frameworks. In contrast, boys' development is more fluid and opportunist in the face of environmental variation, and patterns are more likely to breakdown.

However, effects for girls cannot be ruled out just because they do not react badly in obvious and disruptive ways like boys, and appear far more poised and self-contained. Assumptions about the long-term effects of divorce on boys and girls have had to be revised by researchers who have followed their subjects into adulthood.[38] While, as children, girls seem better adjusted socially, emotionally and academically at each step, disturbing 'sleeper effects' may be present, which cause problems in later life.

Children also 'learn to inhibit aggressive tendencies by identifying with and hoping to please a loved parent'. If extensive daycare experience 'dilutes the intensity of children's identifications with their parents, then the motivation for boys to inhibit their aggressive feelings and actions may be considerably reduced'.[39] The failure to identify with parents and/or experience of rejecting, authoritarian care has an impact on the developing personality that can persist into adulthood. The aggression question is one of those issues which extend beyond considerations of childcare régimes and into matters like the impact of parental absence on early relationships.

SECTION B

THE REALITY OF DAYCARE

We know that successful childcare involves low adult/child ratios, devotion to and interest in the children, and time to talk and play constructively with the children. We also know that much childcare fails to meet these requirements. Demanding children occupy the staff while quiet children are ignored and become withdrawn and detached. The only way to make childcare 'pay', or to justify it in terms of releasing large numbers of women into the workforce, is to have a high ratio of children to adults, but that is associated with the worst results for the children. Childcare staff are often untrained, low-skilled or of low intelligence and change jobs frequently. These problems are ignored by those whose advocacy of childcare is mainly motivated by the concerns of equal opportunities and the re-definition of gender roles. Paedophiles are attracted to childcare, posing further risks to children.

After-school care is promoted as the answer to the problems created by two-earner families, but there is little research into its outcomes, and what there is suggests it can be harmful to children.

Quality Control

The most recent annual report of the Equal Opportunities Commission gave details of a plan under review by British Rail to establish crèche facilities at railway stations. Parents going in to work would leave their children in the morning, and collect them later in the day. The Interplayce company was reported to have developed a Portakabin nursery to set alongside a railway line. A further idea mooted has been for nurseries at car parks, where children could be left while parents caught a company bus to work. The Japanese toy firm Tomy has been reported as interested in setting up 100 or more nurseries which would use Tomy toys and equipment.

Adam Smith Institute[1]

Back to Basics?

When confronted with evidence of negative outcomes of childcare, its defenders claim that these are all associated with low-quality care, and that what they advocate is universal access to high-quality care, which will supposedly be free from drawbacks. This raises the question of how realistic it is to expect such high-quality care to be available to ordinary working mothers. As we shall see in Chapter 13, economic considerations alone might be sufficient to render this a pipe-dream. So, if we can leave aside the university-based show projects which are endlessly touted by childcare lobbyists, what can we say about the standards which pertain in the sort of facilities which mothers are actually using?

From the evidence which is available, it is obvious that 'quality' is not something that childcare establishments and their staff commonly attain. When researchers assert that 'higher standards of quality are imperative if children are to thrive in childcare',[2] *there may be a failure to grasp the seriousness of this statement in view of the knowledge that much available childcare does not reach even the minimum standard required to prevent actual harm.*

How does the information which we have about the developmental needs of babies and small children translate into 'quality care', and how easy or difficult is this to arrange out in the real world?

To further children's development, a small number of constant caregivers not only need to show warmth, affection and consistency to the children, but they should understand the individual child's communications and behaviour. When staff changes have to occur, there should be careful management of transitions. The experiences available must change as children develop and be varied enough to prevent boredom in what is often a very long day. Children make more progress when encouraged to play with stimulating and educative materials, are read to and have an orderly—but not too restrictive—environment.[3]

Unsurprisingly, language develops better if adults have conversations with children rather then just telling them what to do, and when they recast or expand on the child's speech. This is doubly important, because children with verbally richer environments also have better emotional adjustment.[4] Peer talk has little positive influence on language: its structure is poor and its content egocentric. Unfortunately, in centres, peer talk all too easily tends to replace more important caregiver talk.

However, children are adversely affected by the loss of familiar peers, as well as familiar caregivers. Children who can maintain friendships over time tend to have greater social skills and better social adjustment. Although those who go with close friends are less affected by changes, this is unlikely to happen, since moves are governed by the parents' work and financial considerations. Moreover, children separated from friends seem less able to make new friends than children who remain in the same peer group.[5]

However, it cannot be over-emphasized how much of this is closely related to structural aspects of quality. Responsive and stable adult/child relationships and appropriate learning opportunities are not only more likely in a well organised and stimulating physical environment, but where there is a trained and stable workforce, an appropriate group size and high adult/child ratios.

One large-scale national study of 57 American daycare centres typically found that group size was the foremost determinant of the *quality* of the experience of children aged three to five years. In groups of less than 15-18 children, caregivers were more responsive, instructive and affectionate, and children were more involved in classroom activities. In turn, the group size factor plus the training factor were the most important influences on children's *development*.[6] In centres where the workers had been there longer, as well as having more training in child development, children also had better scores for cognitive development compared to children in unstable arrangements—bearing out the Thomas Coram findings.

A substitute caregiver has to learn, as a professional skill, to assess the developmental stage of a baby and how, for example, it is important to respond to the baby's tentative smiles and vocalisation. Parents have difficulty in not responding.

The conditions for good childcare clearly require adequate funding, but one may not guarantee the other. Low levels of communication are on record for centres with good overall quality, and correspondingly more maladjustment among the children than in centres where overall quality was poorer, but the language environment was good.[7]

Some children, particularly the quiet and inhibited who are 'no trouble', may be easy to ignore even in a high-quality centre and can end up neglected compared with their more demanding peers. Observations of children entering daycare show how expressive children receive more and different forms of attention from staff. Infants whose distress at entry tends towards a despair-like immobility and withdrawal receive less attention and, six months afterwards, are more socially detached.[8] Aimless wandering, in which the child is not involved with toys, peers or staff, has been identified as a particular problem in childcare centres. Along with a lack of attachment to any staff, it is associated with adjustment problems when the child is of school age.[9]

Clearly, it takes a lot of planning, resources, expertise, and a constant commitment to maintain standards with careful monitoring to ensure an adequate level of care. A pilot project at Yale University was as close to ideal as a programme could be. Yet it was concluded that:

> When adults have a fair capacity to be parents, their young children do best when cared for mainly by parents ... Group care, even under the best circumstances, is stressful for very young children ... In contrast to the natural family setting and activities, how artificial is the daycare centre and what it can provide. It is very difficult to duplicate in the centre more than a few of the experiences most appropriate for the toddler, experiences that he could have at home without anyone giving the matter a moment's thought ... the child from one to three is not by nature a highly suitable member of a large group ... difficulties magnify as the group increases in size ... separation reactions become more acute as the day lengthens and fatigue decreases coping ability.[10]

However, even the best trained, most sensitive and highly motivated care workers are still doing a contracted job of work. A child's moral standards, sense of belonging and identity can hardly come from anyone but the parents. What is irreducible and irreplaceable is the way in which the 'spiralling strands of development that transform helpless newborns into sociable and socialised small people are plaited into their relationships with known, loved and loving adults'. The permanence, continuity and commitment required is difficult to 'meet outside the vested interests and social expectations of family roles and cannot be adequately replaced by professionalism'.[11]

Finding 'Quality'?

To what extent do *existing* establishments or childminders approximate to the kind of daycare environment we know best facilitates child development? Assessments carried out in 227 daycare centres in five metropolitan areas of the US, as part of the National Childcare Staffing Study, put the average one at a barely adequate level of quality. Only 12 per cent received a rating of 'good'.[12] In Britain, most of the nurseries in the Thomas Coram Research Unit study:

> ... were very isolated and many were under-resourced, which was reflected in poor staff: child ratios, problems with accommodation, poor pay and conditions and instability of caregivers for children.[13]

At the age of 18 months, children had staff:child ratios varying from 1:2.4 to 1:8.5, with an average of nearly 1:5.

Important conditions for 'quality' care are that there must not only be few children per adult, but few changes of staff. Yet, according to the National Childcare Staffing Study, in a one-year period four out of ten US nursery workers left their jobs. Over half of all childminders leave the work every year and there is evidence of similar high turnover in Britain.[14] In work on attachment in daycare, it took nine months for a clear majority (or 67 per cent) of infants to form an attachment to a skilled caregiver. Yet, given the nursery staff turnover rate and the common practice of moving children on to new caregivers every six or seven months, few would have this time with the same person. Further, as this data came from middle-class families and high-ability caregivers, 'the often-stated concern for infants' vulnerability in childcare ... may be understated.[15]

It is also common for observers of daycare to remark on the discrepancy between the numbers and qualified staff on paper, and the reality. Qualified staff may spend little or no time in classrooms and unqualified aides may be left to cope with large numbers of children. The Thomas Coram Research Project describes how Jamie's mother thought that a day nursery would ensure that he was looked after by qualified staff and that his development would be helped by spending time with other children. On paper there were seven full-time and five part-time staff—half with qualifications. In practice:

... there was often only one member of staff in the [toddler] room. This was partly the result of the poor morale of the staff who made little attempt to conceal their dislike of the job and therefore seized any opportunity they could to leave the room and go on 'errands'. As a result there were many times when one adult was left with as many as fourteen children. Additionally, there was so little attempt by the staff to engage with the children by talking to them or playing with them ...

Staff turnover ... was quite high and in the fifteen months that Jamie had been there he had been cared for by six different people. As there was also quite a high rate of sickness ... he had contact with considerably more than this because of all the temporary replacements ... [with] no qualifications or experience of looking after children.

The lunchtime routine was particularly difficult for toddlers.

They were left [on potties in the corridor] ... whether they had 'performed' or not and apart from instructions to 'sit down' or 'stop fidgeting' there was little or no conversation. The children then moved from the corridor to the tables... and were expected to sit quietly 'reading' ... waiting for the food to arrive. Staff did not eat with them but supervised and told children off when they were too restless.[16]

Because a centre's day has to be longer than the normal working day to allow for parental commuting, the use of shifts automatically doubles the number of people dealing with a child. Holidays, sickness, in-service training and courses all increase the number of strangers, who are 'filling in for the known caregivers who are already filling in for parents'.[17]

In Britain, most workers in local authority and, increasingly, private nurseries have a Nursery Nurse Examination Board (NNEB) qualification, a two-year course for which there are no entrance requirements. Most students start this at 16 and qualify at 18. It is within easy reach of low ability girls. In local authority nurseries, senior staff increasingly have social work or higher qualifications, particularly since these deal with disadvantaged and handicapped children. Most childminders have no training at all, although an increasing number of local authorities now offer short courses.

However, this is superior to the situation in other parts of the European Union where, despite all the claims about the fabulous childcare on tap elsewhere, it is uncommon for staff to have any qualifications at all. In the United States, each state has its own childcare regulations, and ratio regulations for infants in centres range from 1:3 to 1:8 (only three prescribe the former) and, in 80 per cent of states, no specific training is required to care for children.

> The overall regulations ... are so minimal that the possibility of having a 'qualified' staff is virtually nonexistent. ... In a majority of states, the existing regulations allow these very young children to be cared for by a staff that would have a mean age of 18, has not graduated from high school, and has no previous group daycare experience.[18]

There is no general information on quality or any overall monitoring system in Britain for the provisions in which women are everywhere being urged to leave their babies. Peter Moss, one of Britain's most vociferous equality activists and childcare advocates, candidly admits that, given:

> ... the diffuse nature of the private sector, its reliance on parental fees and the variability and general under-resourcing of the regulatory system; and the complexity of providing high-quality environments and experiences for very young children—it would be surprising if services of consistently high quality had developed. Indeed, it would be surprising if a substantial proportion were not seriously inadequate.[19]

Local authority day nurseries are the responsibility of social service departments. Private nurseries must be registered and are inspected (infrequently) by local authority social services departments. These set their own standards guided by recommendations in the Children Act 1989. This advises a staff ratio for children aged two years and under of 1:3, units of no more than 26 children in large nurseries, and at least half of the staff with a relevant qualification. Complaints that local authorities have been taking the recommendations to heart and impeding the growth of childcare have resulted in central government requesting that these be interpreted more flexibly (in effect, taken less seriously) and supervised more lightly.

The Children Act also lays down guidelines for local authorities to consider before they register a person as 'fit' for childminding, ranging from considerations of mental stability to an 'ability to provide warm and consistent care', to basic health and safety requirements. However, the registration system 'is to operate on the basis that the local authority has to be able to demonstrate why they are satisfied that a person is not fit and/or the premises and/or equipment are not suitable', with 'evidence which will stand up in court'. In reality almost anybody who applies to be registered is accepted. Indeed, the authorities sometimes register women who are known to fall below adequate standards in order to keep an eye on them and stop them minding illegally. It is very difficult to 'de-register' a minder, unless there is 'seriously inadequate care', with 'uncaring neglect'; 'gross lack of emotional and physical warmth' or 'grossly inappropriate types of activity and play opportunities'. This must be over an extended period, and it is considered particularly 'inappropriate to do this because of short-term lapses from agreed or intended ratios'.

Industrial Efficiency?

Good intentions about childcare quality have a habit of being engulfed by concerns about the sheer availability and cost. This reveals the contradictions at the heart of demands for mass childcare. Clearly, claims that childrearing at home is outmoded, inefficient and costly in terms of the loss of the mother's labour power, must be weighed against the extraordinary difficulties of rearing children effectively outside the home. At the heart of the argument for the economic advantages of daycare are assumptions that there are economies of scale to be achieved by having one person look after lots of infants, while a mother is only looking after one or two at a time. The 'spare capacity' represented by under-utilised maternal earning power can then be converted into a surplus for herself and the state and even profits for the caring institution. This is virtually inseparable from beliefs that women are 'over-qualified' for looking after children. As the implication is that this can be handed over to someone whose labour is worth less than the mother's own then it is not surprising that childcare workers are at the bottom of the earnings scale. (The worst paying jobs in the UK in 1994 were waitress at £137 per week, sewing machinist at £155.00 and childcarer at £146.00.)[20]

Production line systems fundamental to industrial enterprises are antithetical to the personalised attention, constancy and attachment basic to caregiving and the process of human socialisation.[21] Teams of interchangeable people may be able to clean premises but, while it matters little if floors are swept by different people every week, it matters a lot if children's caregivers are repeatedly changed. The more economies of scale a centre employs, the worse the care, and the poorer the results. This is particularly true for babies. Human young do not come in litters. Even parents of large families have children of different ages. We often hear how difficult, if not impossible, it is for parents of triplets to manage even the basic physical care of three babies at a time. What hope, then, for the childminder in charge of eight, six or even four?

However, if children are to be raised in large groups, then assembly line methods have to be devised to make that possible. In her book *The Daycare Dilemma* Marion Blum provides illustrations of various devices designed and manufactured for American daycare centres. There are the 'double-decker cribs'; two-up and two-down. To make efficient use of space and personnel, they are advertised as enabling the caregiver to keep four babies in open view without constant attention. The children cannot stand up in the first level and, with the sides and the backs closed, they can hears sounds from the other cots, but not see the occupants or who the caregiver is coming towards.[22] Another involves an 'eating facility', or a table with slots in which to place babies to allow four to be fed at once. In Britain, a handcart seating six babies, with three a side, is proudly displayed in a newspaper to illustrate how the City of London is furthering the interests of its female staff.

A central problem in daycare is the effective management and organisation of large groups of young children in a confined space for long hours. If this is integrally linked to mass daycare, then a policy of containment easily emerges. Just what this means is illustrated in accounts of the lives of children observed over a two year period in different centres in the American mid-west. They were not chosen as the best or the worst and, on paper, most would have 'been considered adequate if not good'. To cater for parents working patterns they may, like Mary Moppets' Daycare Centre in Arizona, open from 6.30 a.m. until 1:30 a.m. six days a week. Licensed for fifty children, these 'come and go constantly. The children don't know one another and the teachers don't know them'.[23]

Another, the Lollipop Learning Centre, held approximately 70 children from two to six in a two tier system. Daycare was provided for low income and single working mothers, while mainly middle-class children went to nursery classes offering 'a more cognitive emphasis'. To the outsider, 'the centre had many advantages, in being convenient, offering a full day and requiring no parental participation whatsoever'. It had one certified nursery school teacher in addition to several assistants, aides, and high school students. (The proprietor was a certified teacher, but out much of the time.) It enrolled the maximum number of children possible. This way, the place was filled to capacity and, through spatial rotation, met the licensing code requirements.

As I entered the school this morning, thirty three-year-old daycare children were sitting cross-legged, lining the wall of the corridor outside the art room. The noise was deafening. Children were screaming, crying, and hitting each other. The three teacher aides stood by impassively and did not intervene. One little girl lay on the floor sobbing and calling, 'Mama, Mama', but no one took any notice of her. As the nursery children emerged from the art room, the daycare children stood up and rushed in, shouting and pushing each other.

When one considers the fact that two-thirds of these children spent ten hours a day, five days a week, at the school, the need to form relationships with

other significant adults becomes a critical issue. A great number of the children
... tended to cling to the teachers and aides. Many cried for their parents during
the day. However, despite the evinced need for significant attachment, the
children were not able to form any long-term relationships with adults. ... In
one and a half years I observed six changes of staff in the daycare and five in
the nursery school.[24]

With the children simply 'contained within an atmosphere of chaos,
confusion and impersonality',[25] and unable to form meaningful relationships with any staff member, how did they see the world? The older
daycare children were either hostile or indifferent to the adults, 'while the
younger tended to struggle toward the formation of an attachment despite
the frequent rejection and subsequent departure on the part of the staff'.[26]
The children were tabled for a 'cognitive lesson' each day. However:

> Much of what the staff aides attempted to 'teach' to the children was crudely
> inapplicable to their developmental level or did not capture their interest. Apart
> from TV which was considered educational ...[typically] one aide attempted to
> read a book while two others patrolled the room... Two children were hitting
> each other, two were screaming, and three or four were running around trying
> to escape the aide. ...[One aide] showed the children a picture of a coffee pot
> adjacent to a drum and asked, 'is the coffee pot a drum?' No one answered. The
> aide replied: 'No. Is this (pointing to a drum) a drum? Yes. Why? Because he
> pounds on it. Is a house a park bench? No. Why? Because you can't sit on it.
> Buttered toast is not a toy. Do you think it is a toy? No. Why? Because you can't
> play with it.'

> The above conversation was conducted as an entire monologue, in which the
> aide both asked and responded to her own absurd questions.[27]

Again, while the nursery school section of Lollipop Learning Centre
boasted a tightly planned curriculum, geared to early cognitive skills,
reading readiness and conversational French, the reality was drilling, rote
and repetition, and the making of impressive displays to put on walls or
give to parents, where the children just coloured in easy bits or put their
names on the exhibits.

No service can (or should) run on an unrestricted budget, but in daycare
keeping costs low has a serious impact on the human and physical
environment of the child. Plentiful American evidence suggests how 'for-
profit childcare services are past masters at living on the edge of
compliance when it comes to regulations related, for example, to training
or staff ratios. One way is to hire the minimum number of trained staff
allowed and structure the classes in 'accordion style':

> A few children arrive between 7:00 and 8:00 and are placed in a room with one
> caregiver. At 8:00 more children arrive, so the group is divided and two
> caregivers are now required ... By 9:00, most children have arrived, four groups
> are created, and perhaps as many as six caregivers are available. At the end of
> the day the accordion folds back up ... From the child's perspective, it is possible
> to experience five different groups of peers and at least that many different staff
> during a single day.[28]

In turn, if multi-use of one space is disallowed for health reasons, the children may play, eat and sleep in relays. As they are constantly 'rotated' around the premises this ensures maximum utilisation of all facilities at any one time.

If childcare is a business, then the profit motive is bound to dominate questions of space, time, staff services, children's experiences, and the overall social and physical landscape. Overwhelmingly, worldwide evidence is that 'for profit' provisions tend to be the low-quality provisions. While there is much glossy deception involved in selling the product, the outcome of a system in which children are 'instrumental resources, the parents are consumers ... is frequently an abusive childcare system.' With the insignificance of the child in many 'childcare' institutions described as alarming:

> ... it is not ... human development ... that is fostered, but rather how many children can be contained within the structure for the least amount of money ... it is under these conditions that a profit turnover can be increased and it is these very conditions which produce fragmentation, hostility, violence and severe forms of alienation, contributing to the overwhelming experience of anomie within the life-world of the child.[29]

In texts like *Women and Paid Work*, writers obsessed with equal employment outcomes wax enthusiastic at the 'success' of 'more aggressive enforcement of equal opportunities laws' and tax deductions for childcare in putting more American mothers into full-time jobs.[30] The other side of the coin, involving not only the financial crisis of the American family, but the many horrifying accounts of life in childcare centres and at minders, go unmentioned.

Since childcare is such a labour-intensive enterprise, any increase in the staffing levels or their salaries to attract qualified and better workers drives up the costs and reverses economies of scale. Given the prohibitive costs of running a good centre, particularly for babies, and the need to keep fees reasonably low, good daycare is almost a non-profit commodity. Without very substantial subsidies, nurseries must compromise on accommodation and equipment, staff levels, staff pay and conditions, cover for absent staff, etc., as the private nurseries in London did in the Thomas Coram Research Unit study.

Daycare of a high or, at least, reasonable quality is more often found in the public sector in western countries. In Sweden the cost of a place has been at around two-thirds of the average wage. (The national government and the municipalities each contribute around 45 per cent of the costs.) However, attempts in Sweden and Denmark to increase provision have meant an uphill struggle. Expansion tends to increase, not decrease, costs, create shortages (particularly of trained or competent personnel) and militates against the maintenance of standards. Although daycare became the largest single item on many Swedish municipalities' budgets in the 1970s, and the construction of a network of care facilities proceeded apace (with the number of nursery places increasing tenfold between 1960 and 1980), the timescale for national coverage of all pre-school age children was continually revised. By 1987, only 19 per cent of under-threes were in municipal nurseries, and this rose to a third of under-sevens (the age for formal schooling) by the 1990s (although the figures are much lower for children of two-parent families compared to those of lone parents). Over 50 per cent of under-threes received no substitute care at all. In the 1980s the move away from detailed regulation of nursery conditions by the central government meant that group size began to creep up and space contracted, reflecting harsher economic conditions and pressure to expand daycare.[31]

An Unskilled Job?

Often, the 'professionalisation' of childcare is blamed for the complexities, 'artificiality' and difficulties of providing for children outside the home. According to this analysis, the ambitions and pretensions of obstructionist bureaucrats, or the obscurantism of 'experts' out of touch with the way in which ordinary people have reared children through millennia, stand in the way of cheap, available, and even better childcare.

Childcare is certainly an area where one frequently encounters attitudes that are contemptuous of childrearing and barbarous towards children. This is seen as a low-grade, irrelevant activity, which any idiot (literally) could take care of: 'Can't you use empty garages/Nissan huts and get some unemployed teenager/pensioner to baby-sit for some pocket money?' For those who see the world in gender terms, issues of programme quality and child development may be seen as devices to impede the advancement of women. For the free market devotee, rules and inspections are unwarranted obstacles to the entrepreneur providing a much needed service. The worst fears are confirmed by the demands of the local social services that there be enough 'differentially abled' dolls, or black Lego persons with approved negroid features.

Exponents of both the private daycare market and the public sector often take in each other's washing, and both miss the point. Many who speak of public investment in high-quality childcare see this in terms of the promotion of social change by altering value systems, family behaviour, attitudes and perceptions of sexual identity. The development of the child is subsidiary to these concerns, just as it is seen as unproblematic by the entrepreneur who believes that protection is largely superfluous, in contrast to almost every other consumer area.

Ignorance abounds. A lady who runs a private nursery complains about 'petty rules' that can 'put nurseries out of business', and that 'nothing is safe' from the social service inspectors policing the Children Act. 'Instead of a jug of water for children to wash their hands she must have hot and cold running water with thermostatically-controlled tap', just as child-minders were apparently advised to use an outside tap for rinsing potties, not the kitchen sink.[32] It does not appear to be appreciated that hygiene precautions are necessary to prevent infection, which is why shops, restaurants and hotels are expected to observe strict and detailed rules to protect customers from disease. Similarly, while adult/child ratios are basic to the care children will receive, we find the childcare provider jibbing at a reduction in registration from 60 to 40 children:

> Staffing ratios were previously one to ten. Now they are one to eight for three-to-fives. I have stopped taking under-threes because the new ratio represents an increase of 50 per cent on the wages bill, which is lunatic.[33]

There is also the very serious question of protecting children from abuse. Paedophiles gravitate towards jobs with children. Cases like that of Jason Dabbs, a male nursery nurse at two council nurseries in Newcastle, who indecently assaulted up to 60 children before being detected, point to the need for strict guidelines and supervision of staff who work with pre-school children.[34] At present, while staff in public nurseries must be vetted through police records (a poor guide anyway), the same does not apply to the private and voluntary sectors, where only the owner has to be checked out.

Critics of centre-care often favour childminding as a more natural environment for the child, who spends the day in the home of a 'motherly' woman, who can 'also make forays ... into the ordinary life of the community'.[35] Since mothers and grandmothers have been raising children for centuries, there is no reason to insist on qualifications or training. Many daycare providers agree, especially childminders: 'the most common response by far is that once your've been a mother yourself you know how to handle children, you have nothing to learn'.[36]

However, relatives do have a blood or legal tie to the children and usually love those they are minding. In contrast, the childminders Brian Jackson categorized as *maternal minders* 'invariably have a weak sense of how a child might grow educatively', while those who take in other people's children not only for income, but companionship for their own children, 'may treat the strangers very much as second-class children'.[37] As we have seen, minders often do not establish a relationship with the minded child. This process occurs normally when the child is one's own, but when it is someone else's child it has to be worked at, and many minders are not aware of this need.[38] The minder easily falls between two stools. While not acting like a mother to her charges, she may also not be trained or motivated to provide what a nursery nurse provides as part of a work role. It may be thought perfectly adequate simply to keep the child fed, clean and warm and that this constitutes 'quality care'.

Time To Go Home?

'Did he have fun at his club?' asked Mr Clive Soley, the Labour MP for
Hammersmith and committee chairman. Nodding, he replied: 'I like to play
outside. I like making models. I like to play the games: and I have lots of
friends'. 'Would you be cross if it wasn't there?' Mr Soley continued. 'Yes', came
the emphatic answer.
'MPs are told about childcare benefits by an expert, aged seven'
The Daily Telegraph[1]

After-school care for older children, whether to age 12 or 14, is now
promoted, like childcare in infancy, as another essential and unmitigated
good. Again, this development is occurring in the absence of much
investigation of the effects on children. Penelope Leach believes that they
are being advanced without much regard for children as people at all.
Would adults like to spend their holidays or non-working time in the office
or factory?

Most small children already find the school day stressful; many find the
buildings, and the groups within them, uncomfortably large. To those who are
only just coping with a short day supported by familiar teachers, a longer day
finishing with a different adult must be intolerable. And even somewhat older
children who can cope with these programmes often do not want to: 'We like to
play with our friends after school. We want to go home'.[2]

When parents are unavailable, the alternatives to after-school care, or
a minder, are latchkeys or 'self-care' where, to say the least, 'no study has
clearly indicated that self-care is related to positive outcomes'.[3] At young
ages safety is likely to be the primary concern and, as children get older,
it is unsupervised peer involvement, associated as this is with problem
behaviour, for both girls and boys. A large scale study in Los Angeles and
San Diego showed a significant positive relationship between level of
substance abuse among adolescents and time spent in 'self-care' after
school.[4] In turn, Laurence Steinberg's sample of a cross section of 865
adolescents from schools in Madison (Winconsin) showed how those who
were at home alone were less susceptible to peer pressure than those at
a friend's house, or who were 'hanging out'. The same applied to those
whose parents knew their whereabouts, even when they spent their time
in contexts where adult supervision was low. However, adolescents with
fully employed mothers, or from single-parent and step-families, were
more likely to be unsupervised, whether at home or at a friend's house, or

to be 'hanging out'—independently of socio-economic status.[5]

While a child who is securely at home alone is least likely to get into trouble or keep dubious company, this still may not be an entirely satisfactory solution considered in humane terms.

> My mum and dad both work full-time and we live out of town so they never get home till about 8 o'clock and its awful.
>
> I feel so miserable just wandering about the house on my own. I don't feel scared or anything, just lonely and sad. Once though, I did get a fright when a man came to the door selling stuff and wouldn't go away. Now I don't answer the door at all.
>
> I just wish that they would think about how lonely I am. Sometimes I only see them for about an hour each day. I just wish that one week things could be different.[6]

As it becomes available, parents may use after-school care when they believe that their children need adult supervision, or company in the hours before they return from work. The effects are not a foregone conclusion. There is the possibility that children from some backgrounds may do worse than if they were at home with mother, or compared with being at home alone. Others, especially those who may be more prone to anti-social behaviour, might do better. Difficult children will not be roaming free to do mischief—although this may be at the cost of contaminating others.

This may go some way to explain the somewhat contradictory results from the very limited American studies which deal with after-school care. Data from the National Longitudinal Survey of Youth, on children aged eight to ten, showed that those in the care of mothers after school had higher ratings for anti-social behaviour, anxiety and peer conflict compared with children in other adult care, and scored lower on an IQ test.[7] (Although latchkey children also had more behaviour problems.) However, this finding was entirely accounted for by the negative outcomes for children from single parent households, where they received little comfort, support and supervision.

Research which concentrated on the after-school arrangements of white, predominantly middle-class eight-year-olds from a suburban school system tells a different story. Children returned home to their mothers, attended care centres, stayed with childminders or baby-sitters, or went home alone or with siblings. Significantly, the children who attended centres received more negative peer evaluations (relating to aggression, sharing, co-operation etc.) made lower academic grades, and had lower scores for basic skills and intellectual abilities than either mother-care or latchkey children. Those who went to minders also had more negative peer reports, but were otherwise similar to the mother-care or latchkey children.[8]

Even here, it is difficult to tell whether any detrimental effects are related directly to after-school care, as after-school care children are more likely to have been in infant daycare as well. However, in the far-reaching Vandell and Corasaniti study of the effects of daycare on Texan children,[9] the emotional well-being of children was closely related to going home to mothers after school, rather than to an alternative arrangement, even when earlier childcare experience was taken into account.

The quality of many after-school programmes is low. They may have large numbers of children, a small number of staff and limited activities. Children are often kept amused by videos and computer games. One young boy described a holiday play scheme in a London borough to me as 'television, plasticine and playground', and hated going because of the bullying. If such schemes were better organised, with supervision for homework, for example, then they would constitute a structured extension of the school day, needing to employ para-educational staff.

In spite of the fact that non-parental agencies are supposed to take over the rearing of children for greater and greater parts of the day and the year, The Children Act 1989 *only requires local authorities to regulate daycare and supervised activities for children under eight years old.* Its principle recommendations are that there should be a sufficient staff *in total* to maintain a 1:8 ratio, with half the staff having some form of qualification in teaching, youth or social work, a toilet facility for every ten children and 2.3 square metres of space per child.[10]

As there is little interest in outcomes, it is not surprising that nothing has been done to discover the conditions and activities most likely to meet the needs of children or adolescents in 'out-of-school' care. For example, should staff be allocated to particular children or teenagers—considering that they may spend little time at home with a familiar adult? The Children Act casts the staff as essentially passive. It is simply:

... desirable for people working with children in out-of-school or holiday settings to develop skills in observing what the children are doing and to assess the implication in terms of child development and planning future activities.[11]

If 'providers' of out-of-school care merely maintain control, or ensure basic safety, how is this to be done? Somewhat alarmingly, open access facilities—where the children come and go at will—are welcomed in the Children Act 1989 as a 'valuable resource because they add to the variety of the services available and offer children as they grow older more scope to develop confidence and social skills'.[12] There is nothing on how numbers, which could include gangs of youths, are to be managed, except that providers are somehow 'to ensure that the overall numbers do not put children at risk of injury or accident. The five- to seven-year-olds are more vulnerable than the older children particularly when the facility becomes crowded'.[13]

Uncertainty about which rules to apply to out-of-school care is combined with lack of a clear definition of the role or status of school-age assistants. They do not have an identity as childcare workers, as staff working with pre-schoolers do. While they may work in a school building '... they are not

teachers; indeed, in some school-based programmes, regular classroom
teachers make it quite clear that school-age staff are second class citizens'.
Yet: 'They are often called upon to help children with homework or to act
as a liaison between the child or family and the school. Furthermore,
children often refer to them, quite naturally, as teachers.' In turn, while
they supervise leisure, 'they are not really recreation leaders either'.[14]

When it comes to the school years, the eagerness to replace parents
seems to be combined with an extraordinary vagueness about who or what
is supposed to take their place.

SECTION C

EDUCARE

The campaign for childcare has become entwined with that for early education, as it has been claimed that children who begin their formal education at young ages do better later. However, this campaign really has more to do with the needs of working mothers than their children. Small children do not benefit from long periods in group situations, whether it is called childcare or early education. The small advantages which early education seems to give some children may not be long-term, and it may only be children from very disadvantaged homes who benefit at all. Parental input is the most important factor in child development. However good pre-school education becomes, it will not be able to compensate for the problems children experience as a result of family breakdown and, particularly, fatherless homes.

The discussion of both childcare and early education has been compli-cated by repeated references to lavishly-funded 'show projects' which bear little relation to what can actually be achieved for ordinary parents and their children. None has been more frequently cited than the Perry Pre-School Project, which is supposed to have demonstrated that for every dollar spent on pre-school education, seven dollars was later saved in social services costs. However, as the Perry researchers themselves were at pains to point out, it was absolutely untypical. The resources were lavish and the Project relied as much on home-visits as on centre-based programmes. If Perry tells us anything relevant, it is that parents play a vital role in the success of any pre-school intervention programme.

A Head Start?

*We all know that giving children the opportunity of nursery education
improves their life chances. Investment in the early years of a child's life pays
enormous dividends for both child and society. We should be aiming to break
down the traditional barriers between childcare and education, and to create
comprehensive and integrated services which are grounded in the needs of
children and that have a clear educational focus.*

Margaret Hodge, *The Daily Telegraph*[1]

The belief that children in daycare are getting something over and above
what they could get at home from parents is clearly dependent upon the
way in which this has acquired an 'educational' image. As parents are not
expected, or do not feel knowledgeable enough, to provide schooling for
older children so, similarly, they may also feel that early education is
something which they are hardly equipped to provide, but which it is
advantageous for their child to receive.

The growth of nursery education has become an educational priority
which figures on the agenda of all political parties. The 1989 Education,
Science and Arts Committee urged central and local government to ensure
its 'steady expansion', with the goal of free places for all three- and four-
year-olds. Similarly, The National Commission on Education report
Learning to Succeed wanted education (whether in nursery schools,
classes, playgroups and daycare settings) for 85 per cent of three-year-olds
and 95 per cent of four-year-olds, and the Labour party is planning such
an entitlement.

The Major government was persuaded to proceed with a voucher
scheme for four-year-olds, under which parents would receive £1,100
towards the cost of nursery education provided by private, voluntary and
public schemes, mainly paid for by re-cycling the £548 million current
(1995) expenditure on nursery education by local education authorities
(LEAs).

More Is Better

Pre-school education has usually meant children over three in kindergar-
tens, playgroups or nursery schools, which provide the under-fives with
the skills, knowledge and social competence thought necessary for
achievement in later schooling.[2] However the view is now being advanced
that children can never have enough of school, or never have it early
enough, so that if there are benefits at four, there will be even more if
'education' starts at three, two or one.

Most important is the promise to kill two birds with one stone, with 'a comprehensive approach to integrate education and care into a seamless service for children under five'.[3] With pre-schooling seen in terms of measures to obviate the 'stress and guilt induced in working, and would-be working, mothers',[4] it is widely assumed that a national system of nursery education is the same as a network of crèches that enables mothers to work. Anyway, according to the Education, Science and Arts Committee, nursery education has become necessary *because* mothers work, and because rising divorce rates and the growth of lone parents means that public services must take over more of the rearing of children that previously fell to families.[5] The National Commission on Education's report *Learning to Succeed* employs much the same reasoning.[6] It is continually suggested that other countries are embarking on earlier and earlier mass daycare with long hours in order to promote child development while women are in full-time employment.[7]

However, the aims of furthering maternal employment and early education are distinct and a measure which facilitates one may do little or nothing to foster the other. Discussion of the desirability or the effectiveness of early education becomes difficult when the two issues are conflated. The numbers of disturbed children with language problems in the childminding studies of Bridget Bryant and colleagues in Oxfordshire, or of B. Mayell and P. Petrie in Inner London, do not point to much educational benefit from the frequently unhappy hours the children spent with often unresponsive and ignorant women.[8] Clearly, when a child spends 11 or 12 hours of his waking day 'in the care of indifferent custodians, no parent and no educator can say that the child's development is being promoted or enhanced and common sense says that children are harmed by indifference'.[9]

In turn, local authorities in Britain have been 'pushing down' the school admission age, and taking more under-fives into full-time primary education (or 47.3 per cent in England in 1992, and 62.1 per cent in Wales), when available evidence suggests that this may militate against later school success.[10] Classroom organisation, curriculum objectives and teaching styles designed for one age group are being applied to younger children. To this we can add unsuitable class sizes, problems with outdoor play, inappropriate ratios of adults to children, and an overlong school day. When H.M. Inspectors surveyed nursery and primary schools in the mid-1980s, only a small number were working in a way suited to the needs of under-fives.[11] This policy, often contrary to the interests of children, is widely exonerated on the grounds that they are safely 'at school', while mothers can work. Everyone is happy—except the children and teachers reporting distressed and confused pupils who, at most, should be in specially designed, short day, nursery programmes.

A fundamental problem with the notion of 'educare' is that it is trying to serve conflicting ends. Nursery schools, nursery classes and playgroups are essentially oriented to the educational needs of young children.

Children attend for only a short period, perhaps two or three hours a day, and are gradually introduced to a new world, often on a staggered basis. The advantages of long as against short, and frequent as against occasional, periods of attendance depend upon the individual child's maturity and the number of sessions he can cope with. The pattern of attendance suits the needs of the child, not those of adults, whether working parents, employers, policy makers or ideologues.

Even so, this is largely irrelevant to babies. Certainly, a 'curriculum' is necessary if non-relatives are going to care competently for other people's children. But this—as we saw—largely amounts to the professional systematization and application of everyday parental practice. While it is often envisaged that a group situation would be ideal to stop a toddler from becoming bored at home, this:

> ... does not mean that he is bored of being adult-centred but only that he is ready for new activities. He finds other children fascinating and will enjoy spending time playing near and alongside them, but that does not mean that he is ready to make real friends and be their classmate ... he, too, wants to paint and climb and sing and cook, but, unlike those three-year-olds, his enjoyment and his learning depend on adult participation or at least adult support and commentary. And, far from being even a replacement for that individual adult attention, a group of other toddlers—each as needful of the adult as himself—introduces competition and social stresses he is not yet capable of dealing with.[12]

Children go into daycare when mothers get a job. A small child may just be beginning to enjoy play with other children, and might be able to sustain it for 30 or 45 minutes. But children are in care centres for eight, ten or twelve hours—having to engage in social relations for periods of time that would stress the most gregarious adult, and are ten times longer than what many child development experts consider enough for the pre-school child.[13] Even if specifically educational provisions, or a school-oriented curriculum, are grafted onto daycare, there is a point of diminishing returns, and finally a time in the nursery day at which no educational benefits could possibly accrue to the child. 'By afternoon, restlessness, tearfulness, whininess, or lassitude become endemic. Even the most expert teachers have problems in sustaining the programme and restoring harmony', where what we see is a 'longing for mother and home'.[14]

The 'preoccupation ... with cognitive learning—what a child learns to do, at what age' may ignore 'the affective side ... derived from the experience of love, obtained hour after hour, and not marred by repeated disappointments and losses'.[15]

What Do They Get?

Home and school offer different kinds of experience. Any advantages which young children in pre-school may sometimes show over those who do not attend largely relate to very specific forms of social and intellectual knowledge and skills.[16] It is not due to differences in the amount, but the kind, of attention.

After all, even caregivers in reasonable or good centres and teachers in nursery schools do not, on average, interact more with children than people at home, or provide more stimulation. A systematic educational approach is the likely candidate. The intellectual emphasis, combined with the presence of educational materials, and the influence of institutional regulations, create an environment that facilitates the development of school-related aptitudes or skills.

Just as it will not ensure a daycare infant's development, so there is also nothing of educational benefit for a child in simply being with extra-familial adults and a group of peers each day. An emphasis on free play, or open and fluid programmes, is also not associated with gains. As observed in British pre-school institutions in the mid 1970s, where there was no avowed educational aim or programme in operation, the least talk is addressed to the children, the lowest amount of information given, and the least time spent showing children how to do things.[17] What is important are purposive or goal-directed play experiences, which can lay foundations for literacy and numeracy, rather than simply materials and supervision for what may be time-consuming but undemanding or meaningless activities. Where there are more prescribed lessons, guided play sessions, and more direct teacher instruction, children can be expected to perform at a higher and more complex level.

However, it is clear from many observational accounts of the 'educational' or 'formal activities' provided by daycare centres that these are often inappropriate for the children. For example:

... the toddlers were asked to sit at a table and thread small beads on to a string. They found this very difficult as they were mostly too young to have the necessary manual skills, or the ability to concentrate for any length of time. The adult in charge did not sit down with them but told them to get on with it while she looked in a cupboard for some more string ... the children were frustrated and began throwing beads at each other ... there was chaos. Two children were crying, one very withdrawn child had gone ... to a corner of the room where she was sucking her thumb and rocking back and forth, and the remaining three had half-heartedly joined in the bead throwing.[18]

Moreover, even where the practice in pre-schools may be more 'educational' than typical practice in homes, this is not a *necessary* difference between the two environments. Where daycare provides the context for early education, there may be possible detrimental effects of one to offset against the other. Since it is not a foregone conclusion that there are necessarily any educational pluses for some children when they go to 'educare', the overall balance might be negative.

Two Large-scale Studies

Two large-scale studies suggest that this is the case. Many of the 2,387 American children aged between one and four in the 1986 National Longitudinal Survey of Work Experience of Youth[19] had experienced some form of regular childcare beginning in the first year of life. After controlling for factors like family structure, family size, education, employment and income, the only advantage of going to more formal, or educational provisions, was for three- to four-year-olds on one cognitive test, the Peabody Picture Vocabulary Test. However, this applied to girls only, who might be able to cope with 'relatively more hostile environments from an early age'. There was no similar effect for boys, and children with health problems did better intellectually when they remained with their mothers. Non-healthy boys also did better on physical and social development when they had exclusive early maternal care.

Similar conclusions emerge from a study[20] of the long-term effects of childcare and maternal employment on 333 six- to twelve-year-old middle-class Seattle children. Home-based care was typically used by working mothers in the first year of life, with centre-care or pre-school dominating for three- to four-year-olds. The centres or pre-schools attended were of average to high quality, with better educated staff than the generality of American centres. Time spent in facilities with an educational content was only associated with better intellectual skills for Afro-American children. The suggestion is that it provided reading materials and activities helpful to later academic achievement for middle-class black children who were less likely than their white counterparts to receive these at home. Otherwise, mothers of children from all ethnic groups who had attended centres reported raised levels of difficult, aggressive behaviour.

What Gains and For How Long?

When it comes to heavily disadvantaged children, there is little difficulty finding reports of early intellectual gains associated with pre-school provisions—particularly when they have been the beneficiaries of the experimental early educational or nursery stimulation programmes which have burgeoned in the US. A dip into the literature yields numerous studies like the following:

- In the work of Margaret Burchinal and colleagues[21] 151 children were randomly assigned either to a group which received an intensive, university-based intervention programme from babyhood, or one which went to community-based 'quality' daycare projects of varying durations. Others had parents who chose little or no centre-based daycare. (98 per cent were black, and 80 per cent had single mothers).

  University-based intervention was most successful in improving the intellectual performance of these very disadvantaged children in the pre-school period, although at least a year at a 'quality' centre also helped.

- An early intervention project at the University of North Carolina, for infants at high risk of delayed development due to the circumstances and low intelligence of their parents,[22] used a teacher ratio of 1:4 for two-year-olds and 1:6 for three- to five-year-olds. Very experienced staff received intensive training in maximising communication 'modelled on what a nurturant and developmentally encouraging mother might establish with her child'.[23] Family support was also given to children who received the programme and some who did not, covering skills relevant to effective parenting and household management. The average age at entry was nearly two years, although some did not enter until much later. Other children in the control group went to a less intensive programme of 'quality' community care, for varying lengths of time—with or without parental education.

At four-and-a-half, those children who had been to the experimental programme plus family education scored highest, followed by those in the 'quality' community care facility. As elsewhere, a period of at least a year seemed to enhance intellectual development almost as well as participation in an intensive experimental programme from babyhood until five.

- Alice M. Gordon argues that low-income children are particularly handicapped at school by the failure to communicate effectively. Accordingly, disadvantaged children in a daycare group received language input from specially trained teachers using the kind of reflective, problem solving, creative and abstract talk that middle-class mothers are more likely to have with their children.[24] As a result, the children entered school functioning at a more adequate level in formal adult/child conversation compared to non-intervention groups.

It seems that, on the whole, short intervention periods in the year or so before entering school are almost or as effective as longer, earlier periods, and short sessions, with limited hours per week, are as effective as longer days. However, the differences in intellectual test scores between attenders of special pre-schools or intensive nursery stimulation projects and non-attenders tend not to be permanent. Although there are exceptions, they often last for only a short time after starting ordinary school. It is generally not appreciated how a temporary enhancement of intellect often amounts to a postponement or attenuation of the 'decline' which often occurs with high-risk populations after 18 months.

However, early intellectual gains, even if they are unlikely to be retained, may help disadvantaged children adapt better to the demands of schooling and contribute to long-term improvements in performance and commitment to school. Moreover, evidence suggests that reductions in special education placement, or being held back a grade (under-performing children do not necessarily move upwards with their year in US schools), or social disabilities like unemployment, crime or welfare dependency—*where these can be associated with early education programmes at all*—may be more important over the long term than the rapidly fading early intellectual gains.[25]

The evidence on the longer term impact of early educational and nursery stimulation programmes tends to be organised into study sets. Prominent among these is the Consortium of Longitudinal Studies,[26] where 11 projects which originated between 1962 and 1972 collected information on the subsequent development of as many of the original children as possible. (Five of the projects had been able to randomly allocate children to either a programme or the control group.)

Where significant differences in IQ at an early age had been recorded in favour of children who had been in the programmes, these had generally evaporated by mid-childhood. With tests of reading and maths for children aged up to ten, in only three projects were the results significant and this significance disappeared over the years. Four of the projects reported results ten years or more after the intervention. These showed how, averaged across these projects, only 13 per cent of programme children, as compared to about 31 per cent of controls, had ever been placed in special education. In turn, 32 per cent of experimentals compared to 47 per cent of controls had been kept down a grade by the end of secondary school.

When we come to the social factors, only a couple of the programmes suggested that the frequency or consequences of teen pregnancy, like early termination of education, were somewhat reduced. Two of the studies showed similar (but somewhat stronger effects) for lower crime and recidivism among programme subjects. Information on employment from four projects provides results favouring programme groups, although 'the reasonable conclusion is that weak evidence links quality programmes with employment', as it does for lower rates of welfare dependency.

Overall, the results of the Consortium 'do not support extravagant claims'.[27] Many of its projects obviously had no or little enduring effect on most aspects of development. Other series of studies only include projects which reported long-term effects, indicating that there is much research into the effects of early education which is inconclusive. Studies which show little or no positive effect from attendance at pre-school institutions, short- or long-term, are less likely to be published or, if they are, they are soon forgotten.

How Far Ahead?

Evidence about Head Start may be as or more valuable than that from exemplary programmes. It is a large-scale, community-based, pre-school programme, as well as also being home to a variety of model and demonstration projects.[28] In 1993 there were 1,370 Head Start grantees serving over 714,000 children (mainly below the poverty line) in the 50 states, Puerto Rico and the Pacific territories. Each programme includes six components: early childhood education, health screening and referral, mental health services, nutrition education and meals, social services for families, and parental involvement. Although all programmes must adhere to national performance standards, they are encouraged to adapt to local needs. Parents are also encouraged to take active roles in classes and each programme is administered by a Policy Council, half of whose members must be parents of enrolled children.

The accumulated research on Head Start shows that this also has short-term effects on IQ, school readiness and achievement tests. These decline as children pass through school and none are educationally meaningful after the first year. The impact on special education placement and other measures of long-term effects are less than with 'model' projects. Of the few vigorous studies of long-term effects, a couple showing less special school placement, or children being retained in grade longer, are contradicted by others showing no benefits. There is little or no evidence of any effects on social measures. However, Head Start is difficult to evaluate, not least because of the high geographical mobility of the poor. Moreover, if suggestions are correct that Head Start children are more disadvantaged than those on the waiting lists for places, this could have led to under-estimations of the effects.

The British Experience

When it followed up subjects born in 1970, the Child Health and Development Study[29] found associations between attendance at pre-school institutions and increased test achievement on school-related abilities and skills at ages five and ten. While the differences explained by the main pre-school placement were substantially reduced after adjustment for family size, neighbourhood and social class, children with no pre-school experience were more likely to score below average. Attendance at local authority day nurseries was also associated with lower scores in five of the seven tests. The children did not differ in their overall scores from those children with no pre-school experience, or who started attending infant school before five. Similarly, children who went to nursery classes in primary schools had lower than average scores in some tests, and disadvantaged children seemed to do particularly badly. In contrast, children who attended local authority nursery schools achieved higher than average scores in all except one test, with the highest scores being for the reading and maths. Those who attended hall playgroups had above average mean scores on all the tests and were comparable to the LEA nursery school children in their five-year tests and ten-year reading and maths scores. Children who went to small playgroups held at home had the highest scores in every test but one (maths). When mothers helped at the pre-school institution, children had better vocabulary at ages five and ten, were better at reading and maths at ten and were assessed by teachers as having better communication skills.

There was no relationship between the *amount* of pre-school education (sessions per week or duration in months) and the measures of children's abilities. The attainment of children who attended a couple of sessions a week was not significantly different from that of others who attended more than five. However, children who spent more than five sessions a week in a pre-school placement were more likely to show anti-social behaviour than non-attenders or half-time attenders. The persistence of behaviour problems at the age of ten was, as we have seen, particularly associated with day nurseries. There was no evidence that pre-school education had a positive effect on social behaviour.

While they had the best test results, it is nonetheless difficult to decide whether home playgroups were 'singularly effective in promoting children's cognitive development' or whether, despite all the controls, 'they still represented a highly selected group of children of above average ability'. The children were in small groups, with a higher ratio of adults, which were least likely to have children with behaviour or social problems, being located in rural or well-to-do areas. This 'combination of a homely atmosphere with a small number of children from socially advantaged, and probably stimulating, home backgrounds in home playgroups may well provide the optimal learning environment for very young children'.[30]

Playgroup or Nursery School?

It has clearly been difficult to separate the institutional and home background effects on children's intellectual and educational progress. Without close parental involvement to make them ideal environments for early learning, playgroups per se may not be so effective in delivering short-term results as other more formal or structured pre-school provisions. Other work which has taken close account of social class in relation to attendance at either nursery school or playgroup found that being a member of an advantaged social group gave children a lead over average children of four to six months at age seven. Going to playgroup gave an advantage of approximately two months and attending nursery education an advantage of four to six months—something which would be of particular help to disadvantaged children.[31] These effects seem to match inspection grades for nursery schools and playgroups.[32]

Similar results were obtained by a Newcastle University analysis for the Audit Commission of children's learning on entry to infant school (involving 2,678 pupils from 71 schools in 11 different local authority areas).[33] Pupils with a nursery education scored significantly higher than those who did not take part, even if they had been to playgroup.

No type of pre-school provision consistently out-performs any other type educationally. However, since playgroups in working-class areas are often characterised by limited resources and passive supervisors, there is a question mark over their ability to provide the pre-school education that might best help children from less advantaged backgrounds.[34] Working-class children from nursery education have been shown to be more 'ready' for school in their first term at reception class. They give less attention to free play and more to 'educational' tasks, initiate more contact with teachers and concentrate better alone. They are more likely to play in purposive and creative ways than playgroup children and to show more social competence in joining in, or suggesting, activities. These differences diminished over time as, six months later, the playgroup children were seen to be catching up.

An Advantage For Life?

Information on *long-term outcomes* for early education is even thinner on the ground than that for the short-term. Some of the lessons we are able to draw from what is available are similar to those from many American projects for specifically disadvantaged children. Certainly, early gains may be deceptive. After all, when Douglas and Ross presented their evidence in 1965,[35] children who had attended nursery schools and classes had slightly higher scores than non-attenders for intelligence and school performance at eight years, but lower scores at 15. There was a small increase in deviant behaviour among the attenders.

Data from the 1970 British cohort study on the basic skills of 1,650 21-year-olds points to the insignificance of pre-schooling for later numeracy and literacy and the overwhelming impact of family background—although attendance at day nurseries was associated with very low skills. At first sight, there is a suggestion that those who had no apparent difficulties with reading and numeracy were more likely to have had some kind of pre-school educational provision than those whose skills were very poor (or 87 per cent to 76 per cent for literacy). Those who attended playgroups tended to do best. However, the difference is slight (61 per cent of those with very poor skills had been to playgroup, compared to 69 per cent who had no difficulties). In contrast, local authority nursery schools or classes did not seem to give any edge to performance in adult life, but rather the reverse (19 per cent of those with very low literacy had been in a nursery class, compared to 14 per cent with no difficulties, and the figures for nursery schools are 16 per cent and eight per cent respectively).

Again, this hardly means that playgroup 'out-performs' nursery schooling, in the long as much as the short-term. As the researchers comment: 'Pre-school provision outside the home does not feature as important independently'. The effects of different types of pre-schooling on adult skills are probably mainly to do with the social and economic situation of the family, and the choice this implies. Middle-class parents have traditionally tended to opt slightly more for pre-school playgroups, while working-class children go to nursery school.[36]

As attendance at pre-school provisions has expanded, along with childcare generally, we would expect to see some beneficial impact on overall school performance if the results are anything like their enthusiasts claim. Yet the findings of Tom Gorman and Cres Fernandes (in *Reading in Recession* for the National Foundation for Educational Research) point to a decline in overall performance over the period 1987-1992 in 24 schools,[37] with a similar fall in a nationally representative sample. Evidence from other directions tells the same story. For example, the Secondary Heads Association survey of intake tests for 455 state and independent schools tells of a sharp and accelerating drop in the reading abilities and overall educational attainment of 11-year-olds between 1991 and 1994.[38] Teaching methods are invariably blamed, and these may, indeed, bear much responsibility.

The authors of *Reading in Recession* have also listed other possible contributory factors (all of which have been related to literacy and numeracy skills in the literature) in the pupils' backgrounds. These are: the considerable increase in lone parents and male unemployment; the pressure on mothers to go out to work and the increase in the use of daycare facilities, to which can be added the increased pressure on primary schools to accept four-year-olds, when the curriculum and structure are inappropriate.

It is factors like maternal education, parental involvement and parents' social and economic position which have the overwhelmingly strongest association with children's educational attainment—at any age.[39] The:

> ... parents' role in skills acquisition is critical, especially in the early years before formal education begins ... Mothers can be effective enhancers of their children's vocabularies, and can improve their visual-motor skills thorough reading to them and playing with them. Or, they can impoverish their children's development by failing to provide the critical inputs at the right time.[40]

The child is likely to do particularly badly when parental disinterest is coupled with 'early exposure' to day nurseries where: 'these background features add up to a degree of either neglect by parents of their children's basic education, or ... early feelings of inadequacy in contributing positively to it'.[41]

What the child brings from the family background to the classroom is of critical importance. This relates to the occupational class and housing of parents, the degree of contact they have with the school and the interest they express.[42] If anything, the marked effect of parental interest on school performance increases as the child's school career progresses. As seen in the Newsons' work on child development in 700 Nottingham families, the rate of father involvement in middle childhood was closely associated with both school success and low rates of law-breaking.[43]

Much the same applies to skills in specialist, as well as basic, subjects. In sciences,[44] over a half of pupils' variation in achievement has been accounted for by 21 factors grouped into five blocks: home background, pupils' ability, school influences, teaching practices and pupils' attitudes. The most important factor was the socio-economic status of the home, measured by factors like the parents' jobs, education, and books at home.

Within Reason

Given the primacy of the relationship between home background and attainments, and the general 'paucity of evidence, and inconsistent results' from studies, suggestions that nursery education is going to have a big impact on educational performance, let alone social problems, are, to say the least, 'premature'.[45] Barbara Tizard's conclusion from her review of 1975—that this could not possibly close the class gap in achievement or prevent educational failure—is echoed later by those presenting the evidence from the Child Health and Development Study, who emphasized how 'It is important ... to recognise that *large* long-term effects attributable to early education should not be anticipated.'[46]

It is certainly far-fetched in the extreme to suggest that pre-schooling could overcome the cumulative disadvantages that children face in a world of family fragmentation. It is unlikely that it could compensate for the de-investment in children resulting from the decline in marriage and the way that smaller generations are becoming disproportionately the products of fatherlessness, broken relationships and poverty.

While there is a tendency to advocate additional years of pre-school experience as the way to improve short- and long-term effectiveness, the evidence is that there is little or nothing to be added by extending either the years or hours of nursery education beyond a half-day for one year. [47] Most non-handicapped children seem to reach a threshold of performance, or achieve most of the benefits, in this time, after which there are rapidly diminishing returns.

Whether or not children are going to benefit from, and build upon, investments in pre-school education is heavily dependent on the early and enduring efforts of parents, as much or more than upon the initial institutional provisions themselves. For children from more advantaged homes, pre-schooling is an expression of parental educational interest. Where this is lacking, or not so developed, one of the most important tasks of pre-schooling is to galvanise parental involvement by providing a focus or stimulus for parental effort. A home may not be a school, but school depends on home.

We are looking at pre-schooling from the wrong end if we think that this can either substitute for, or dispense with, parental input. Unfortunately, as this is 'not much good for parents in full-time work',[48] an engineered decline in parental involvement is inherent in many plans in which the professionals take over the childrearing as parents get on with earning. Demands for pre-schooling may be premised upon the shrinking role of parents, but it needs them as its principal actors if it is going justify itself—however it is provided.

The Perry Pre-school Project

We are persuaded that the gains made by children who receive high-quality pre-school education will reduce the need for remedial education at a later stage, help to ensure that we do not waste talent, and perhaps also reduce the social costs which arise from youth unemployment and juvenile crime.
National Commission on Education[1]

We have had occasion to refer several times to the lavishly-funded, show projects which are cited endlessly by childcare lobbyists in justification of their own position. The project which overshadows all the rest in the Consortium of Longitudinal Studies, as well as Head Start and just about every other pre-school and care facility, is Perry Pre-School, in Michigan, USA.[2] It closed its doors 25 years ago, to become the 'plentiful evidence' for assertions that—were full-time nursery education-cum-childcare available for all—the result must be an almost miracle generation of successful, responsible, high-achieving people. Under headings like *Nursery teaching can save a fortune,* we are told that: 'A national scheme of education for the under-fives would produce huge economic benefits for Britain', because:

> A long-term study in Ypsilanti, Michigan ... had shown that such pre-school programmes more than paid for themselves, returning seven dollars to the public for every dollar invested. The children who went through the programme were much less likely to become criminals or to require support from social services.[3]

The hope for the High/Scope Perry Pre-school Project, as with other experimental programmes, was that it might break a cycle in which children's school failure often begins with poor intellectual performance. This leads to a negative disposition towards learning, to special education placement and low school achievement, and finally to continuing poverty as adults, because of high male unemployment, single parenthood and welfare dependency, often combined with involvement in violent and drug-related crime.

Accordingly, the study asked whether high-quality, active learning programmes that supported children's cognitive and social skills with individualised teaching could provide both short- and long-term benefits to black children of low intelligence, living in poverty. There were 123 children originally assigned to either a programme or no-programme group. Due to losses, the programme group eventually contained only 58 children. Two waves of programme children entered at either age three or four. Around half the Perry subjects were from families on welfare, compared to one fifth of all black American families. Their families were twice as large and homes twice as crowded as those of the general black population. One half of fathers were unemployed, and one half of the families in the study had single mothers (compared to a third of blacks overall in 1970). Their IQs were in the range for the borderline mentally retarded, while the IQs of the control group ranged between 80-85, the middle range for black children in the 1960s.

The programme used consistent supervision by consultants specialising in the High/Scope curriculum as well as systematic on-site staff training. Staff had a very low turnover rate. (Perry teachers were paid ten per cent above the standard teachers' pay scale.) It involved a daily 2½ hour classroom session, with four teachers serving 20 to 25 children. (While it has been found that similar pre-school programmes can be effective with eight children per teacher, effectiveness declines substantially when the number of children exceeds ten.) Perry also had a high level of outreach to parents as partners, with a weekly 1½ hours home visit to each mother and child.

It should already be clear that twelve hours of teaching a week, with a highly intensive learning programme, cannot be equated with daycare, and neither are the results applicable to ordinary nursery school provisions. It cannot be 'evidence that daycare has a long-term anti-poverty effect on the children who attend'[4]—simply because it was not daycare.

For almost three decades the project followed and assessed the children through ages three to eleven, at ages 14-15, at age 19, and at age 27. Those in the programme had significantly higher scores on general literacy at age 19, and had spent significantly fewer years in programmes for educable mental impairment (with 15 per cent vs 34 per cent in the control group spending a year or more in such programmes). They completed a higher level of schooling compared to the controls (71 per cent to 54 per cent completing 12th grade or higher); they had a significantly lower percentage receiving social services at some time in the previous ten years (59 per cent vs 80 per cent); they had significantly higher monthly earnings at age 27 (with 29 per cent vs seven per cent earning $2,000 or more per month), significantly higher percentages of home ownership (00 per cent vs 13 per cent); and fewer arrests by age 27 (with seven per cent vs 35 per cent having five or more arrests), including significantly fewer arrests for drug dealing (7 per cent vs 25 per cent). In turn, significantly fewer of the births to programme females were out of wedlock (57 per cent to 83 per cent). The same effects were found for those participating for one or two years. There is no evidence that the programme would have had more or similar effects if it served children aged three years and under, or those of a later age.

The cost per pupil per school year was a total of $7,252 in 1992. If, over the lifetime of the participants, the pre-school programme returns to the public are estimated $7.16 for every dollar invested, this is *in relation to the prospects for low IQ, disadvantaged black children in the American inner city*. It does not mean that a similar return, or anything remotely like it, would be made for middle-class British children, or even for the average working-class child.

The Perry researchers have cautioned 'overgeneralisers' who claim that Perry 'establishes the long-term benefits of Head Start or state-funded preschool or childcare day programs', particularly when they do not consider the quality of these programs.[5] Furthermore, they emphasize that, even for the sample of very deprived, inner-city black children, the improvements were incremental, not radical. They also insist that Perry is not a cure for poor or deprived backgrounds and that, as for breaking individual cycles of disadvantage:

> ... pre-school programmes are only part of the solution. If the nation is to really confront poverty and its related problems of unemployment, welfare dependence, crime, and drug abuse, much broader social-policy action is needed.[6]

Most importantly, *Perry is not only unusual, it is virtually unique. No other programme has recorded similar effects on teen pregnancy, crime, welfare and employment and other social outcomes*. Indeed, two projects run by the Perry researchers using different curriculum models to High/Scope, or a traditional nursery school and the Distar model (with its greater emphasis on direct instruction), did not achieve the same results. Indeed, by 15, children from the Distar had engaged in twice as many serious delinquent acts as did those in the other two groups.[7]

Perry researchers L.J. Schweinhart and D. Weikart managed to sift out a number of other American studies (some were also from the Consortium mentioned above) which had produced evidence of statistically significant, long-term benefits of pre-school interventions. There were seven intensive long-term projects (with under 500 study participants, but tight experimental designs), and four extensive long-term studies (with over 500 participants but relatively loose, quasi-experimental designs). Higher intellectual performance scores, seen during the programme, persisted through to the age of ten in two projects (and had disappeared by 12-14 in one of these). In four of the intensive studies and one of the extensive studies significantly fewer programme group than non-programme group members ever had special education. In one of the intensive studies and two of the extensive studies significantly fewer programme group than non-programme group members ever had to repeat a grade, and the programme group had a significantly higher rate of high school graduation. In two studies only females had higher graduation rates. Only one found significantly less probation records for programme participants aged 13-16. Overall, girls benefitted more than boys.

However we account for the success of Perry, what must not be overlooked is that it not only offered a high-quality, developmentally appropriate curriculum, but attempted to continue the programme in the child's home. Because of the home visiting aspect:

... it is simply impossible to attribute the impressive effects ... to only the centre-based programme. Even if you could, this does not mean that they could be reproduced in the kind of projects that would characterise a programme of national scope.[8]

Working Through Parents?

Enthusiasm for institutional answers to childhood deprivation in particular, and the promotion of child development in general, has clearly led to a disproportionate amount of emphasis being placed on the centre aspect of the Perry experiment, to the virtual complete neglect of the home aspect. This fixation on a distorted version of Perry has also distracted attention away from the continued search for effective early intervention programmes. We now think we know all that we need to know about furthering the interests of disadvantaged children, and children every-where. This is unfortunate for, as experimentation has quietly proceeded, it has increasingly demonstrated the key role of parents. Early education itself does not compensate for poor parents; it depends, for its own effectiveness, on working with and through the home. Parents may provide a vital connecting link between a pre-school programme and any longer term improvements by supporting their children throughout the school years. The other studies which the Perry researchers have identified as having produced evidence of lasting benefits of pre-school interventions often focussed as much or more on home visits than classes for children which, in some cases, only involved a one-to-one session each week, or ran for only part of the year. These seemed as effective or more effective than programmes at infant development centres or year-round nursery classes during childhood. To these we may now add a number of programmes, all emphasizing interventions to increase parental involve-ment, which have achieved significantly beneficial results in the medium term (see Appendix 1).

Where parents of children in disadvantaged circumstances are poorly educated themselves, it may be desirable to try to improve their own low educational level along with their attitudes towards schooling. British work on the acquisition of basic skills has pointed to the role of family literacy programmes, which involve both parents and young children, as a two generational way to tackle the poor standards of both.[9]

SECTION D

THE IMPACT ON THE FAMILY

Children who have been in childcare are more likely to have insecure relationships with their mothers. Insecure relationships with parents can lead to lack of social skills in other relationships as well as difficulty in dealing with stress later in life.

The decline in support for the family in the fiscal system, coupled with male job insecurity and low earnings, has forced most mothers into the workforce, with longer hours for fathers. There is little recognition that becoming a parent is exhausting and demands major lifestyle changes. Media images of high-achieving women for whom motherhood makes scarcely a blip in their careers are unhelpful.

'Quality time' is a concept which meets the requirements of adults, not children. The need of children for parental attention cannot be manipulated to fit in with work schedules. The stress and exhaustion of double-income couples affects their parenting abilities, as well as their relationships with each other. The guilt which working mothers feel may not be a cultural construct but a natural indicator of the tension between the demands of parenthood and career.

Childcare is said to lower the risk of depression for mothers, but depression is not associated with caring for children but with poverty. Poor mothers may feel better when they have increased income. For better-off mothers going out to work, especially full-time, may increase the risk of depression. Depression and strain are increasingly the lot of parents —whatever their work arrangements—owing to the removal of fiscal and cultural support for the family. Poor parents make anxious parents.

The New Man is an unhelpful myth. Men are judged to be good fathers if they share caregiving tasks, but research indicates this is of little relevance. Nor does more time spent with children by fathers mean better outcomes, if the father is having to make up for an absent mother. If men take over housework women may feel reduced in status, as they regard household management as their prerogative.

The children of working mothers are often disadvantaged in their education, particularly boys. The effects become more severe as the mother's working hours increase.

Semi-attached?

The Attachment Question

> *Children in daycare show the same degree of attachment to their mothers and the same degree of security as children with full-time mothers. This is just as true of children who have been in daycare from the earliest weeks of life as of those who began daycare for the first time at two or three years of age.*
>
> Sandra Scarr and J. Dunn, *Mother Care: Other Care*[1]

The question of early attachment represents the arena in which the childcare battle has been most bitterly fought.

Prominent among the studies which Jay Belsky had in mind in 1986 when he spoke of extensive non-maternal care as a risk factor in early childhood development[2] was that of B. Vaughn and colleagues[3] who had reported in 1980 on a low-income sample. Infants who entered out-of-home-care prior to their first birthday were significantly more likely (47 per cent) to have insecure-avoidant relationships with their mothers by 12 months, and also at 18 months, compared either with home-reared counterparts, or those whose mothers started work later.

The study was later extended.[4] By 24 months early daycare also seemed to be having a negative effect on children who were secure as infants, making them vulnerable and prone to similar problems to those of insecure infants as a whole. More difficult parent/child relations for the early work group were further borne out at three-and-a-half years. The securely attached infants who had attended daycare before 12 months were more negative and poorly adjusted compared to those who had remained at home.[5] Indeed, while only the insecurely attached amongst the home-reared children had difficulties when they started school: 'The daycare children, regardless of attachment classification, and the home-reared insecure children all had similar high behaviour problem scores'.[6]

In comparison, P. Schwartz looked at middle-class infants in Chicago and Michigan in 1983.[7] She found that avoidant behaviour towards mothers was significantly greater at 18 months of age for those who had been in full-time daycare before nine months than for those who had been reared at home for the first 18 months of life, or who had been in only part-time daycare. (Only 32 per cent of infants in the home-reared group were moderate to high on avoidance, compared with 50 per cent in the part-time group and 82 per cent in the full-time group.)

Similarly the 1984 study of Joseph L. Jacobson and Diane E. Wille[8] involving 93 upper middle-class white infants aged between 16 and 21 months, showed a far higher rate of anxious attachments (61.5 per cent) for those in non-parental (mainly childminder) care for over 20 hours per week, compared to those with little or no daycare (31.4 per cent) or with daycare of limited hours (22.2 per cent).

The more temperate objections to Belsky's citation of these studies included criticisms about using children from disadvantaged and poor backgrounds, or ones who had poor childcare, which made it invalid to base a generalised argument on these. Belsky's case was dismissed as just 'one individual's interpretation of research on infant care that is at best, selective, and at worst, misinterprets the available data.'[9]

It may be true that attachment problems with childcare children do not crop up in every study,[10] or may be limited to boys,[11] or may be related to different lengths and hours of alternative care. The fact remains that such findings have continued to come in since Belsky first voiced his misgivings.[12] What is clear is that there is no relationship between attachment problems and the type of substitute care used, whether this is centre, childminders, or 'in-home help', such as nannies, or *au pairs*, or between the outcomes and the class and education of the parents.

One such study was by Jay Belsky himself and colleague Michael J. Rovine. Two longitudinal studies of infant and family development showed how infants in intact working- or middle-class families, with 20 or more hours of substitute care per week, had more insecure and disturbed relationships with their mothers.[13] The rate was 43 per cent for those with extensive non-maternal care and rose to 49 per cent where there was extensive non-parental care (i.e. when care by fathers was also excluded).

Sons of mothers who were employed on a full-time basis of 35 hours per week or more were also more likely to be insecure in their attachments to their fathers than other boys. As a result, more were insecurely attached to both parents (29 per cent compared to the seven per cent who spent less than 20 hours per week in non-parental care). Other work[14] has also found that 12 month-old middle-class boys whose mothers worked full-time had significantly higher rates of insecure relationships with fathers than boys whose mothers provided care, and were more likely to be insecurely attached to both parents.

Four of the number of studies which had appeared by 1988, involving low-risk infants and using similar, high-quality research techniques, were used by Belsky to obtain an overall rate of insecure attachment of 41 per cent among children in out-of-home-care, compared to 26 per cent in home-care.[15]

This selection was criticised for being narrow and excluding research with ambiguous results, or which did not confirm the association.[16] However, when one critic attempted to set the record straight with her own review of data from 16 studies, she had to concede that this still showed how 'infants whose mothers work full-time during their first year are consistently and statistically significantly more likely than infants of mothers who work part-time or not at all to be classified as insecurely attached', even if the difference had been reduced to 38 per cent, compared with 29 per cent.[17] Other sceptics used 13 studies in which the children were almost all white first-borns from generally advantaged family backgrounds, and regular non-maternal care averaged 32.6 hours of paid work a week.[18] Insecure attachments were significantly less common in infants with exclusive maternal care than among those who experienced non-maternal care for more than a few hours per week, whose avoidance was also higher.[19]

Clearly something is going on, and it may be 'incontestable and unavoidable that some degree of association between avoidance and daycare exists',[20] or that 'there is *more than enough* evidence to ... seriously entertain the possibility instead of explaining it away and thus dismissing findings that may be ideologically disconcerting'.[21] Indeed, the meta-analysis of worldwide childcare literature by C. Violato and C. Russell estimated that regular non-parental care increased the risk of children developing insecure bonds by 66 per cent. They noted that if this increase were related to disease due to environmental factors, it would be considered extremely serious and result in public health initiatives.[22]

Who Is Vulnerable?

Poor daycare will, of course, contribute to risks, and parents with poorly attached children may be more likely to enrol them in lower quality childcare, with more children per adult. More nurturant families, with greater social support, are associated with higher quality childcare, so that children who enter stable childcare arrangements are more likely to be the ones with the most secure maternal attachments.[23] Children who are attached to their caregivers are more competent and positive with peers and other adults. A secure attachment in care can buffer the discomfort of parental departures, and may even go some way to compensate for lack of a secure attachment to the parent.[24] However, good daycare, in itself, does not *necessarily* enhance the security of the parent/child relationship.[25] Instead, we find that children who are insecure with their mothers tend to engage in lower levels of play with their caregiver regardless of how attached they are to her.[26]

Again, we must bear factors of self-selection in mind. Mothers who are prepared to sacrifice their additional income or employment opportunities may also be especially patient and sensitive with their young babies. However, self-selection also works the other way to reduce the numbers of potentially insecurely attached children in daycare.

Boys are more likely to be removed from center-care to home-care, or to receive more attention from mothers who do not return to work.[27] Mothers who prenatally express a desire to return to work, but do not do so, are far more likely to have sons, while those who work full-time are far more likely to have daughters.[28] Because infant boys 'are already developmentally delayed compared to girls, their abilities to regulate their attention and emotion and find order in the world are particularly in need of help from a sensitive healthy caregiver'.[29]

This connection between a mother's work decisions and the infant's temperament, vulnerability, health or other difficulties has been disputed, and it has also been denied that mothers' assessments of their children's needs have any objective foundations. Instead, the mother's perceptions supposedly express the preferences of a male-oriented culture, or the unwarranted importance attached to boys by parents with a 'traditional view of gender roles'.[30] Thus, a more 'plausible explanations of why mothers of sons might want to stay home' is given as 'the seductive nature of the mother/son relationship, the greater investment of parents in sons, or the greater value that society places on boys'.

However, the particular susceptibility of boys to stress in early life is seen over and over again in many different contexts. For example, Frank L. Mott's investigation showed how formal childcare environments had a marginally beneficial effect on some intellectual skills for girls at four.[31] While boys hardly gained from any non-family environment, those with health problems were far better off socially, physically and emotionally when they stayed with their mothers.

If around a half of daycare infants *do* establish secure relationships, then what are the moderating factors? There are suggestions that infants exposed to long hours of parental separation are not only more likely to be insecure if they are boys, but if they are characterised as fussy or difficult, or if their mothers are limited in their interpersonal sensitivity or less satisfied with their marriages, and if their mothers have strong career reasons for working.[32]

What is central to attachment theory is that a sensitive, responsive caregiver is important to the development of a secure attachment. Insecure, ambivalent attachments and avoidance by the infant are associated with unresponsive, uninvolved caregiving, linked to relatively low maternal availability and sensitivity. A baby's irritability is particularly likely to interact with a lack of maternal responsiveness to produce an insecure attachment, where the mother finds her life stressful and where she feels that support is lacking.[33] Thus, if the parent is less available because of stress or other reasons, and if the infant is less resilient in the face of inconsistent care, then he is at greater risk for an insecure attachment. This means that, of course, that there are other factors which can cause or contribute to the risk of insecure attachment, whether or not there is also daycare—as when, for example, there are non-intact families, or maternal depression.[34]

In view of this, increased rates of insecure attachments have been attributed simply to the lack of responsiveness and sensitivity among mothers who work outside the home full-time. There may be a higher incidence, not only of stressed, but also rejecting mothers. Women who dislike or are indifferent to their babies may not only be more inclined to work, but their career priorities and a heavy workload could lead to rejection or distancing of the child, as would preferences for an 'independent' baby. Parental attitudes and values both influence decisions on whether or not to work full-time and use daycare, and are, in turn, affected by these.

Interestingly, one study which did not find insecure attachments related to full-time, non-maternal care—or anyway, not when this started in the first six months of life—addressed questions of self-selection (as well as care quality).[35] The 45 children involved were from a longitudinal study to examine the effectiveness of early educational intervention on the development of deprived children. This allowed for the random allocation of children to daycare of a high quality for 30 to 40 hours a week, independently of mothers' work. Maternal sensitivity emerged as the key factor in the security of attachment, although the numbers of infants in the sample who received exclusive maternal care was very small.

Nevertheless, considering the independent link to long hours of alternative care found in so many studies, the possibility cannot be dismissed that the risk of insecure attachment is also likely to be *increased* 'when infants from relatively well-functioning, intact families are reared in these particular circumstances'.[36] Moreover, as we have seen,[37] even daycare infants who are classified as securely attached as infants can become unsettled by pre-school age and have the same problems of insecurely attached children due to inconsistent care. Mother/child relations may undergo a deterioration as the child becomes more negative, and the dissatisfied mother more hostile.

The 'Strange Situation'

A common criticism has been that the standard 'Strange situation' test of infant attachment is not suitable for daycare children. This is based on the way that secure infants greet a parent positively following separation, approach her (particularly if they are distressed) and are comforted when they are upset. It involves a sequence in which the infant is exposed to an unfamiliar place, an unfamiliar person, parental separation, and the experience of being alone. Those with insecure relationships either avoid contact, or actively and angrily resist the parent's overtures. (Other tests, like ones involving co-operation between child and parent on simple tasks, are more suitable at 24 months and over.)

It is claimed that daycare children, being used to repeated separations, will experience all this differently from parent-care children. They are less concerned about separation, but their tendency to maintain distance has been mistaken for avoidance, resulting in faulty judgements about insecurity, when 'independence is more valued and encouraged in children in employed-mother homes'.[38] As daycare children are used to other people, they are less likely to be as interested in their parents, or as put out by strange people or surroundings, than home-reared infants.[39]

Indeed, 'greater physical distance from mother and apparent avoidance may, in fact, signal a precocious independence', or early and advanced maturation.[40]

However, the 'Strange situation' test has held up well as a measure of attachment, and attempts to replace it have been unsatisfactory.[41] The familiarity argument cannot account for many indications of insecurity, or why the hours in daycare should matter, and why children with certain backgrounds—known to increase vulnerability to other stresses—should be disproportionately affected. The notion that the high levels of avoidance and insecurity among infants with extensive daycare backgrounds simply mean that they are less stressed and more independent has been tested.[42] Two groups of 12 month old infants, *both* with insecure/avoidant attachments, were compared in 'reunion with mother' episodes. Yet, it was the half with the most non-parental care who whimpered, cried more, explored and played less than those with less non-parental care. (They were scored by raters blind to their attachment classification and childcare history.)

In fact, it is securely attached infants who are better able to tolerate brief separations by 18 months,[43] just as it is home-care infants who tend to show least concern when temporarily separated from mothers, including those in the Thomas Coram British sample.[44] Secure attachment seems to be the foundation for greater self-confidence and trust.

Having to reluctantly acknowledge the findings on attachment as statistically significant, critics are then apt to challenge their practical importance. Either the degree of disrupted relations may not have reached the (unspecified) level at which they might be prepared to admit a 'real' problem exists, or the significance of poor early attachments may be disputed. Thus, having insecure relations with parents does not necessarily imply that the children involved 'are emotionally insecure in general', since 'attachment is a relationship, not a global personality trait'.[45] Agreed. But this does not mean that the quality of a child's relationships is irrelevant for development, or that the outcomes of insecure parent/child relations are benign. Is it being claimed that attachments (to anybody) are unimportant and dispensable? If so, how are we to explain the fact that children who are securely attached to both their mothers and alternative caregivers are more competent than those insecurely attached to either one or both?[46]

What some research points to is that insecure daycare infants may be less socially withdrawn and more confident than insecure infants in home-care.[47] This is not unexpected, as daycare providers may sometimes compensate to some degree for poor relationships with mothers. Home-reared insecure children are likely to be isolated with inattentive and unresponsive mothers, who are disproportionately single parents. But this says nothing about the differences between outcomes for secure and insecure infants generally, nor does it negate the findings that higher levels of insecure infants are found in daycare samples. Nor does it negate that fact that, in the main, it is well known that insecure attachment '...is related to a set of ... outcomes which most developmentalists would regard as less than desirable'.[48]

Do Secure Relationships Matter?

As it is in early personalised contact that the skills are acquired that can be used in other settings, it is not unreasonable to suppose that secure infants might also differ from their insecure counterparts as they grow up. This could affect how they relate to others, how others relate to them and how they feel about themselves and their relationships.

Children with secure attachment histories are more socially competent with peers;[49] tend to be less socially withdrawn and hesitant, and more self-confident and tolerant of frustration. In contrast,[50] when the mother/child bond is insecure or ambivalent, the child is less willing to explore the environment, more inclined to be fearful and more likely to withdraw from social activity. As being cared for oneself increases the possibility of expressing concern for other people, secure children are more sympathetic to the distress of others. They are less likely to be judged by anyone in their early school years to have serious behavioural problems, while being less emotionally dependent on teachers.[51] However, they are also better at getting help and capitalising on adult assistance, or using attention and direction in ways that promote further intellectual and social development.

The available studies show how children whose attachments to both parents are insecure tend to be the least competent.[52] There are also suggestions that boys may be more adversely affected by insecure relationships than girls, and that infants judged insecurely attached at both 12 and 18 months of age will be the ones most likely to show longer term effects. Not every study shows the same pattern. While the strength of the associations has been disputed, as have the mechanisms responsible for these linkages between early relationships and later socio-emotional functioning, even critics of the research acknowledge the general trend in the literature.[53]

Of course, the connection of early attachments to outcomes is governed, at least partly, by the child's later experience with mother, father and others.[54] Those who develop problems may also receive less supportive care from their parents after infancy, or other stresses. A minority of infants in general samples show some insecurity of attachment, whether due to environmental or neuro-biological processes, or a mixture of both. How these difficulties and their possible implications are resolved or 'outgrown', compensated for, or aggravated by, later experience or biological development is by no means fully explored or understood.

Even so, high levels of positive maternal involvement during the first two years of life have been linked to low levels of behavioural problems at four years, even when the mother's behaviour towards the child at the later age is taken into account. Similarly, maternal acceptance and responsiveness during the infant and toddler years predict high levels of considerateness at age ten.[55] In turn, the emotional quality of the mother/child relationship at age four has been significantly correlated with mental ability at four, school readiness at five to six, IQ at age six, and school achievement at age twelve.[56] These associations are strong even when the mother's IQ, socio-economic status and the child's earlier mental ability are taken into account.

Later problems are more likely to occur in proportion to the cumulation of stressful life events on top of a poor attachment in infancy.[57] Longitudinal research involving children born on the Hawaiian island of Kauai in 1955 and followed up to 18 years[58] showed how the more that stressful events increased, the more were counterbalancing protective factors needed to insure positive outcomes. However, chances of a better outcome were enhanced if the child received plenty of attention from their primary caregiver during the first year of life. Boys who are insecurely attached in early life deal less well with later life stresses. This vulnerability meant that 40 per cent of the poorly attached males in, for example, the work of M. Lewis and colleagues, showed various signs of psychopathology at six, compared to only six per cent of boys who had been securely attached.[59]

The emotional bond with parents is a central and critical element in human development. If substitute care during the first year increases the likelihood of insecure parent/child attachments, then *at the very least* this means that the child is more susceptible to the effects of stressful events encountered later.

Stressed-out Parents

Today, guilt is inflicted on mothers who consider working and leaving their babies in others care. Not only do friends and relatives suggest in subtle and not so subtle ways that we neglect our children if we choose to work after motherhood, but we have built-in sources of guilt that give each of us nightmares.

Sandra Scarr and J. Dunn, *Mother Care: Other Care*[1]

As childcare affects children, so employment effects parenting. Attachment, like other outcomes, depends, as we have seen, on parental work patterns, parental behaviour, parental attitudes, family structure and the home environment, as well as upon the nature of the child and the care provided while parents are away. Most obviously, where we have dual income households or fully employed parents, there are time constraints.

Parents are giving much more time to earning a living and much less to their children than they did a generation ago. (The amount of 'total contact time' between parents and children, is calculated to have dropped 40 per cent for the USA during the last quarter-century.)[2] A primary cause of this decline has been the enormous shift of mothers into the labour force. To this we may add the extension of fathers' hours of employment. Almost two-thirds of respondents to a Parents at Work survey of their membership (overwhelmingly mothers in white collar jobs) routinely worked longer than their contract hours: 42 per cent might work over 50 hours a week and 27 per cent of the full-time workers worked over 60 hours when busy.[3]

The more hours mothers are employed, the less time they can give to 'primary care activities', which includes playing with or talking to children, or helping with their homework if they are older. In early life attachment is promoted by prompt attention to distress, appropriate stimulation, and the parent's synchronisation of their responses with those of the infant, as well as warmth and general responsiveness. This might be 'intuitive parenting', but it is vulnerable to disruption if relaxed time is not available in which to learn the infant's particular signals and responses.[4] Moreover, time for parenting in the period following a birth may be essential, not only to the development of the infant, but the whole family system as well.[5]

It is not usually until the age of three months that the baby's patterns of eating and sleeping become regular enough for parents to plan accordingly. For a baby with colic, or one who is premature, this process may take much longer. Others are nervous or very jumpy and can get highly agitated and disturbed, even by small changes of environment. Some may also have unusual medical or educational needs, as well as difficult temperaments.

The mother herself must regain her physical strength and normal activity level after childbirth. There are uncommon women, bruited about in the media, like the one who 'took off only the equivalent of a long weekend [from work] to have her babies'.[6] As many or more women are likely to be excruciatingly tired and weak in the weeks after birth. They may have had operative deliveries, complex labours, or they might be prone to post-natal depression or changes in mood and energy that take some time to return to normal. All members of the family may be affected by interrupted sleep and providing for someone who makes their needs known by crying. People who have had no experience of babies until they acquire one of their own often do not realise that these are far from being compliant bundles who can be conveyed around like unprotesting bags of sugar.

It is not exaggerating to say that parents who return to work before important transitions are satisfactorily accomplished may find themselves lacking the endurance, tolerance, patience, and enthusiasm to fully enjoy and respond to their infant's developmental needs. Attachment may be discouraged as inappropriate, inconvenient or painful. Some parents may even begin the detachment process before birth:

> ... when both parents anticipate the pressures of having to return to work 'too early' (in their own words, 'before three months'), they seem to guard against talking about the future baby as a person and about their future role as parents. Instead, their concerns are expressed in terms of adjusting to time demands, to schedules, to lining up the necessary substitute care. Very little can be elicited from them about their dreams of the baby or of their vision of themselves as new parents.[7]

Certainly, if parental insensitivity is increased by spending less time with the infant and not knowing his or her signals very well, so repeated separations of the child from a parent may make it difficult to develop and maintain stable relationships. The security of attachment between mothers and infants at one year can be predicted from the quality of contact at three months and the mother's time with the baby, as a study of American first-borns demonstrated.[8] Both of these factors make an independent contribution, so that time is, in itself, linked to security of attachment, even apart from the mother's behaviour and attitudes. As many of these mothers were employed at three months, work was the main reason for spending less time with the infant.

Cramming attention into a 'happy hour' or 'quality time' may not be very relevant to small children, for whom it is 'impossible to schedule togetherness times'.[9] How do you 'make a tired baby stay awake for a day's worth of cuddling', or 'persuade a one-year-old who wanted you to play with him this morning to take his one and only chance and play right now?'[10] Moreover, if the mother monopolises the child's attention during her short time at home, this may displace the father, by taking over the time he would otherwise have had with the child.[11]

Clearly, children can become objects to spend some time with, when the parent can fit this in, rather than people requiring relationships. However, what parents may want after a weary day is for the child to sleep well until it is time to get up for the centre or minder again. Yet, night times are the only chance children may have to get the parental attention they have missed all day.

> If she naps, one set of parents told the teacher, 'then we have her up half the night'. In another centre, a mother was told that her child, usually a non-sleeper, had in fact slept that day. 'Well, Peter', said his mother, 'you didn't get much out of this afternoon's program, did you?' The mother's message, to both the child and his teacher, was that sleep was not an appropriate activity for a young child.[12]

Even if the husband increases his share of household tasks (and total workload) each working parent must put in more hours to meet basic responsibilities. Dual earners must attend to household work, children, and family leisure in the short period that remains after both have put in their time at work and commuting. Fending off reports of adverse daycare effects, one exponent candidly admits that:

> ... two full-time jobs, work and motherhood, would lead to more rejection of every additional burden, including the baby. Other mothers might foster insecure attachments in their infants, not because they are away all day at work, but because they have to do chores and tasks that compete with the infant when they are together ... Many working mothers feel overworked and tired; they feel life is hard; they are rushed and harried. It is not unreasonable that these mothers would be less accessible to their infants. The reason their infants might not be so securely attached, in other words, is not that 40 hours of care is hard on infants but that 40 hours of work is hard on mothers.[13]

In the Parents at Work Survey, 72 per cent of the mothers claimed to be exhausted by the end of the day, and the incidence of insomnia, depression and other stress related symptoms was high.[14] This is borne out in the study by Pamela Daniels and Kathy Weingarten of American couples, where the price of holding down two demanding occupations, one at home and the other away, was 'constant fatigue and overloaded circuits': in no other situation was so much conflict so consistently reported.[15] A recent British study also conveys this sense of being constantly rushed.[16] For all the dual-earner spouses, the problems of combining parenting with employment led to immense pressures and conflict, as well as shortage of time in which to accomplish anything. Mothers had lower levels of job satisfaction than all other groups, with many regretting that they could neither enjoy their children nor their careers.

Parents who have low occupational status, work commitment and aspirations and take the child to non-home based care arrangements feel the greatest stress.[17] The widely publicised dual-career couple, who are highly committed to high status, high paid, careers and can afford child-care at home 'may be relatively protected from the negative impact of work-family pressure'.[18] The chairman of a company who has 'a nanny and a couple at home to cook dinner'[19] is in a different world from the woman who takes a child to the minder or nursery at 7.00 a.m. before going into the cornflake factory.

Diane Hughes' and Ellen Galinsky's study underlines how, if balancing job and family responsibilities is extremely difficult for most parents, the period before children enter school is the hardest of all, with 'one out of two male employees and two out of three female employees ... having a hard time managing'.[20] With the demands of work and childrearing at their most incompatible, it is 'the time when stress, anxiety, and perhaps defensive withdrawal from the child are most likely to occur'. Even with older children: 'approximately two out of every five employees, male and female, were feeling conflicted and torn by all they had to do'.[21] Again, mothers with children under 18 had the highest stress levels, more psychosomatic symptoms and greatest work-family interference.

The Role Of 'Guilt'

We frequently hear that the only real problem with maternal employment is 'guilt'. As a product of antiquated social attitudes about mother's role and children's needs, this makes mothers feel pulled in different directions and unable to take proper advantage of employment opportunities. This 'guilt' appears even more maladaptive if it really is true that putting occupational fulfilment first benefits children.

The investigations of Margaret T. Owen and Martha J. Cox clearly connect early resumption of employment with low investment in parent-hood.[22] This, together with the long hours worked by early returners, badly affected the security of mother/infant attachments, and lowered the quality of parenting generally. Interestingly, while other work relates high commitment to work vis-a-vis parenting to less strain for mothers,[23] this may not necessarily be in the children's interests, since such circum stances may also be ones of poorer parent/child attachment. Middle-class women with low commitment to work experience less strain when their jobs are not professional or managerial in nature. Work that is less scrutinized by others and less demanding may generate less pressure. It is the women with a high commitment to work but low commitment to parenting who have less role stress in higher status jobs. Thus, if work is important to personal identity, the employment that involves high esteem may generate less stress, but may mean less sensitive parenting. Women who feel less 'guilt' or anxiety about leaving their children, or have few if any misgivings about putting their work first, may make their own lives easier, but whether they make better parents is another matter.

Such findings reveal a basic conflict between parenting and the demands for equality of achievement in the workplace at each point in the lifecycle. As recognised by establishment feminists, the latter will be undermined by women themselves so long as they put more value on their family and reduce strain by taking less responsible work. The choice is less investment in children and more investment in work, or more investment in the family and less in work. However, this choice is bound to be reflected in the developmental outcomes for children. This should lead to a re-assessment of claims that employment necessarily makes a woman a 'better mother to her child' because it must 'enhance a woman's life, providing stimulation, self-esteem, adult contacts, escape from ... housework and childcare, and a buffer against stress from family roles'.[24]

While, in one study, the daily separation of mother and child led to enhanced mother-initiated physical contact upon reunion,[25] others have reported that parents in dual-wage families provide their babies with less stimulation, and suggested that this was due to the 'overload experience' of these couples.[26] However, attitudes to work also come into this. Elsewhere, children whose mothers were reluctant to put them into daycare had better development in terms of co-operativeness, compliance, persistence and socially constructive behaviour, than the children of mothers who did not hesitate.[27] (The higher levels of conflict in the families of securely attached infants had much to do with the mothers' difficulties or misgivings about daycare.) Moreover, parental contact and involvement with the centre was strongly associated with both the quality of attachment to parents and caregivers.

Mothers Go Mad

The costs of this enforced dependency [of mothers in the home] can be measured in human, as well as economic terms; a number of researchers have studied its effects on the mental health of mothers and their children ... the worst adjusted and most unhappy women were mothers at home who wished they could be employed. Another study ... found ... children of depressed mothers avoided them and shunned attention also from other adults. Such studies cast serious doubt on the conventional wisdom that a mother's care in the home is invariably the best care for young children.

Equal Opportunities Commission[1]

How are the reports about the pressures on dual income families to be related to claims that mothers out of the workforce are at risk of depression?

The corollary to the message that children do fine in daycare is that mothers go mad at home. In 1994 the press seized upon what was described as the first British investigation into the 'hidden cost of home management'. According to one commentator, it proved that working at home was: 'Far from the easy-paced routine, it is a kind of institutionalised, low-grade torture'.[2] The public were not to know that this was based on 146 questionnaires given to mothers with children at one primary school, of which 94 were returned. This does not make those who replied representative, either of mothers at the school, or of the general population. (The researchers noted that they had overall poorer mental and physical health than national norms).[3] There was no independent, or objective, assessments of health, and no enquiries about past health or pre-existing problems. There were no controls for economic circumstances or for marital status, although both are powerful predictors of well being.[4] Divorced and other lone mothers, whether employed outside the home or not, report lower feelings of well-being than married mothers, and they and their children have significantly less satisfactory adjustment on measures of stress and psycho-social functioning.[5] Clearly, such findings could have been seriously distorted for a host of unknown reasons.

Lynne Murray's studies provide a more vigorous appraisal of maternal depression and its effects on children. Post-natally depressed women commonly experienced difficulties with their partners, lacked support from their families, tended not to have confiding relationships with other women, and commonly experienced financial hardship or housing difficulties.[6] They had more problems with their babies and were less sensitive and attuned to the infant's signals. In turn, their infants were more likely to be insecurely attached at 18 months, to have increased rates of behavioural problems and to do badly on cognitive tasks. The mothers continued to find their children difficult to manage as they grew up, even when current and recent depression or parental conflict were taken into consideration. At school the children showed more behavioural problems and these were associated with insecurity of attachment in infancy. Boys, in particular, were more likely to have problems, including hyperactivity.

Other work on a North London sample also showed a significant association between maternal depression in the first year and lower intellectual attainment at four, even with low birth weight or impaired infants removed from the study.[7] Further work in South East London has underlined that those most at risk are boys, especially in lower class families,[8] while girls appear to be relatively protected from the deleterious effects of their mother's illness. Maternal depression had a profound effect on both perceptual and verbal aspects of IQ, independently of the boy's birth weight, parents' IQ, the home environment, marital conflict, or the later quality of mother/child relations, or the child's behavioural problems.

Data from the Child Health and Development Study allows us to examine in some detail the associations between mothers' *employment* and their susceptibility or otherwise to depression.[9] Certainly, mothers who had non-manual jobs had a lower depression score than mothers who had never had a job outside the home. However, the difference was not significant for part-time manual jobs, while full-time manual employment was associated with a slight rise in depression. However, the big differences in maternal depression were associated with socio-economic status. It was the socially disadvantaged mothers in employment who had lower depression scores compared to housewives, while poor women who had given up their jobs were the most depressed of all. Employment reduces the risk of depression in women with a particular vulnerability to this condition, but the vulnerable mothers are also those defined as disadvantaged.

For more 'advantaged' mothers, or those not under so much financial pressure, the depression scores of those in non-manual jobs were much the same as those of housewives, whereas manual employment, particularly full-time, carried a greater risk of depression. Thus, socially 'advantaged' women at risk of being depressed may *increase* the likelihood if they take up employment, particularly on a full-time basis. The data provides no support for the idea that respite from childcare itself, as when the child attends a nursery or playgroup, reduces the mother's risk of depression.

Other reviews of the evidence have come to much the same conclusions.[10] Depression in employed wives is greatly *increased* if they work full-time, as are all health problems among mothers of young children unless they have the financial resources to pay for help in the home. Margaret T. Owen and Martha J. Cox described how anxious mothers were when they worked 40 or more hours a week compared to those who worked part-time or not at all,[11] while non-employed mothers were no more depressed or less well adjusted than employed mothers. Maternal anxiety was the direct result of long working hours and, to the extent that 'maternal employment raises anxiety, there may be an indirect relation to child outcome'.[12] While mothers who decided not to work had the highest ratings for life satisfaction (despite financial sacrifices), the full-time employed mothers were overwhelmingly dissatisfied with their employment status compared to the non-employed and the part-time groups. Although their jobs were of various types (e.g. laboratory technicians, nurses, managers, lawyers) it was a living standard dependent upon two salaries that compelled them to return to their jobs soon after the birth of their babies.

In reality, women are least depressed and most satisfied when their employment status is consistent with their own and their husbands' preferences. There is a terrible slight of hand in the suggestion that, because some women are unhappy at home when they wish to be employed, it means that all mothers are unhappy when they are non-employed and are better off at work. Arguably, employment will only decrease a woman's depression if it means job satisfaction and not too much additional pressure, role strain or fatigue. It is opportunist to suggest that these women are depressed simply because they are not working and that, furthermore, this means that maternal care is somehow not right or even menacing for young children.

One-earner families are heavily represented in the poverty statistics. Both the continually demeaning and dismissive references to mothers at home, and the economic squeeze on families with one main earner, have contributed towards the isolation and demoralisation of homemakers. 'Money cannot buy love, some object. The lack of money cannot produce love either, whereas the lack of resources can rob people of their ability to care'.[13] Without reasonable financial security it becomes difficult for parents to provide an environment in which children can flourish.

This must be related to suggestions that parenthood may have generally negative consequences for the psychological well being of adults: *men as well as women*.[14] Parents report that they are less happy, less satisfied with their lives, worry more, as well as having higher levels of anxiety and depression. What is more, the gap between people with and without children seems to have been increasing in recent decades. It appears that, as the relative economic position of parents has declined, so the subjective benefits of parenthood have also fallen. The increase in women's employment opportunities has not only increased the opportunity costs of childrearing, but the decline in men's job opportunities and income, due to labour market and tax changes,[15] also means that parenthood brings greater economic strain as well as more marital conflict. The rising opportunity costs of raising children are also changing attitudes about parenthood. As this comes to be viewed more negatively, they play a role in lowering the relative well-being of parents. After reviewing the evidence, Sara McLanahan and Julia Adams overwhelmingly attribute the decline in well-being to financial and time constraints, as well as the increase in marital disruption and female-headed families. Their analysis is directly at odds with claims that mothers' satisfaction and happiness is increased through being fully employed and able to support their children independently of men. Here, maternal employment reflects a shortage of family resources to meet increasing demands:

> ... the change in women's labor force participation has been critical in the relative decline in mothers' subjective well-being ... working has substantial psychological benefits for women without children. Working mothers, on the other hand, do not receive equivalent benefits from work, and therefore their well-being has declined relative to that of non-mothers. Mothers clearly face a dilemma: If they work, they reduce their opportunity costs, but they simultaneously increase the demands on their time.[16]

What Use Is A Father?

*This helplessness in the face of domesticity is ridiculous and depressing. What
happens to the intelligent, professional, hard-working adult that leaves him
unable to cope with beans on toast for two at tea time, get the Hero turtle
costume assembled by bed-time and review his notes for tomorrow's meeting?*
'Dad's still a dud about the house', *The Daily Telegraph*[1]

Men As Mothers

The effects of parents' work on parent/child relations and child development relate to changes in the behaviour of fathers as well as mothers, and
the impact these have on both marital and parental behaviour.

Calls for more childcare are often accompanied by demands that men
should also do more at home to free women for careers. But whatever
household responsibilities men may or may not assume, at present or in
the future: 'it is doubtful that a satisfactory resolution to this struggle
[with role overload] can be obtained simply through a readjustment of
gender roles on an individual or couple basis, given the time demands on
two working parents'.[2]

While fathers experience more stress than men who are not parents,
fathers in dual-earner families are most stressed of all. Furthermore, the
evidence is pervasive that fathers whose wives work full-time show less
sensitive behaviour towards their young children, see them more
negatively, and are more aggravated by them.[3] Sons especially seem to
suffer. Some recent studies show how infant boys in employed-mother
families are not only seen more unfavourably, but receive less attention
from both parents than girls, or children of either sex in non-employed
mother families.[4] This fits with observations that fully employed parents
prefer having girls, as boys are seen to be too demanding of parental time.

As positive involvement with the father is very important for boys'
academic achievement, intelligence and social development, these findings
deserve more attention than they get. As males are more sensitive to
variations in caregiving than females, early group care may not only be
more detrimental to boys, but their well-being may be further prejudiced
at home, since full parental employment reduces both the availability and
sensitivity of both mother and father. This is seen in the longitudinal
Hawaiian study, where boys were both more vulnerable to maternal
employment and the father's absence or lack of involvement.[5]

Yet, while greater participation by men in household work is, first and
foremost, advocated to advance women's job prospects, it is also claimed

that, by another lucky coincidence, this will also be good for the father/ child relationship and child development. Not only is breadwinning depicted as an age-old justification for male control and oppression of women and children, but the man who is the main or only breadwinner is often described as lacking a significant relationship with, or interest in, the children. He is the prototype absent father:

> Father's conventional role as provider is unquestionably the reason that he is regarded as an outsider not only by members of his own family but also by experts who have long since dismissed the possibility of his making any significant personal contribution to family life.[6]

According to Anna Coote, Harriet Harman and Patricia Hewitt: 'the traditional emphasis on men as breadwinners' has 'effectively exiled them from their children'.[7] At most, they are described as being interested in doing only the 'fun things', like playing sports, taking children out or reading stories, while avoiding the 'real' day-to-day work involved in caring for a young child.[8]

Against them is pitted the 'involved' father, who is unconcerned about his own job prospects and has abandoned the provider role. As David Blankenhorn has pointed out, this helps 'explain our contemporary cultural obsession with stay-at-home Dads, Daddy trackers, and fathers on paternity leave'. Such men are exceedingly rare statistically, but, as 'an élite image of the New Father, they are ubiquitous'.[9] This father embraces the view of employment held by women, where work and family are not overlapping domains, but conflicting domains. If role strain means that mothers tend to have more ambivalent attitudes to employment than fathers, which results in their more sporadic, contingent commitment to work outside the home, there must be role strain for men too.

An unwarranted equation is often being made here between primary caretaking tasks, like preparing food, changing nappies, cleaning and clearing up, and father involvement, where the former are used as a measure of the importance of fathers to children. Yet 'servicing operations' —while necessary to physical well-being—may have little bearing on father/child attachment or the child's social, intellectual, moral or emotional development. This being the case, it is possible that increased paternal participation in the former could be counter-productive when it comes to the latter.

This was dramatically brought out in a study of Mexican fathers who were more affectionate and companionable than mothers, and much more likely to be encouraging their children and participating in shared activities, but low on primary caretaking in what is often seen as a highly 'macho' culture.[10] There is certainly an association between high levels of father involvement, secure attachment and enhanced toddler development, and this is particularly true with regard to children's problem solving behaviour, especially for boys. However, whether fathers take responsibility for caregiving (feeding, changing, arranging babysitting) is weakly related to variations in child development, compared with the amount of time they spend together. 'This supports previous work suggesting the central role of the father as playmate rather than care-giver'.[11]

However, *under certain conditions,* the sheer amount of time that fathers spend with babies is actually associated with less secure fa-ther/infant relationships. What is true is that fathers who are positive towards their infants are motivated to spend more time with them, and this increases attachment. But it may simply be a compensation for mother's lower involvement and a sign of stressed families. Hence, when fathers spend more time with infants simply because the wife's job means she is less available, or because it is necessitated by the demands of the home situation, it does not follow that this makes for better father/infant relations—more likely the reverse.[12]

Such observations apply to role reversal situations where the father stays at home and the mother becomes sole breadwinner. Data from the National Longitudinal Survey of Youth on early maternal employment and childcare arrangements showed how early father-care was particu-larly detrimental for the development of three- or four-year-old boys in low-income families.[13] It might be assumed that father-care would always be benign like grandmother- or other relative-care. But many fathers who are the main care-providers for infants are probably unemployed, with problems of low self-esteem and emotional well being. While role reversal cases are presented in the media as wonderfully successful models, most couples in this situation are not there of their own choosing, and usually revert to more traditional arrangements given the opportunity. Findings from the most recent sweep of the National Child Development Study show that the highest levels of both personal and marital satisfaction were recorded for those living in 'traditional' families, where the man has a clearly defined position as the main earner. The highest levels of dissatisfaction, for men and women, were found in role-reversal house-holds where the wife worked and the husband stayed at home.[14]

Marriages Of Convenience

Insofar as job pressures and a heavy workload create stress, they affect marital as well as parental relationships. More father participation due to the wife's job demands may mean more marital problems, without any necessary gain in father/child attachment. Clearly, we should not:

> ... argue simplistically for the virtues of father involvement, without considering possible unintended, negative consequences of the push for such involvement, consequences that may not bode well for the marital happiness of some dual-earner couples.[15]

If each spouse is encouraged to minimise their own responsibility for childcare and other domestic work, and tries to offload the burden onto the other, this may become an important source of stressful negotiation or open conflict, with some fathers said to be involved with their children because of 'coercive marital exchange'. The implication is that different marital processes may underlie father involvement in dual and single-earner families. Certainly, dual-earner fathers seem to be less satisfied with their work, marital relationships and personal lives than are single-earner fathers.

Building on research which shows how husbands' increased involvement in family work is associated with conflict, one longitudinal study of marriage looked at a number of aspects of father involvement for dual-earner and one-earner families, with one child aged under 25 months. While the two groups did not differ in social background, fathers' work hours, sex role attitudes, or perceived parenting skills, there were lower levels of marital conflict in one-earner than in two-earner families. While the two groups of men were similar in the extent of their leisure or play activities with their children, the more that the dual-earners did with the child, the less positive they felt about their wives, so that 'marital negativity' was 'consistently, positively, and strongly related to paternal involvement in childcare'. While men in one-earner and two-earner families were indistinguishable in terms of love for wives shortly after marriage, dual-earner fathers report loving their wives significantly less two years later. In contrast, for single-earner families, no aspect of fathers' involvement was associated with reports of poor marital relations.[16]

Feeling comfortable about involvement in childrearing or childcare tasks is an important factor. While the nature or degree of men's participation is subject to change over time, it may be counter-productive to push the pace beyond what people are able or willing to assimilate. Even in a study of 50 high status dual career couples, where fathers provided 38 per cent of the overall childcare at home, and expressed a desire to spend even more time with their young children, nearly half insisted that they found it difficult to do the kind of childcare tasks which are customarily performed by women. Much the same proportion of women said how difficult is was to relinquish their authority over childrearing.[17] This is hardly surprising, considering how most mothers like to have ultimate control over how they manage their children.

Working Mothers and Their Children

... children may even become smarter once their mothers are out of the house. A 'higher IQ', writes Ms. Shreve in her 1987 book, Remaking Motherhood *is only one of the benefits that the children of working mothers may come to enjoy. Others include 'better social adjustment ... more expansive sex-role ideology, greater self-esteem, greater confidence in one's ability, a more positive view of women, better educational progress, more vocational options and a potential for greater economic independence'.*

The Wall Street Journal[1]

According to the Equal Opportunities Commission:

> ... concern in the United States about the possible plight of children of working mothers prompted a number of studies ... They concluded that there were no consistent effects of the mother's employment on any aspect of child development.[2]

This is grossly misleading. Lack of an entirely *consistent* package of effects in each and every study does not mean that there have not been a number of adverse findings, in Britain as well as in the United States. The finding that sons of employed mothers score lower on intellectual measures occurs frequently enough to warrant serious consideration. In a series of Canadian studies, the ten-year-old sons of middle-class employed mothers obtained lower scores on mathematics and language achievement tests, and a comparable group of English speaking (but not French speaking) four-year-old sons also had consistently lower IQ scores than either daughters of employed mothers, who showed only a very slight drop, or children of non-employed mothers.[3]

Similarly, while research on 500 American four-year-olds showed no overall effect of maternal employment, more detailed analysis revealed that boys from high-income families with working mothers had lower scores for cognitive development. Furthermore, those whose mothers worked in the first year had the poorest levels of cognitive ability.[4] As boys are more vulnerable, such negative effects may be because of their experience of unstable care arrangements or less attentive care in infancy. (Some girls did a bit better in terms of cognitive ability when a very particular comparison was made between those whose mothers returned to work in their second year and those whose mothers did not return to work at all.)

More has been made of the way in which, in the Canadian series and elsewhere, the daughters of working mothers are more career-minded and have less stereotyped sex-role attitudes. It seems to be regarded as most important that girls should have the approved outlook on work, or that both sons and daughters should have 'a role model of a competent woman ... for their later lives'. Boys development gets scant consideration, so long as they 'respect women's rights and achievements [and] how better can they learn that women can be as accomplished as men than by living with an accomplished mother?'[5]

However, some studies show *adverse effects on the attainments of both sexes*. In a large American sample of children from primary age to 16, from the High School and Beyond Study involving a random sample of 15,579 students, maternal employment was consistently linked to lower maths and reading scores for white children from two-parent families.[6] The more the mother worked, the stronger the effects. The negative effects of working full-time over the child's lifetime are greater than the negative effects of working part-time or full-time at some stage. (For blacks the results were ambiguous, with adverse effects only for the reading scores of teenagers of lone parents, while primary-age black children with single, employed mothers had somewhat higher reading scores.)

A similar picture emerges from the analysis of the intellectual development and behaviour of American three- and four-year-old white children from the 1986 assessment for the National Longitudinal Survey of Youth (NLSY).[7] Maternal employment in the first year had detrimental effects on both measures, regardless of sex or poverty, with the effect falling dramatically if employment was postponed to the third year. (Just as white and black four- to six-year-olds from the same study were significantly more non-compliant when their mothers had begun full-time employment in the first two years of life.)[8] Under ten hours a week was least detrimental, but there was a slightly larger effect when mothers worked 10-19 hours compared to where they worked over 20. (Children in the middle range may have had more experience of *ad hoc* and unstable care arrangements.)

The results from the British National Child Development Study suggest that the five-year-old children of mothers working outside the home had poorer social adjustment at school than children of mothers who were not employed. While employment in the pre-school years had ceased to have a measurable effect on adjustment at seven,[9] those whose mothers had worked full-time had poorer reading and arithmetic scores at this age than children of mothers who had not been employed or who had part-time jobs. The highest scores on vocabulary tests were achieved by children of at-home mothers and the lowest by children of mothers in full-time manual work, followed by children of mothers in part-time manual work. Even children of mothers in non-manual employment or working from home had slightly lower scores than those of housewives. In turn, children of

mothers in full-time manual or non-manual employment, and those who
had recently left employment, had higher anti-social behaviour scores
than those of housewives. Those of mothers who worked part-time,
manual or non-manual, had only slightly higher scores than children of
non-employed mothers.

Where we consider the children *of working mothers* only, here we find
that those who have the most favourable development and environment
have mothers who not only have high occupational status, but seemed to
have managed to square the circle by having little stress from dual
responsibilities and are available to their children. In turn, employed
mothers may tend, on average, to have higher educational aspirations and
put a greater emphasis upon qualifications than those who keep entirely
out of the workforce. But, as work hours increase, even positive educational attitudes and high occupational status may fail to counter-balance
the negative effects of high anxiety and less time in which parents can
give attention to the children.

As Adelle E. Gottfried and her colleagues found, once the number of
hours that mothers of five-, six- and seven-year-olds work start to rise
beyond 30 or so a week, the negative relationships to development
emerged: lower achievement scores on intelligence tests, lower ratings for
reading and lower educational stimulation at home.[10]

Whether the worrying findings on older children are attributable to
events in the pre-school years, or are maintained and even engendered by
the two full-time jobs pattern in the school years, is unclear. Certainly, all
is not right.

SECTION E

PUBLIC POLICY IMPLICATIONS

All demands for childcare mention 'high quality', but universally available high-quality childcare has not been achieved anywhere. The supposed gains to the Exchequer which would result from getting mothers back to work can only make sense in the context of cheap—i.e. poor-quality— childcare. Even at the most optimistic assessment it is doubtful if there would be any net gain from offering free or subsidised childcare; it would be more likely to show an overall loss. Many single parents have no qualifications and would only get low-earning jobs—assuming they can find employment.

Also, assumptions about the number of mothers who would go back to work if childcare were available may be wrong. The majority of people, including working mothers, believe that small children should be cared for by their parents. While all demands for employment policy relate to getting mothers into the workforce, little attention is being paid to the loss of human capital and productivity involved in the under-employment of men.

Equality activists want equal outcomes in employment, not freedom of choice for mothers, even if this means pressurising women into lifestyles they would not have chosen for themselves. High-earning professional women, who have the most choice about balancing career and childbearing, prefer to take time off from their career while children are small.

Countries which have tried to provide universal childcare have backed off and turned to subsidising maternal leave instead. The argument that national output increases as mothers enters the workforce involves a statistical sleight-of-hand: all that happens is that services which had been provided free now have to be paid for, so that activity enters national output figures. Meanwhile family life becomes more fragile. The emphasis on mother's earning capacity, which can be increased by childcare, ignores the fact that children are the earners of the future, and their earning capacity is dependent upon the investment of time which their parents make in them. If the social infrastructure provided in the home were to be replaced by paid agencies of the social services it would consume any supposed gains from getting mothers into the workforce.

The demand for childcare is part of a wider trend to downgrade parenthood, which has resulted in reduced resources being allocated to parents of dependent children. Having children has come to be associated with poverty and lower levels of personal satisfaction. Policy should be directed towards restoring the viability of parenthood, and making sure that parents who wish to look after their children at home are not discriminated against. Freedom of choice for mothers should include the freedom not to go out to work, if that is what they prefer.

Chasing a Chimaera

In the late 1970s, I would often get telephone calls from women anguishing over issues surrounding going to work and providing alternative care for their infants or young children. As these women told their stories, two things were clear. First their circumstances were impelling them to work. Second they were basically calling for reassurance, for permission. They worried that daycare might harm their infant and wanted an expert to tell them everything would be all right. I did ...

But I rarely get calls like this anymore. Although women still call me frequently, they now commonly ask for permission of another sort. They ask for permission to stay home. They have been told or have read that babies are unaffected by daycare and that it is foolish to jeopardize their career by staying home.

L. Alan Sroufe, *Early Childhood Research Quarterly*[1]

Childcare may be the terrain of the ideologue and the dogmatist, some against, most for. The evidence makes it a prevaricator's paradise. Is childcare harmful to small children? Is early education advantageous? As we saw, it all depends—on the sex, age, health, temperament and maturation of the child, as well as the parents and the family and, not least, the type, duration and quality of the alternative caregiving environment. What we certainly must do is drastically rein in extravagant claims being made for its benefits.

First of all, we need to be more aware of the growing body of research suggesting that many children in substitute care are negatively affected in some, or many, ways. At the very least, we must recognise that 'the existing evidence is such that blanket statements about the benign effects of infant daycare on social competence, especially in males, may be premature.'[2] Overall, daycare is inferior to parental care. The idea that 'a substitute mother can be the same as a real mother is at best double-think, at worst nonsense'.[3] In many, or most, cases, shifting care outside of the home means a falling quality of care. This is particularly likely to be true for middle-class children. However, infants whose families are under economic stress may also be at special risk, not only because of the cost of proper care, but because the strain can undermine the parents' capacity to be available to and supportive of their offspring.[4]

Much of existing daycare is also clearly inadequate when it comes to providing a healthy environment for development, as high-quality care is very expensive. The irony is that we are urged to expand daycare enormously when, if proper standards were enforced and we refused to tolerate provisions which are clearly unconducive and even detrimental to development, the number of places would, in all likelihood, fall.

Affordable Care Is Low-quality Care

The singular difficulties and cost of providing good quality care, with its highly involved and trained staff, small group size, caregiver stability, and low infant to caregiver ratios, should surely demonstrate how 'affordable, universally available, good-quality, easily accessible childcare' (to use the popular mantra) is a chimaera, unrealisable in the real world. Affordable care is *low-quality* care. Universally available *high-quality* care is achievable nowhere on earth.

The fantasy gains currency from the way in which the old social and economic supports have gone. Since parents cannot afford to care for their children, childcare seems inevitable, as the something *out there* which will perform the task instead. This is all on a par with the mirage of the man in the desert who imagines that a spring of accessible, free and pure water *must* be behind the next dune. At the same time, we cannot accept that there might be limitations on adult choices; so, somehow, society has got to relieve people of the mundane caring that gets in the way.

However, although the word 'quality' trips out as part of the familiar incantation in many of the grand plans of childcare, in practice it has little or no bearing on recommendations, which are subordinated to the one, over-riding aim of getting more mothers to work. The demand for free and universally available daycare from birth onward is a women's issue, not a child issue.

Presenting their calculations of the returns from maternal employment Heather Joshi and Hugh Davies make the astonishing statement that:

> Whatever their precise magnitude, there are likely to be intrinsic benefits to children in the childcare provisions envisaged here. Legislation already exists to protect children against poor standards of care. It should go as read that the facilities hypothesized in this paper are of a standard to benefit children directly.[5]

The suggestion is that any provision that meets minimum registration requirements must be like Perry Pre-school! Moreover, their claims that 'the revenue gain to the exchequer may exceed the costs of 100 per cent subsidy' have to be read with one eye on the small print. Then it will be seen that the 'gains' not only take a long time to realise, but relate to cheap childminding, with after-school programmes only for primary children: 'secondary school children fend for themselves'. Even in the case of this 'low cost' childcare, 19 per cent to 25 per cent of the hypothesized gains to the public sector take ten years to accumulate (62 per cent or 71 per cent after 20 years). Their alternative of 'high cost' childcare (a day nursery with an educational input at a cost of £5,400 per child a year for 1991) shows a loss almost as high as its ultimate gain after ten years, and a Swedish style 'high cost' system 'overshoots massively'.

Hence, it is a mistake to assume that claims for big returns to the Exchequer from investment in childcare must relate to 'quality' childcare. Even what, at first sight, appear to be suggestions for improvement are all too apt to be swept aside in the push for expansion. In their *Childcare in a Modern Welfare System* (for the Institute of Public Policy Research) Bronwen Cohen and Neil Fraser speak of children's access to the 'social, educational and long-term economic benefits' of daycare, in which 'stability and continuity' are provided by 'properly trained and paid workers: low staff turnover, secure staff/child relationships' etc., However, while standards 'should be clear and vigorously enforced', they are also apparently to be 'minimal ... local authorities should be able to develop their own guidelines ... taking account of local needs and conditions'.[6]

What Are The Real Gains?

Anyone who believes that there are gains to be made for the public purse from childcare is under a delusion. Indeed, there may be stronger limits to the capacity of subsidised care to get mothers 'back to work' than its exponents acknowledge. Not only Bronwen Cohen and Neil Fraser, but also Sally Holtermann for the National Children's Bureau,[7] seem to have been extravagant with promises about the billions that would accrue to the nation if their recommendations were implemented. In the Equal Opportunities Commission's *Parents' Employment Rights and Childcare*, Holtermann herself, as one of the authors, speaks of those who 'may have somewhat overestimated the extent to which, with greater availability of childcare, women would work longer hours'.[8]

In this EOC publication, plans for a more limited expansion of subsidised childcare are put forward simply for low earners and lone parents. If individuals and employers each paid a third of the cost, the price to the state is estimated at £922 million a year (1992) while the flowback to the Exchequer would be about £1,080 million per year. It is candidly admitted that this depends upon the high taxation of low-income households which, were it reduced, would mean that 'the flowback to the Treasury would be less', while more money in the pockets of parents and less in the state's would weaken the case for childcare subsidies![9]

That 90 Per Cent

The magic number of 90 per cent of lone parents desperate to work is bandied about in support of these claims as if it were an incontrovertible fact. However, the actual figures in the relevant survey are that 28 per cent of lone parents wish to work now or 'soon' and 63 per cent 'later'. The 90 per cent is all 'in due course', often after the children have grown up— so it can hardly be that the 'lack of available and affordable childcare prevented them from doing so'.[10] Those who cite childcare as an enticement to make them work 'sooner', or an obstacle to returning to work are a decisive minority of unoccupied lone parents (or 26 per cent). Taking into account those who wished to make changes, whenever, there would be an overall decline of lone parents on Income Support of 23 per cent.[11] For all lone mothers of children under five, there is a 'preferred' employment rate of only 40 per cent, much of it part-time.

Evidence like this has led the Employment Department to characterise even the 'revised' EOC figures for the gains from *targeted* childcare subsidies as 'over-optimistic' about the extra numbers in work, their earnings levels, and the deadweight costs. Many mothers who already work would qualify for the subsidy, which alone turns the proposals into a net cost to the Exchequer. While Holtermann claims that an extra 132,000 lone mothers would enter employment, evidence only points to a 'potential response' of around 90,000; plus an additional 100,000 married women, rather than 285,000. Moreover: 'These more realistic figures are still based on the rather questionable assumption that all of the subsidy would be effective in inducing all these mothers into the labour market, and that they would all find jobs'.[12]

Not least, the vast majority of single mothers finish school at the minimum age and, like many women in low earner couples, only a minority have any educational or vocational qualifications. This must be added to the more general, if scarcely mentionable fact, that mothers are less sensitive then men, especially fathers, to work incentives. In the old Soviet Union it was eventually realised that it was counter-productive to push low-income mothers into the workforce, especially considering the high cost and poor quality of much daycare.[13] What then are we to make of arguments that big subsidies have to be offered to mothers whose earning potential is low to get them into work, the reason for which is to reverse the 'inequity' women suffer in lost earnings by having children, when special training will also have to be offered in order to make their employment worthwhile?

Researchers from the Institute of Fiscal Studies now calculate that, even if the state paid childcare costs, only 70,000 women would take jobs and 130,000 would increase their hours (representing 20 per cent of full-time employees and 15 per cent of part-timers).[14] This would involve about seven per cent of lone parents and five per cent of women in unwaged couples, as the move would primarily affect existing two-earner couples. The net cost is still £900 million despite benefit savings and higher tax revenues, and this does not take into account greater use of formal childcare by mothers who do not change their labour supply. If subsidies are means tested, the figures fall to 60,000 new employees (45,000 would increase their hours). A £10 voucher, costing £170 million net, might encourage 30,000 new entrants to work and 50,000 to increase labour supply, but what does £10 per week buy in terms of childcare? The researchers admit that their data does not provide information that 'could enable us to determine the quality of care received by a child'[15] (although they think it 'iniquitous' to refuse a child opportunities to improve his life chances!).

Any notion that crèches will pay for themselves by transforming mothers into ambitious, full-time careerists, is moonshine—not least because it is based on arrogant and ignorant assumptions about what other people want and dictatorial notions of how they must live. The most that is likely to happen is that more mothers would use subsidised childcare to work longer part-time hours. Hard pressed secondary earners are as resistant to increasing their hours or responsibilities and losing flexibility as they are anxious to take work which will boost family income. Already, part-time employment accounts for much of the employment created over the last decade as well as the growth in women in paid work since the 1970s, who in turn account for most of the growth in the workforce.

It is, in any case, a misconception to ever suppose that childcare, or the transfer of domestic tasks to the market sector or collective, could put mothers on an equal footing with childless women or men. Households in which caregiving takes place need a lot of management. Moreover, the mothers' 'feelings for their children still exist ... finding time for loving them limits their availability for advancement and never having time for anything puts the mother/worker at the top of the stress table'.[16]

Childcare As The Final Solution

One has a certain sympathy with radical feminist Shulamith Firestone who believes that: 'Daycare centres buy women off'. In her ultimate revolution, complete freedom and perfect competition for women means artificial reproduction, with the end of attachment, genetic children and childhood as a life phase.[17] As such, the residential institution has often appeared as the final solution to all the demands of caregiving, as developed in China, the old Soviet Union, Romania and the German Democratic Republic.

By encouraging mothers to work, while paying unemployment benefits to men who don't, the state may not be getting two workers for the price of one, as equal opportunities activists promise, but only one or even half for the price of two.[18] The state may not net in more taxes, even if it raises these, if companies push out full-time workers and restructure jobs so that they can be filled by more contingent, cheaper workers. The obverse of such feminisation of the labour market is the reduction of men's productive contribution.

While there is talk of women getting 'breadwinner incomes', the market will not pay everyone at the kind of level which men had when they dominated it. It is obvious why business is so keen both to have publicly funded daycare and more Family Credit for low wage earners, since this will lower both the costs to workers themselves and firms' wage bills by throwing production costs onto the state.

Who Cares About Men?

Equality activists take no account of the implications for revenue of losses in the male capacity to provide which may easily follow from further female employment drives and childcare subsidies, particularly if these are expressly targeted on lone parents. The contribution of male workers is assumed to be constant, although the notion of men as family providers is roundly condemned and the express aim is to make women able to support themselves and their children independently. The increased number of men without families to support will have reduced incentives to enter or stay in the labour market or increase their earnings, and are far more likely to become dependent themselves.

There is already a weakness in government tax revenues, as the gap between what the government spends and the income it receives is, if anything, widening. The change to a feminised workforce, with much flexible, part-time and casual work, may not be an unmitigated good, and it is arguable that this may be holding back national output, as well as depleting tax revenues. The most productive type of worker is the full-time male between the ages of 35 and 65, and the failure to keep skilled, mature men in full-time jobs, as well as high unemployment among young men, represents an inefficient use of labour. A lack of subsidised childcare services is blamed for initiating 'a downward occupational spiral which results in an irrevocable life process'[19] for women, but the effect of labour market marginality on male life chances is, it seems, of no consequence, and there is little concern about the depreciation of men's human capital.

It might make as much or better economic sense to retrain older workers, as well as paying more attention to the problems of unemployed and under-employed men. Their taxes would then take the pressure off young families, instead of placing more burdens on mothers to leave their infants. Furthermore, the knowledge that employers would value them in their middle and later years, despite a work break, would do much to help women make decisions about work and family.

When families push more labour onto the market to cope with economic insecurity, couples expend twice the effort to get where they would have previously have been on one main income, and are unable to co-operate to exploit any division of labour. Encouraging or coercing mothers to work by making it progressively more difficult to stay at home simply means more dissatisfied parents struggling with work patterns they regret. This is unconducive to the interests of the child if it undermines marital stability and parental care. The failure to provide adequate time for parenting, especially during critical times in a child's life, produces these hurried, worried parents raising hurried, worried children.[20] Moreover, when child well-being is increasingly undermined by the evasion, refusal or difficulty of fathers to provide for their children, how does the disparagement or condemnation of breadwinning possibly motivate men to support their offspring? What 'frequently burdens young mothers today is not the ideal of paternal provision, but rather the erosion of that ideal'.[21]

What Parents Really Want

... perhaps the most moving letters of all are the letters I have received from
couples with small children on very low incomes who say the emotional stress
is sometimes intolerable. Then there are those who have written of their pain
of leaving a nine-week-old baby in somebody else's care. Others write and tell
of their heart rending decision to chose between their baby and their mortgage.
Some have even decided to lose their houses in order to look after their baby
themselves. None of them saw cheap childcare as the answer.

Kathy Gyngell of Full-time Mothers[1]

Childcare Of First Resort

Despite claims that it is only the lack of 'affordable, accessible childcare'
which consigns children to the care of their parents, there is evidence that
a majority of people still view parental care as ideal at pre-school age.[2]
Care by the mother is particularly preferred for babies and toddlers. Thus,
97.2 per cent of non-employed American mothers favour parental care for
children under one, as do 64.3 per cent of employed mothers. (For children
aged between one and two the figures are 92.8 per cent and 62.1 per cent,
and for those over two it is 83 per cent and 52.8 per cent.) Furthermore,
79 per cent of women thought that the roles of wife and mother were more
important than that of a worker outside the home. Similar figures were
obtained from the 1985 wave of the National Longitudinal Survey of
Youth,[3] where the majority of parents considered care by close kin to be
best for young children under three.

Given the strong preference in favour of the family as the rearer of
children, it is understandable that, when asked to choose what work
arrangements they think best for families with children, nearly 80 per
cent of British people opt for the mother being at home when the children
are under five. Only three per cent want two full-time jobs. As children
grow older, the emphasis passes to part-time work for the mother.
Similarly, when asked 'should a woman work when her children are under
school age', over half said that she should not, while a third said that she
should work only part-time.[4] There is little support for notions that women
with young children *ought* to work.

Who Is Being Forced?

Official pronouncements on women's needs tend to emphasise mothers
who work, rather than those who are not in the labour force at all (which

includes half of all mothers of under-fives). Moreover, the notion is perpetuated that all working mothers need substitute childcare, and that all children not being accommodated in formal arrangements are somehow suffering in inadequate arrangements. Yet many mothers do not need daycare at all, not least because they arrange work schedules so that there is always a parent or grandparent at home with the children. Furthermore, 92 per cent of married women with children say they work part-time because they do not want a full-time job.[5] Indeed, it seems that 70 per cent of the five million women of working age who are economically inactive do not want a job, and a half cite looking after their home and family as the reason. Claims made by bodies like the Equal Opportunities Commission that 'Lack of childcare and limited employment rights force many women to leave work completely after a baby and restrict them to part-time jobs when they return to work'[6] are wide of the mark.

If anything, it is the mothers in employment who are more likely to be the victims of economic compulsion than the mothers who stay at home. One poll showed that 62 per cent of employed mothers of infants would have been at home if money were not the problem (and 82 per cent in the lower income bracket).[7] Overall, about two-thirds or more of British or American dual-income families want a parent at home,[8] and the experience is international. Surveys in 120 diverse enterprises in ten former Soviet Republics showed that three-quarters of women working full-time preferred part-time work, especially where there were children.[9] Under the impetus of a strong equal rights movement, Denmark pursued the policy of full maternal employment and invested heavily in daycare centres. Yet Jacob Vedel-Petersen, Director of the Danish National Institute of Social Research, observed in 1989 that this ran:

> ... counter to what most women want. When we asked mothers which overall structure they prefer, the answers accumulate around 1½ jobs in the family ... only an insignificant minority prefer two full-time jobs with the children in a daycare center all day. This preference has been noted in several investigations ... in contrast, actually, of a growing number of women in full-time jobs, including women with small children. In other words, the gap between desires and realities has steadily widened. This aspect has never been a subject of serious debate in Denmark.[10]

Childcare does not seem to have been the subject of open debate before being developed anywhere. Yet the evidence we have seen shows how the arrangement where one parent provides the whole or the bulk of care for pre-school children, and then perhaps incrementally increases their participation in the labour force as children go to school, is associated with the least problems. If parents find work interesting, then their satisfaction may benefit the family without cutting into the child's time at home.

In contrast, the widely advocated pattern of early, full-time work, is overwhelmingly associated with adverse reports. It is doubtful whether most families can function with both parents following the traditional male work model. At most, one breadwinner can subordinate other roles to work for most of the time, with another breadwinner playing an ancillary, less demanding role. For both persons to be career dedicated, couples would have to stop having children, as more are already doing, or else household services, as well as childcare, would have to be provided from outside sources on an unprecedented scale.

Parents usually have different priorities from equality activists, who are publicly financed to campaign for equal outcomes in the marketplace. The latter laments as irrational and negative the 'belief that young children should be cared for at home by their mothers ...' or that 'the main role of the "good father" is to support his family financially'.[11] However, the majority of parents find their family life more important and satisfying than work, and they see earning opportunities in terms of improving the security of family life. Mothers' 'choices about market work are constrained not by routine household drudgery, but by complex, often satisfying, and highly energy absorbing caregiving work at home', and 'they refuse to give up the personal caregiving activities they value in life'.[12] If mothers put their families first, it is hard to see how this is 'to the detriment of women',[13] if it is doing what they themselves value. Differences in earnings reflect differences in the approach of parents to work, not just discrimination, or the division of labour by gender. Despite the difficulties and disadvantages of one-income families, the numbers of children cared for at home remains surprisingly high.

What we have more of are 'dual earners', rather than 'dual-career' families. Anyway, the notion of 'dual-careers' no more takes account of structural economic constraints, than women's preferences, or household work.[14] This is because the model rests on increasing female access to high level professions and managerial positions, when there will always be a limited supply of well-paid, developmental careers in the occupational structure. Even many highly educated mothers would rather not engage in their own career in the childrearing years. No doubt many childless women do not 'anticipate quite so heavy a commitment to family', and so sharp a reduction in working hours, if and when they become mothers. No doubt many female students anticipate spending more time on the job than with their families. No doubt the expectations of men about their working hours are more consistent with outcomes over time than are women's. However, this does not make women's appraisal of future priorities from a childfree standpoint the more 'correct' perspective, compared with the reassessments they make once they actually become parents. As the one-time deputy editor of the magazine *Marie-Claire* put it:

> Until I had Joe, I always wanted a career as well as children and I assumed I'd be able to manage the two. But I didn't have a clue. If you don't have sisters or friends with children, you don't know what it is all about. ... No one in the editorial team had had a baby ... [but] I kept hearing about women who had

worked right up until the day they gave birth and gone back to work two weeks later. The realisation that I couldn't go back to full-time employment came when I started to try and organise childcare. I remember pushing Joe round the park, and each time I thought about it I'd start crying. It was a feeling of grief and utter desolation. The idea of being separated from my baby was more than I could bear.[15]

Women in élite positions are more likely to be single and childless, or divorced, since it means they are better able to pursue careers without interruption. There is not a shred of evidence to support the claim that, once childcare arrives, more women will have children—rather the contrary. Everywhere the experience has been that women will not have babies in order to leave them in the crèche.

The Scandinavian Experience

This is nowhere better illustrated than by Sweden's experience, which is probably the most concerted attempt in history to engineer equality between men and women in every sphere, with massive public re-education, economic incentives and social pressures. The equality drive in the 1970s included changes to tax and housing assistance which made it almost impossible to support a home on one income, while subsidised daycare assumed priority as the main form of help for parents.[16]

By the 1980s Sweden led the Western world in women's employment, with an estimated 85 per cent of mothers of under-sevens in the work-force. It also had the highest percentage of women who worked part-time or were only nominally in the workplace (being registered sick or unemployed). As part-timers increased from one third to 45 per cent of employed women, the average number of hours worked actually dropped —accounted for by the increased employment of those in the primary childrearing age group. If the idea was for mothers to combine parenthood and employment by doing both at the same time, rather than in sequence, another unintended effect was to increase the rate of childlessness, and drive down family size. As in the former socialist countries, the necessity for two wage-earners was accompanied by birth rates significantly below replacement level.

According to a national poll for the Swedish government in 1987, 80 per cent or more of mothers regarded it as ideal to be able to care for their children at home, at least until they were three.[17] By the late 1980s, mothers could qualify for extended periods of parental leave, much of it paid. Those who had two or more children sufficiently close together might remain on leave from work for five consecutive years or longer, and, on return to work, had to put in no more than six hours to qualify as doing a full day's work. With role conflict reduced to manageable levels, the birthrate ascended sharply to replacement level.[18]

Norway has moved in the same direction, giving parents 42 weeks of paid leave at 100 per cent, or 52 weeks at 80 per cent, of pay. Finland now offers a cash benefit to parents of under-threes as an alternative to a place in a childcare project. Denmark has also introduced a sweeping new parental leave law which is expected to reduce the demand for childcare places. Any parent gets at least six months paid leave after maternity leave finishes and they can have a further six months with their employers consent. Local authorities can supplement the generous flat rate payment and most are likely to do so in order to reduce the demand for services for young children.

Trends In Europe

A trend towards longer hours in pre-school educational institutions in Europe has to be balanced by the movement away from care for infants. Even the expansion of programmes for toddlers is marked by ambivalence, or concern about quality and cost. If pre-school education is increasingly universal, publicly funded and operated so, in France, with a long tradition and much experience, about 95 per cent of children aged three to five are in écoles maternelles, (which run a developmentally appropriate curriculum for four days a week). In Italy, about 90 per cent of three- to five-year-olds attend some kind of pre-school, but less than half of mothers are in the workforce at all. In turn, 75 per cent of German children aged three to five are in part-time educational programmes. At the same time, under ten per cent of under-twos in France, five per cent in Italy, and only two per cent in Germany are in pre-school or public nurseries of any kind. Overall, the trend of recent years has been towards extending maternity leave in some form to make it possible for a parent to be at home until the child is at least one-and-a-half or preferably three:

> The rationales offered for these policies include the extraordinarily high costs of satisfactory out-of-home infant care, a belief that young children are better off if the mother stays home for awhile, a desire to encourage low-skilled women to stay out of the labour force in a period of high unemployment, and an interest in facilitating a better balance between paid work and family work, especially for women.[19]

However, even parental leave provisions hardly come cheap, as these invariably mean making up the parent's wages for an extended period, and there is a tendency for them to give way to more traditional forms of family support. (In Sweden, the costs of unemployment and welfare provisions, together with declining tax revenues, has pushed the budget into massive deficit, and put pressure on the parental leave programme.) The process occurred in the old socialist territories, and is now exemplified in Slovenia (formerly part of Yugoslavia), where the monolithic emphasis on childcare and full-time maternal employment was first modified by a parental leave system, which is now being replaced by family allowances and tax reliefs.[20]

Putting A Price On Love

One solution to role overload for the employed mother is to buy as much help
as you can possibly afford, even if it means foregoing other pleasures—which
you probably do not have time for anyway ... *Unless you are on the poverty*
line, money spent on cleaning help, fast foods, and other self-saving tactics
will be money well spent. Fish and chips or pizza a couple of nights a week
will not kill anyone. (emphasis added)

Sandra Scarr and J. Dunn, *Mother Care: Other Care*[1]

Can Money Buy Everything?

Are mothers wrong to put their work secondary to the welfare of their
families, or misguided in finding the latter a source of satisfaction? Is
caregiving work really a minor or comparatively useless pursuit? Does it
make a more or less important social contribution than work in the
market sector? Do we attribute the social product just to those who work
in market production, while ignoring and devaluing reproduction and
human care without which no society could continue?

Claims that full maternal employment represents an immense gain in
productivity or economic well-being rest, to no small extent, on the entry
of previously unpaid services into the money economy. Of course, where
one spouse earns while the other maintains the home and family, national
productivity statistics only reflect the output of the earning spouse. If both
go out to work and as a result have to pay for childcare and for someone
to clean their house, Gross National Product (GNP) includes both parents'
earnings as well as those of the caregiver and cleaner.

However, this does not increase the services rendered; it merely puts a
monetary value on them. When people buy takeaway food instead of
cooking it themselves, nothing is there that would not have existed before,
as one woman fries burgers while another minds her baby. In turn, much
of the money which the state takes in taxes from earning mothers goes
straight out again to cover some of the functions that people once
performed as part of their everyday life.

In the process women move from 'home-production' to doing similar
work for the government or service industries, or staffing the administra-
tions than manage it. The steady increase in service jobs, in both the
public and private sectors, which makes women available for the market,
is part of a self-fulfilling process. For Denmark, the number of female
homemakers declined by 579,000 between 1960 and 1982 as the number

of employees in the Danish public sector grew by 532,000, with most of the growth in daycare, care of the elderly, hospitals and schools.[2] Similarly, in Sweden, the numbers in public employment tripled between 1960 and 1980, much of it in the welfare sector. Claims by feminists that opportunities have increased for the exercise of female power have to be seen against a background of women becoming increasingly dependent upon the state, both as welfare clients and as welfare workers. By 1980, 70 per cent of the 17.3 million social service jobs at all levels of American government were held by women and could account for much of female job gains since 1960.[3] Some is due to the expansion of formal education and medicine. However, personal service tasks, like childcare, may be done less efficiently because the objects of attention are non-family members, in whom nobody has a personal stake.

It has tended to be the case that women choose work in the personal service field because this is congruent with work in the domestic sector. Ironically, the disapproval and disincentives surrounding home-based childrearing may encourage girls to gravitate towards paid caregiving. One in five girls aged 15-18 asked, on behalf of City and Guilds, to pick from a list of careers which included science, law, building and acting, chose a 'career' in childcare. The only difference from the parental generation seemed to be that no girl wanted to become a housewife. However: 'the rocketing popularity of child-minding/nursery nursing may be down to the fact that this has become an acceptable stopgap and euphemism for girls who really want to run a home and look after children'.[4]

While 'cashing out' services may *add* little or nothing to the sum total of production, this does not negate their existence or importance. Modern historians and sociologists like to see housewives, past and present, as engaged in demeaning, monotonous and pointless work that produces nothing of intrinsic value. However, paid employment can double the workload while diminishing what is produced at home.[5] 'Unwaged work' is depicted as archaic and worthless, but the truth is that this is the most significant factor affecting the quality of life of all, as massive amounts of unpaid labour necessarily underpin industrial economies. While it does not feature in GNP, domestic work clearly makes a vital contribution to the functioning of the market sector. Not least, it increases the productivity of present and future wage-earners. Economists have sometimes dealt with the increased prosperity of working-class households in the first part of the twentieth century without taking into account the investment of personal resources in improving living standards. We see this in the dramatic improvements in child health between 1890 and 1930, a period in which a tremendous interest and popular effort went into developing domestic knowledge and skills.

Time given to the care and welfare of husbands and children is now expressly condemned for detracting from the woman's personal accumulation of income and 'human capital'. Men are depicted as exploiting her labour to maintain or enhance their own earning power. There is no recognition of collaboration or mutual support for mutual benefit. Yet, the wife's conscious investment in the husband's work performance, or marketability, in the childrearing years is undertaken, not least, to increase her own options through the enhancement of their *joint* resources, with his increasing income seen as generally benefiting the family.

Children The Producers Of The Future

Given the rejection of any value or motivation beyond a self-centred, one-generational concern to maximise personal gain, there is no acknowledgement that the performance of children depends upon the altruistic commitment of parental time and resources. The idea that the economy must be operating below capacity if women are caring for children rather than earning wages neglects the fact that those children are the generators of future wealth, and that their productivity depends upon a considerable investment by parents in their upbringing. Moreover, whereas an adult can retrain or revitalise their vocational skills, there may be no 'second chances' where children's development is concerned.

In his book *The Causes of Progress* Emmanuel Todd describes how economic development proceeds from cultural development, where literacy and the 'modernization of the mind' are not simply the products of material wealth, or even of formal education. They depend upon the prolongation and enrichment of the human learning process, in which the key variable is family life. Where mothers bring their own increased educational resources to the system of inter-personal relationships, this furthers the development of complex civilisation and economic advancement.[6]

If personal caregiving is fundamental to the sort of life that people find valuable, they are also valued in this sphere precisely *because* what they do is unpriced: 'uncompensated civic work remains a huge factor in the generation of self-worth and community respect for *both* men and women'. But:

> Wherever care is shifted into the market economy, it is paid but poorly paid *work* and, like other low-income service jobs, open to the least skilled workers. By contrast, for as long as care remains in the gendered economy of kin/community services, it is *work but not a job*, and the grammar of pay, inequality, and feminisation on these issues does not rule in the care-provider's self-concept, because it is fulfilled in a gift relation that it would be entirely incongruous to imagine in contractarian terms.[7]

There is, in any case, a limit to which types of caregiving can be transferred to state institutions or commercial ventures. Given the huge value of the input, the social infrastructure provided by the home would involve very significant investment if it had to be provided by crèches, nurseries, counselling, nursing, hospitals, health centres, canteens, policing etc. The family's early attachments are also the basis of human culture, and childrearing lies at the heart of the relationships, obligations and responsibilities which sustain a moral economy on which both state and market depend, but cannot generate. However, both industrial capitalism and the growth of state power have made it difficult to protect the boundary between the competitive market and the altruistic economy of the family.[8]

Historical Measures To Protect The Family

Historically, various devices have been constructed to shelter the family from full immersion in the industrial economy. One was the 'living wage', which endeavoured to provide men with earnings which could support a family as well as themselves. Competition between family members for work, with its downward push on the wage rate, was discouraged through restrictions on child and female labour.

Other mechanisms involved tax allowances on the old principle of 'ability to pay', which assumed that taxation should not only reflect the level of income, but the number of people dependent upon it. Family allowance schemes have also been widespread, whether operating at the level of firms, industries, professional associations, local authorities or the state. Equal pay and opportunity policies once tended to go with compensation for families through various forms of allowance schemes. This reflects the way that past generations of feminists were often the leading advocates of measures to foster the special contribution of mothers, as well as the entry of women into the professions and politics. They also realised that women's occupational advance and family protection were not necessarily opposed, while the entry into the market of necessitous or hard-pressed secondary earners was in nobody's interests.

Whatever the means, compensatory measures which counter the disadvantages of families in the waged economy also safeguard the value of time spent in childrearing, and help define this, not as worthless and demeaning work, but socially approved work that contributes to the greater good of the community. The arrival of children is a stressful and demanding time for parents, yet there is little recognition of the fact that time for parenting may be essential for the well-being both of the infant and the family system. While the emphasis is placed on the need for pre-schools to overcome educational disadvantage, the attention which a child receives at home—the biggest influence on children's attainments—is being squeezed by financial disincentives against parents either staying together or giving time to their children. Indeed, the responsibilities of parenthood are scarcely recognised at all now in the tax system, and the tax reforms of the 1980s were targeted at single, childless people, whose tax burden fell.

Thus, a couple on average earnings with two children paid 22.5 per cent of their income in direct taxes in 1995/96 (i.e. income tax and National

Insurance, counting Child Benefit as if it were tax relief) compared to 9.0 per cent in 1964/65 and 20.9 per cent in 1978/79. One reason why family taxes have increased so much is the abolition of the child tax allowance and the family allowance in the late 1970s. They were replaced by Child Benefit when both were at their lowest level, and this, in its turn, was frozen for much of the 1980s. The married couples' allowance, worth half of the basic personal allowance up to 1990, was frozen in value and then heavily cut, so that its cash value fell to £4.97 per week in 1995/6. National Insurance, which makes no allowances for dependents, has risen steeply while council tax (which replaced household rates) makes couples pay 25 per cent more than singles.[9]

Childrearing has become increasingly associated with poverty, poor living standards, stress and lower levels of psychological well-being. These trends ensure a feedback effect on child welfare and the desire for children. As it becomes both more untenable economically (and increasingly disapproved of) to rear children at home, so there are more parents under pressure who must necessarily make whatever childcare arrangements they can find. At the same time, the massive media campaign to smooth the path of women to work involves getting us all to accept lower standards of childrearing. Parental freedom is compromised. They must spend large percentages of their earnings, or have them involuntarily removed, so that this money can be translated into minimal wages for others to provide childcare, which is often of a far lower standard than the child would receive at home.

However, since many of the problems of parenthood result from a lack of family resources (time and money), these are amenable to public solutions.[10] A family of two or three children, spaced two or three years apart, means full-time parenthood for ten or twelve years at the most. It should surely be possible to plan for this short segment of the lifecycle, which represents less time than most able-bodied people spend in retirement, for which increasingly lavish provision is made. In the light of the difficult position of the family in the equal wage and opportunity economy, some of the thought, planning and finance that now goes into the construction of pension schemes, whether private, state or employer-assisted, needs to go towards the re-creation of family allowance schemes, to help modern parents at the most heavily loaded point in the lifecycle.

Freedom To Choose

It is certainly best all round if parents can *choose* whether or not they wish to work outside the home. For a variety of reasons, some women prefer to arrange alternative care for their children. This is their right. However, out of consideration for the welfare of children, no government should encourage or coerce mothers into employment unless it can indeed ensure that childcare of a proper quality is widely available. By its nature, this is likely to remain a very scarce and costly commodity. In turn, it is also necessary for the law to afford more protection to the marriage contract. It will then become more rational to invest in marriage as the place in which to securely co-operate in the rearing of children.[11]

Subsidised childcare also means that not only do families who do not wish to use these facilities receive no direct benefit, but also that they are paying through taxation for other parents who put their children into third party care. Tax relief that allows parents to write off a proportion of their childcare expenses provides no assistance to families who do their own caring. Whatever else might be said about families with a mother at home, they are every bit as deserving of relief as families with employed mothers.

Conclusion

The Daycare Juggernaut

Coming out against (daycare centres) now would be like coming out against the automobile ... Daycare is a fact of modern life, no longer a debatable issue ... Whether for it or against it, whether one thinks it is healthy or not, it is inevitable. Daycare is like a roller coaster that cannot be stopped.
Marion Blum, *The Daycare Dilemma*[1]

The campaign for daycare is like a juggernaut racing downhill. It carries an unlikely band of fellow-travellers—feminists and advocates of 'alternative lifestyles', together with industrialists, trades unionists, left-wing academics and right-wing government spokespersons. There is an almost universal consensus in the media that the mass provision of daycare is both desirable and urgently required. Any alternative viewpoint is regarded as almost too absurd to mention.

And yet, as we have seen, the case for daycare is far from watertight. The research findings into the effects on children, mothers and fathers of a system which transfers responsibility for childrearing out of the home and onto third-party carers should at least give pause for thought. If the movement has become unstoppable, as some of its supporters like to claim, we should be aware of what we are letting ourselves in for.

We are calling for the mass institutionalisation of the youngest, and most vulnerable groups of the ordinary child population, as a 'better' form of child rearing, at the same time as we are increasingly aware of how unsatisfactory and dangerous institutions are even for older 'problem', neglected or unwanted children.

Calling for a national childcare strategy, Margaret Hodge, Labour MP for Barking, complained that 'for too long, the early years of a child's life have been seen as the private concern of the parents'.[2] Yet she admitted that Islington Council, under her leadership, had failed children in the care of its homes, after a government report had severely criticised the council's response to allegations of abuse and sexual exploitation. Malcolm King, the chairman of social services in Clwyd, North Wales, recently stated that: 'The evidence emerging is that children's homes were a *gulag archipelago* stretching across Britain—wonderful places for paedophiles but, for children who suffered, places of unending nightmares'.[3] (In Clwyd at least 100 children were sexually abused over 20 years, of whom 12 subsequently died.) Similar stories have, and are, being told of other areas, but none seem to dim the bright hopes held out for the collectivisation of the care of the under-fives.

The Abolition Of The Family In Utopia

It appears to be taken for granted that, given a committed 'national childcare strategy', all the necessary knowledge and resources exist to speedily achieve full 'equality of opportunity'—not only between women and men, but 'between children themselves'.[4] This would 'nurture human capital and unleash new power into the economy ... as the Government would be helping nurture better educated and more socially amenable future generations'.[5] Childcare exponents are obviously unperturbed by the way in which the twentieth century is littered with the wreckage of such dreams, which have so often floundered in a mess of unforeseen complications, unintended consequences and misery.

The childcare campaign is now the leading example of the way in which, as Bryce Christensen observes,[6] the demands of Utopians have insinuated themselves into contemporary politics via welfare issues and equal opportunity programmes. Whether Utopia is represented as a dream or a nightmare, and whether it is fantasy or plan, key elements from Plato's *Republic* onwards have been comprehensive childcare, along with full female employment, promiscuous sex, and the demise of the family.

In the work of New Left philosopher Herbert Marcuse, leading inspiration of the 1960s counter-cultural revolution, the individual will only achieve the 'gratification of freely developing needs' as he sheds the restraints of marriage, gender roles and family life. Yevgeny Zamyatin had Bolshevik Russia in mind when *We* was published in 1924 and, in this predecessor to Orwell's *1984*, children are cared for from birth in the Child Rearing Factory. In Huxley's *Brave New World* the word mother is 'a pornographic impropriety', children are cared for by officials who programme them for lives of hedonism and conformity, as the ruling élite encourages promiscuity and recreational drug-taking. In both works, rebellion takes the form of the re-assertion of the mother/child bond.

Parental care, as a relic of the pre-scientific age, receives particular emphasis in *Walden Two* by behaviourist psychologist B.F. Skinner. In his preface to the 1976 edition Skinner complained that the potential of home-reared children was squandered because of all the mistakes and errors of incompetent parents. Group care abolishes the division between home and school. This not only meant that blood relationships could be happily forgotten; it would also destroy 'prejudices regarding the occupations of the sexes' and foster the 'complete equality of men and women' in all forms of work.[7]

Changes in family law and welfare policy currently being promoted in the West are much the same as those enacted soon after the 1917 Russian revolution by the Bolsheviks in order to dismantle the family: easy divorce, abolition of the distinction between legitimate and illegitimate births, and collectivised child rearing.[8]

It seems that what we learn from history is that we do not learn from history. Perhaps we might at least try a little harder to respond to objective research findings, rather than the demands of interest groups. We might also pay more attention to what parents and children actually want. Career success for individuals is ultimately a private matter, while the well-being and development of children and families is basic to the future of everything. More effort needs to go into creating the circumstances under which families can optimally raise their children. It might appear to be the responsibility of parents to provide the healthy, secure, loving, disciplined and nurturant infancy and childhood which is every child's due. However, they cannot do so unless the wider society creates the conditions and policies which enable them.

In the interests of fairness, if for no other reason, all parents should receive recognition, including those who choose to care for their children at home. If the government has any duty to facilitate the successful rearing of the nation's children, it would do well to enhance the opportunities for parents to care for their own children. This is in line both with most people's aspirations and with what we know is best for the welfare of most children.

Appendix

Working Through Parents

One particular programme which actually reported a retention of IQ gains for low-income children at eight years, as well as better school performance and school attendance, involved intervention with the family as a whole from before the birth of their first child until 30 months after.[1] Families were given a range of medical and other services (important in the US where there is no national health service comparable to Britain's), visited regularly and could, if they wished, use daycare or a traditional nursery school. With family support and a flexible programme, changes in the programme parents' behaviour, compared with that of parents in the control groups, may have been crucial to its success. As they recognised their role in influencing their child's development, the parents acquired more control over their lives.

The role of continuing parental support is also seen in the effects of the Child/Parent Center Pre-school programme in Chicago on children up to ten years. Here, 757 low-income, inner city black children aged three and four were enrolled in this variant of Head Start.[2] (They are part of the comprehensive Longitudinal Study of Children at Risk.) The pre-school project was a half-day programme designed to promote children's school readiness and reading/language skills. As with Head Start, it emphasised the provision of comprehensive services to families. Unlike Head Start, it provided for several years follow-up services as the children went through primary school. The central philosophy was that parents are the critical socialising force in children's development. Direct parental involvement of at least one half day per week was expected in order to enhance parent/child relations and attachment to school. This may have entailed acting as classroom aides, attending school events, accompanying field trips, attending meetings on behalf of the child, or organising resources.

While the children were not randomly assigned to the programme, a sophisticated strategy was used to detect possible selection bias and unmeasured variables that might affect the relationship between pre-school and child outcomes. Significant differences in achievement in reading and maths persisted up to the age of ten and even increased somewhat over the years, compared to the many studies showing the effects of pre-school on achievement fading to insignificance. There were also the familiar favourable effects on grade retention and special school placement. Parental involvement, which increased both the parent's and the child's commitment to school and learning, was again identified as a vital component that mediated the impact of pre-school on later adjustment. The children whose parents were most involved benefited the most and increases in parental involvement persisted into the school years. In contrast, and as found elsewhere, longer spells of pre-schooling conferred no additional benefits as the children moved through primary school.

A similar story is told for the Parent/Child Development Center programmes for low-income black children in Birmingham and New Orleans, and Mexican American families in Houston. These target children from 12 months, and make extensive use of parents as inter-venors with their own children. A follow-up at seven to ten years showed that the treated subjects significantly outscored untreated controls in both reading and maths, although no significant differences were recorded for grade retention or special education. Again, recent data from the follow-up of children in the Carolina Abecedarian Project, through to age 12, showed how disadvantaged children of low intelligence were particularly likely to maintain gains in IQ and academic achievement when pre-school intervention which emphasized parental involvement was followed with support in the early school years from Home School Resource Teachers.[3]

Where parents of children in disadvantaged circumstances are poorly educated themselves, it may be desirable to try to improve their own low educational level along with their attitudes towards schooling. British work on the acquisition of basic skills has pointed to the role of family literacy programmes, which involve both parents and young children, as a two generational way to tackle the poor standards of both.[4]

Notes

Introduction: 'The Key to Utopia'

1 *Employment Gazette Historical Supplement*, Vol. 102, No. 10, Employment Department Group, Government Statistical Service, October 1994.

2 *Employment Gazette, ibid.*

3 Phillips, A., 'More Women are Looking at Babies and Seeing a Sticky Ball and Chain', *The Guardian*, 17 June 1996.

4 Currie, E., 'Childcare: The Allowances that go Begging', *The Times*, 1 March 1990.

5 'Employers for Childcare', *Good Childcare, Good Business*, May 1993.

6 *Mind the Children*, London: Adam Smith Institute, 1989, p. 5.

7 Cohen, B. and Fraser, N., *Childcare in a Modern Welfare System*, London: Institute for Public Policy Research, 1991, pp. 90 and 105.

8 Carlson, A., 'Beyond the "Family Wage" Quandary', *The Family in America*, Vol. 8, No. 12, Rockford, Illinois: The Rockford Institute, December 1994.

9 Hancock, B., for the Equal Opportunities Commission, in *The Daily Telegraph*, 18 July 1989.

10 From Barukov, O., *Socialist Cities and Socialist Reconstruction of Life*, quoted in Mace, D. and Mace, V., *The Soviet Family*, London: Hutchinson, 1964, pp. 142-43.

11 *Mind the Children*, London: Adam Smith Institute, 1989, p. 25.

12 Kon, A., 'How We're Learning the Crèche Lesson', *The Sunday Express* 1 March 1992.

13 Cohen, B. and Fraser, N., *Childcare in a Modern Welfare System*, London: Institute for Public Policy Research, 1991, p. 124

14 *Ibid.*, p. 5.

15 Braverman, H., *Labor and Monopoly Capital*, New York: Monthly Review Press, 1974.

16 Drummond, M., 'Will Neanderthal Tories Waste the Women's Vote?', *The Daily Telegraph*, 25 February 1992.

17 Garner L, 'The Price of Taking Home a Pay Packet', in *The Daily Telegraph*, 6 July 1988.

18 General Household Survey, 1992.

19 Joshi, H., Macran, S. and Dex, S., 'Employment, Childbearing and Women's Subsequent Labour Force Participation: Evidence from the British 1958 Birth Cohort', Working Paper, Social Statistics Research Unit, City University, 1995; and Joshi, H., Macran, S., and Dex, S., 'A Widening Gulf Among Britain's Mothers', *Review of Economic Policy*, Vol. 12, No. 1, 1996.

20 Moss, P., *Mothers in Employment*, Vol. 2, Minutes of Evidence, Evidence to Employment Committee, House of Commons, London: HMSO, 1995, p. 176.

21 Ferri, E. (ed.), *Life at 33*, National Children's Bureau and City University, 1993.

22 Estimated government figures for average earnings in 1996-97 are that single full-time employees will earn £250 per week, but that female full-time employees will earn £287 per week and that, on average, men will earn £397 per week. This suggests that single men are earning less than women and family men considerably more than both. Source: Budget Press Release 28th November 1995.

23 Moss, P., *Childcare and Equality of Opportunity: Consolidated Report to the European Commission*, 1988, p. 27.

24 Holtermann, S., *All Our Futures*, Ilford, Essex: Barnardos, 1995, p. 47.

25 Warner L., 'Do Women Really Want to Get to the Top?', *The Daily Telegraph*, 24 January 1990.

26 Michaels, R., chairperson of the Women Returners Network, quoted in Liz Gill 'Counting the Cost of Going Back to Work', *The Times,* 26 March 1990.

27 See *The Times*, 28 June 1988.

28 Benenson, H., 'Women's Occupational and Family Achievement in the US Class System: A Critique of the Dual-career Family Analysis', *British Journal of Sociology*, Vol. 35, No. 1, pp. 19-36.

29 Joshi, H. and Davies, H., 'Mothers' Human Capital and Childcare in Britain', Employment Committee, *Mothers in Employment*, Vol. 3, Appendices to the Minutes of Evidence, p. 507.

30 *Ibid.*, p. 499.

31 Bush, J., 'The Child is Father of the Man', *The Times*, 24 December 1993.

32 *Mothers in Employment*, Vol. 3, Employment Committee, Appendices to the Minutes of Evidence, p. 528.

33 *A Practical Guide to Contracting for Quality Childcare*, London: Working for Childcare, 1992.

34 Information from the Daycare Trust, London.

35 Memorandum from the T&GWU to the Employment Committee, *Mothers in Employment*, Vol. 3, Appendices to the Minutes of Evidence, House of Commons, 1995, HMSO, p. 412.

36 Monk, S., 'From the Margins to the Mainstream: An Employment Strategy For Lone Parents', *Mothers in Employment*, Vol. 3, Appendices to the Minutes of Evidence, Employment Committee, p. 536.

37 Holtermann, S., *Investing in Young Children: Costing an Education and Daycare Service*, London: National Children's Bureau, 1992.

38 Toynbee, P., *The Independent*, 16 June 1996.

39 Holtermann, S., *Investing in Young Children, op. cit.*, p. 29.

40 Holtermann, S., *Investing in Young Children, op. cit.*, p. 74.

41 Holtermann, S., *All Our Futures, op. cit.*, p. 46.

42 *Households Below Average Income 1979-1991/2*, Department of Social Security, HMSO, 1993.

43 Watson, G, 'Hours of Work in Great Britain and Europe: Evidence from the UK and European Labour Force Surveys', *Employment Gazette*, November 1992.

44 Data from general Household Survey, in Harkness, S., Machin, S. and Waldfogel, J., 'Evaluating the Pin Money Hypotheses', Discussion Paper WSP/108, Welfare State programme Suntory-Toyota International, London School of Economics and Political Science, May 1995.

45 Bush, J., 'The Child is Father of the Man', *The Times* 24 December 1993.

46 Memorandum from Save the Children, *Mothers in Employment*, Vol. 3, Employment Committee First Report, Appendices and Minutes of Evidence, p. 564.

47 Ward, C., Dale, A. and Joshi, H., 'Combining Employment with Childcare: An Escape from Dependence', Journal of Social Policy, Vol. 25, No. 2, 1996, p. 223.

48 Lister, R. *Women's Economic Dependency and Social Security,* Equal Opportunities Commission, 1992, p. 68.

49 Gerson, K., *No Man's Land: Men's Changing Commitments to Family and Work*, New York: Basic Books, 1993, p. 229.

50 Memorandum from Save the Children Fund, *op. cit.*

51 Joshi, H., Dale, A., Ward, C., and Davis, H., *Dependence and Independence in the Finances of Women Aged 33*, London: Family Policies Study Centre, 1995, p. 9.

52 *Ibid.*, p. 19.

53 *Ibid.,* p. 27.

54 Ward, C., Dale, A., and Joshi, H., 'Combining Employment with Childcare: An Escape from Dependence', *Journal of Social Policy,* Vol. 25, No. 2, 1996. p. 245.

55 Wagner, D.M., *Taming the Divorce Monster: the Many Faults of No-Fault Divorce*, Washington DC: Family Research Council, 1995.

56 Memorandum from the T&GWU, *Mothers in Employment*, Vol. 3: Appendices to the Minutes of Evidence.

57 Leader, *The Times*, 18 March 1994.

58 O'Leary, J., 'Children Reading Badly at Ten "Suffer for Ever"', *The Times*, 13 September 1995.

59 Holtermann, S., *All Our Futures: The Impact of Public Expenditure and Fiscal Policies on Britain's Children and Young People*, Ilford, Essex: Barnardos, 1995, p. 33.

60 Roberts, I. and Pless, B., 'Social Policy as a Cause of Childhood Accidents: The Children of Lone Mothers', *British Medical Journal*, Vol. 311, 7 October 1995, pp. 925-28; see also McCormick, M.C., Shapiro, S., Starfield, B.H., 'Injury and its Correlates Among One-Year-Old Children', *American Journal Diseases of the Child*, Vol. 135, 1981, pp. 159-63.

61 Roberts, I. and Pless, B., *op. cit.*, p. 925.

62 Grice, E., 'Just a Weary Housewife', *Daily Telegraph*, 29 November 1994.

63 *The Key to Real Choice: An Action Plan for Childcare*, Equal Opportunities Commission, 1990, p. 2.

64 *Social Justice: Strategies for National Renewal*, The Report of the Commission on Social Justice, London: Vintage, 1994.

65 Earl Russell, Liberal Democrat spokesman on Social Security, 'The Threat to Beveridge is Unemployment', *The House Magazine*, 14 May 1995.

66 Wicks, M., 'What Matters is the Care of the Child', *The Independent*, 4 March 1989.

67 Drummond, M., 'Will Neanderthal Tories Waste the Women's Vote?', *The Daily Telegraph*, 25 February 1992.

68 Wicks, M., *op. cit.*

69 The House of Commons Commission has decided to implement a voucher scheme (of £6 a day) in line with those in operation in the National Audit Office and the House of Lords for those with under-fives working more than 15 hours a week.

70 Miller, R., 'Big Firms Join in Call for National Childcare Policy', *The Times*, 6 September 1995.

71 *Employment Committee, Report and Proceedings of the Committee* House of Commons Session 1994-5, *Mothers in Employment*, Vol. 1, 1995, p. xxviii.

72 *Work and the Family: Ideas and Options for Childcare. A Consultation Paper*, London: Department for Education and Employment, 1996.

73 Equal Opportunities Commission, *Mothers in Employment*, Vol. 2, Minutes of Evidence, *op. cit.*, p. 64.

74 See Hancock, B., *op. cit*; and Maggie Drummond (below) as well as any Equal Opportunities or European Commission report on childcare and equal opportunities.

75 Klein, U., 'Returning to Work: A Challenge for Women', *World of Work*, International Labour Office, No. 12, May/June 1995.

76 Drummond, M., 'Who's Holding the Baby?', *Telegraph Weekend Magazine*, August 1990.

77 Marsh, A. and Mckay, S., 'Families, Work and the Use of Childcare', *Employment Gazette*, August 1993, pp. 370-81; see also *Work and the Family: Ideas and Options for Childcare, op. cit.*, which describes 25 per cent of childcare used by working mothers of under-fives in 1994 as strictly commercial; 69 per cent was by a relative (including a spouse); 3 per was by a friend or neighbour. These figures were taken from the British Social Attitudes 1995 Report.

78 *Evening Standard*, 29 July 1991.

Chapter 1: 'What the Research Tells Us'

1 Equal Opportunities Commission, *The Key to Real Choice: An Action Plan for Childcare*, 1990.

2 Deborah, P., McCartney, K., Scarr, S., Howes, C., 'Selective Review of Infant Daycare Research: A Cause for Concern', *Zero to Three*, February 1987, pp. 18-21.

3 Belsky, J. and Eggebeen, D., 'Scientific Criticism and the Study of Early and Extensive Maternal Employment', *Journal of Marriage and the Family*, Vol. 53, 1991, p. 1108.

4 Christensen, B.J., *Utopia Against the Family*, San Francisco: Ignatius Press, 1990.

5 Remark by Belsky, J. at a consultation on 'The Risks of Daycare', sponsored by the Rockford Institute in Chicago, 6 December 1988, quoted in Christensen, B., *op. cit.*, p. 78.

6 Belsky, J. and Steinberg, L.D., 'The Effects of Daycare: A Critical Review', *Child Development*, Vol. 49, 1978, pp. 929-49; see commentary in Christensen, B.J., *op. cit.*, pp. 67-82.

7 Bush, J., 'The Child is Father of the Man', *The Times*, 24 December 1993.

8 Howes, C., 'Relations between Early Childcare and Schooling', *Developmental Psychology*, Vol. 24, No. 1, 1988, pp. 53-57.

9 Belsky, J., 'Infant Daycare: A Cause for Concern?', *Zero to Three*, Bulletin of the National Center for Clinical Infant Studies 6, 1986, pp. 1-7.

10 Belsky, J., 'Parental and Non Parental Childcare and Children's Socio-emotional Development: A Decade in Review', *Journal of Marriage and the Family*, Vol. 52, 1990, pp. 885-903.

11 *Ibid.*, p. 895.

12 Belsky, J. and Eggebeen, D., 'Scientific Criticism and the Study of Early and Extensive Maternal Employment', *Journal of Marriage and the Family,* Vol. 53, 1991 p. 1107.

13 Evans-Pritchard, A., 'Bewildered Little Losers in the Nursery Stakes', *The Daily Telegraph*, 18 November 1991.

14 Feetham, M., letter, *The Times* 18 January 1990.

15 Christensen, B.J., *Utopia Against the Family*, San Francisco: Ignatius Press, 1990, p. 77 referring to Fallows, D., *A Mother's Work*, Boston: Houghton Mifflin, 1985; and Levine, E.M., 'Daycare: Cons, Costs, Kids,' *Chicago Tribune*, 18 September 1984.

16 Moss, P., quoted in *The Key to Real Choice: An Action Plan for Childcare*, Equal Opportunities Commission, 1990, p. 38

17 See, Belsky, J., 'Parental and Non-parental Childcare and Children's Socio-emotional Development: A Decade in Review', *Journal of Marriage and the Family* 52, 1990, pp. 885-903.

18 Such comments are now ubiquitous in publications on daycare or working mothers, for example, Melhuish, E. and Moss, P., *The Daycare Project*, Thomas Coram Research Unit, Institute of Education, University of London, (undated summary of research findings); Moss, P. and Melhuish, E., 'The Daycare Project' in Robbins, D. and Walters, A. (eds.), *Department of Health Yearbook of Research and Development*, London: HMSO, 1990, p. 56.

19 Melhuish, E.C., 'Research on Daycare for Young Children in the United Kingdom' in Melhuish, E.C. and Moss, P. (ed.), *Daycare for Young Children: International Perspectives*, London: Tavistock /Routledge, 1991, p. 158.

20 Blum, M., *The Daycare Dilemma*, Lexington, Mass: Heath, 1983, p. 54.

21 White, L.J., Leibowitz, A. and Witsberger, C., 'What Parents Pay For: Childcare Characteristics, Quality, and Costs', *Journal of Social Issues*, Vol. 47, No. 2, 1991, pp. 3-48.

22 McCartney, K., Scarr, S., Phillips, D., Grajek, S. and Schwarz, J.C., 'Environmental Differences among Daycare Centers and Their Effects on Children's Development in Zigler, E.F. and Gordon, E.W. (eds.), *Daycare: Scientific and Social Policy Issues*, Boston: Auburn House Publishing Co., 1982, p. 127.

23 Faye, D., 'The Problem of Infant Daycare' in Zigler, E.F. and Gordon, E.W. (eds.), *op. cit.*

24 Melhuish, E.C., 'Research on Daycare for Young Children in the United Kingdom', in Melhuish, E.C. and Moss, P., *Daycare for Young Children: International Perspectives*, London: Tavistock/Routledge, 1991; Moss, P. and Melhuish, E., *Current Issues in Daycare for Young Children*, London: HMSO, 1991; Moss, P. and Melhuish, E., 'The Daycare Project' in Robbins, D. and Walters, A. (eds.), *Department of*

Health Yearbook of Research and Development, London: HMSO, 1990; Melhuish, E. and Moss, P., *The Daycare Project*, Thomas Coram Research Unit, Institute of Education, University of London, (undated summary of research findings).

25 Melhuish, E.C., 'Research on Daycare for Young Children in the United Kingdom' in Melhuish, E.C. and Moss, P., *Daycare for Young Children: International Perspectives*,London: Tavistock/Routledge, 1991, p. 150.

26 Hennessy, E., 'Is Daycare Good for Children?', *Nursery World*, 17 January 1991, pp. 12-14.

27 Mentioned in Brannen, J. *et al.*, *Employment and Family Life: A Review of Research in the UK (1980-1994)*, Centre for Research on Family Life and Employment, Thomas Coram Research Unit, Institute of Education, Employment Department Research Series No. 41, 1994; Martin, S., Plewis, I., McGurk, H., Hennessy, E., and Melhuish, E. 'Stability in Daycare and Cognitive Development', unpublished.

28 Hennessy, E., 'Is Daycare Good for Children?' *op. cit.*, p. 14.

29 Tizard, B., *Adoption: A Second Chance*, London: Open Books, 1977.

30 Melhuish, E.C., 'Research on Daycare for Young Children in the United Kingdom' in Melhuish, E.C. and Moss, P., *Daycare for Young Children: International Perspectives*, London: Tavistock/Routledge, 1991, p. 156.

31 Melhuish, E. and Moss, P., *The Daycare Project*, Thomas Coram Research Institute, Institute of Education, University of London, (undated summary of research findings), p. 3; Moss, P. and Melhuish, E., 'The Daycare Project' in Robbins, D. and Walters, A. (eds.), *Department of Health Yearbook of Research and Development*, London: HMSO, 1990, p. 56.

32 Melhuish, E.C., 'Research on Daycare for Young Children in the United Kingdom' in Melhuish, E.C. and Moss, P. (ed.), *Daycare for Young Children: International Perspectives*, London: Tavistock/Routledge, 1991, p. 149.

33 Robertson, A., 'Daycare and Children's Responsiveness to Adults' in Zigler, E.F. and Gordon, E.W., (eds.), *op. cit.*

34 Vandell, D.L. and Corasaniti, M.A., 'Childcare and the Family: Complex Contributors to Child Development' in McCartney, K., *Childcare and Maternal Employment*, San Francisco: Jossey-Bass inc., 1990.

35 *Ibid,* p. 153.

36 Violata, C. and Russell, C., 'Effects of Non-maternal Care on Child Development: A Meta-analysis of Published Research', Paper presented at the 55th annual convention of the Canadian Psychological Association, Penticton, British Columbia, Canada, 1994.

37 Hwang, C.P., Broberg, A. and Lamb, M.E. 'Swedish Childcare Research', in Melhuish, E.C. and Moss, P., *Daycare for Young Children*, London: Tavistock/Routledge, 1991.

38 Andersson, B-E., 'Effects of Public Daycare: A Longitudinal Study', *Child Development*, Vol. 60, 1989, pp. 857-66; and Andersson, B-E., 'Effects of Daycare on Cognitive and Socio-emotional Competence of Thirteen-Year-old Swedish Schoolchildren', *Child Development,* Vol. 63, 1992, pp. 20-36.

39 Hennessy, E., Martin, S., Moss, P., Melhuish, E., *Children and Daycare: Lessons from Research*, London: Paul Chapman Publishing Company, 1992, p. 54.

40 This is because the statistical techniques commonly used may actually exaggerate any original bias. 'This flaw ... is not slight, for it does not produce experimental results that are limited, but results that are uninterpretable.' Frye, D., 'The Problem of Infant Daycare', p. 223 in Zigler, E.F. and Gordon, E.W. (eds.), *op. cit.*

41 See discussion of Gunnarsson, L. in Lamb, M.E., Hwang, C-P., Bookstein, F.L., Broberg, A., Hult, G. and Frodi, M., 'Determinants of Social Competence in Swedish Pre-schoolers', *Developmental Psychology*, Vol. 24, No. 1, 1988, pp. 58-70.

42 Cochran, M., 'A Comparison of Group Daycare and Family Childrearing Patterns in Sweden', *Child Development*, Vol. 48, 1977, pp. 702-07.

43 Lamb, M.E., Hwang, C-P., Bookstein, F.L., Broberg, A., Hult, G. and Frodi, M., *op. cit.*

44 Caughy, M.O., DiPietro, J.A. and Strobino, D.M., 'Daycare Participation as a Protecting Factor in the Cognitive Development of Low-income Children', *Child Development*, Vol. 65, 1994, pp. 457-71.

45 Leach, P., *Children First,* Harmondsworth: Penguin Books, 1994, p. 70.

Chapter 2: 'Better than Home'

1 Kon, A., 'How We're Learning the Crèche Lesson', *The Sunday Express*, 1 March 1992.

2 Infant Daycare Research Report Commission on Social Policy Issues' Legislators Introduce New Federal Initiatives', *Zero to Three*, February 1988.

3 Melhuish, E.C. 'Research on Daycare for Young Children in the United Kingdom' in Melhuish, E.C. and Moss, P. (eds.), *Daycare for Young Children: International Perspectives*, London: Tavistock/ Routlege, 1991, p. 158.

4 Bronfenbrenner, U., *The Ecology of Human Development*, Cambridge, MA: Harvard University Press, 1979.

5 Scarr, S. and Dunn, J., *Mother Care: Other Care*, Harmondsworth: Penguin Books, 1987, p. 29.

6 Koester, L.S., 'Supporting Optimal Parenting Behaviours During Infancy', in Hyde, J.S. and Essex, M.J. (eds.), *Parental Leave and Childcare*, Philadelphia: Temple University Press, 1991, p. 325.

7 Leach, P., *Children First,* Harmondsworth: Penguin Books, 1995, p. 86.

8 Newson, J. and Newson, E., *Seven Years Old in the Home Environment*, London: Allen and Unwin, 1976.

9 Tizard, B., *Adoption: A Second Chance*, London: Open Books, 1977.

10 Howes, C. and Rubenstein, J.L., 'Determinants of Toddlers' Experience in Daycare: Age of Entry and Quality of Setting', *Childcare Quarterly*, Vol. 14, 1985, pp. 140-51.

11 Waite, L.J., Leibowitz, A. and Witsberger, C., 'What Parents Pay For: Childcare Characteristics, Quality, and Costs', *Journal of Social Issues,* Vol. 47, No. 2, 1991, pp. 3-48.

12 *Ibid.,* p. 46.

13 Jacobson, A.L. and Owen, S.S., 'Infant-Caregiver Interactions in Daycare', *Child Study Journal*, Vol. 17, 1987, pp. 197-209.

14 Parmenter, G.R., 1976 reported in McCartney, K., Scarr, S., Phillips, D., Grajek, S. and Schwarz, J.C., 'Environmental Differences among Daycare Centers on Children's Development' in Zigler, E.F. and Gordon, E.W., (eds.), *Daycare: Scientific and Social Policy Issues*, Boston: Auburn House Publishing Co., 1982, p. 127.

15 McCartney, K., 'Effect of Quality of Daycare Environment on Children's Language', *Developmental Psychology,* Vol. 20, No. 2, 1984, p. 259.

16 Lamb, M. E., Hwang, C. P., Bookstein, F. L., Broberg, A., Hult, G. and Frodi, M., *op. cit.;* and Cochran, M.M., 'A Comparison of Group, Day and Family Childrearing Patterns in Sweden', *Child Development*, Vol. 48, pp. 702-07.

17 Melhuish, E.C. 'Research on Daycare for Young Children in the United Kingdom' in Melhuish, E.C. and Moss, P. (eds.), *Daycare for Young Children: International Perspectives*, London: Tavistock/ Routledge, 1991, pp. 152-53.

18 Davie, C. E., Hutt, S. J., Vincent, E. and Mason, M., *The Young Child at Home*, Slough: NFER-Nelson, 1984.

19 Sylva, K., Roy, C. and Painter, M., *Childwatching at Playgroup and Nursery School*, London: Grant McIntyre, 1980.

20 Davie, C. E., Hutt, S. J., Vincent, E. and Mason, M., *op. cit.*

21 *Ibid.,* pp. 175-76; and see Tizard, B., Carmichael, H., Hughes, M. and Pinkerton, G., 'Four-Year-Olds Talking to Mothers and Teachers' in Hersov, L.A. and Berger, M. (eds.), *Language Disorders in Childhood*,

1980, a book supplement to the *Journal of Child Psychology and Psychiatry*, 1982, pp. 49-76; Tizard, B. *et al.*, 'Adults' Cognitive Demands at Home and at Nursery School', *Journal of Child Psychology and Psychiatry*, 1982, pp. 23, 105-116.

22 Stith, S.M. and Davis, A.J., 'Employed Mothers and Family Daycare Substitute Caregivers: A Comparative Analysis of Infant Care', *Child Development*, Vol. 55, 1984 pp. 1340-48.

23 Mayall, B. and Petrie, P., *Minder, Mother and Child,* University of London, Institute of Education, 1977.

24 Moss, P., *Review of Childminding Research*, University of London, Institute of Education, 1987.

25 Hughes, M., Mayall, B., Moss, P., Petrie, P. and Pinkerton, G., *Nurseries Now*, Harmondsworth: Penguin Books, 1980, p. 171.

26 *Ibid.*, pp. 20, 22.

27 Hennessy, E., Martin, S., Moss, P. and Melhuish, E., *Children and Daycare: Lessons from Research*, London: Paul Chapman Publishing Company, 1992.

28 *Ibid.,* pp. 34-35.

29 Mayall, B. and Petrie, P., *Mother, Minder and Child,* Slough: NFER, 1977; and Byrant, B., Harris, M. and Newton, D., *Children and Minders*, The Oxford Pre-school Research Project, London: Grant McIntyre, 1980.

30 Mayall, B. and Petrie, P., quoted in Hughes, M. *et al.*, *Nurseries Now*, *op. cit.*, p. 173.

31 Hughes, M. *et al., op. cit.,* p. 165.

32 *Ibid.*, p. 169.

33 Mayall, B. and Petrie, P, *Mother, Minder and Child*, Slough: NFER, 1977.

34 Hughes, M. *et al., op. cit.,* p. 170.

35 Golden, M., Rosenbluth, L., Grossi, M.T., Policare, H.J., Freeman, H.Jr. and Brownlee, E.M., *The New York Infant Daycare Study*, New York: Medical and Health Research Association of New York City; McCartney, K., Scarr, S. and Vandell, D.L. and Powers, C.P., Daycare Quality and Children's Free Play Activities', *American Journal of Orthopsychiatry*, Vol. 53, 1983, pp. 493-500.

36 Howes, C., 'Relations Between Early Childcare and Schooling', *Developmental Psychology*, Vol. 24, No. 1, 1988, pp. 53-57.

37 Vandell, D.L., Henderson, V.K., Wilson, K.S., 'A Longitudinal Study of Children with Daycare Experiences of Varying Quality', *Child Development*, Vol. 59, 1988, pp. 1286-92.

38 Phillips, D., McCartney, K. and Scarr, S., 'Child-Care Quality and Children's Social Development', *Developmental Psychology*, Vol. 23, No. 4, pp. 537-43.

39 See also McCartney, K., 'The Effect of Quality of Childcare on Children's Language Development', *Developmental Psychology*, Vol. 20, 1984, pp. 244-60; Phillips, D. and Grajek, S., 'Daycare as Intervention: Comparisons of Varying Quality Programs', *Journal of Applied Developmental Psychology*, Vol. 6, 1985, pp. 247-60; and Howes. C. and Rubinstein, J., 'Determinants of Toddlers' Experiences in Daycare: Age of Entry and Quality of Setting', *Child Care Quarterly*, Vol. 14, 1985, pp. 99-107.

40 Howes, C. and Stewart, P., 'Child's Play with Adults, Toys, and Peers: An Examination of Family and Childcare Influences', *Developmental Psychology*, Vol. 23, No. 3, 1987, pp. 423-30; and Clarke Stewart, K.A. and Gruber, C., 'Daycare Forms and Features', Ainslie, R.C. (ed.), *Quality Variations in Day Care*, New York: Praeger, 1984, pp. 35-62.

41 Howes, C. and Stewart, P., *op. cit.*

42 Petersen, C. and Peterson, R., 'Parent/Child Interaction and Daycare: Does Quality of Daycare Matter?', *Journal of Applied Developmental Psychology*, Vol. 7 No. 3, 1986, pp. 18-21.
    Elsewhere, a study of three-year-olds who had been in daycare since 12 months showed that the level of social play with their caregivers predicted their positive responses towards their own mothers, see Kermoian, R., 'Type and Quality of Care; Mediating Factors in the Effects of Daycare on Infant Responses to Brief Separations', paper presented at the International Conference on Infant Studies, Connecticut, March 1980.

43 Howes, C., 'Can Age of Entry into Childcare and the Quality of Childcare Predict Adjust at Kindergarten?', *Developmental Psychology*, Vol. 26, 1990, pp. 292-303.

44 See section with references in Blum, M., *The Daycare Dilemma*, Lexington, Mass: Heath, 1983.

45 Goodman, R.A. *et al.* (eds.), 'Proceedings of the International Conference on Child Daycare Health: Science, Prevention and Practice', Supplement to *Paediatrics*, Vol. 84, 1994, pp. 986-1020.
    Between 1978 and 1986 infestations of *Giardia lamblia,* a common parasite causing diarrhoea, increased among American children by 75 per cent. They also increasingly fell victim to *Cryptosporidium*, an important cause of watery diarrhoea in children attending daycare centres, see Hoelcelman, R.A., 'Parasites in Paediatric Practice'; Richards, Jr., F.O., 'An Overview of Parasitic Diseases in Children in the United States—What's Old? What's New?'; Kenny, R.T., 'Parasitic Causes of Diarrhoea', *Paediatric Annals*, Vol. 23, 1994, pp. 389-90, 392-96 and 414-22.
    Outbreaks of viral A Hepatitis are particularly associated with large (especially 'for-profit') childcare centres, as are cytomegalovirus, respiratory infections, shigellosis, and influenza, see Blum, M., *op. cit.*

46 Black, R.E., 'Giardiasis in Daycare Centers: Evidence of Person-to-Person Transmission', *Paediatrics*, Vol. 60, 1977, pp. 486-89.

    Another study on influenza, which can lead to childhood meningitis and epiglottitis, concluded that daycare children were about 12 times more likely to contract this, see Redmond, S.R. and Pichichero, M.E., 'Hemophilus Influenza Type B Disease: An Epidemiologic Study with Special References to Daycare Centres', *Journal of the American Medical Association*, Vol. 252, 1984, pp. 2581-84.

47 While it poses few problems for men, non-pregnant women and children, cytomegalovirus can cause birth defects affecting the brain and nervous system, sight, hearing and movement. One antibody test showed a cumulative infection rate among daycare children in Alabama of between 70 and 100 per cent, compared with approximately 50 per cent of children generally, see Pass, R.F. *et al.*, 'Cytomegalovirus Virus Infection in a Daycare Centre', *New England Journal of Medicine*, Vol. 307, 1982, pp. 477-79; and Pass, R.F. *et al.*, 'Young Children as a Probable Source of Maternal and Congenital Cytomegalovirus Infection', *New England Journal of Medicine*, Vol. 316, 1987, pp. 1366-70.

48 Katkova, I. in Lapidus, G. W., *Women, Work and Family in the Soviet Union*, New York: M.E. Sharpe, 1982.

Chapter 3: 'Aggression'

1   Sanger, S. and Kelly, J., *The Woman Who Works, The Parent Who Cares*, New York: Bantam Books, 1988.

2   Blum, M., *The Daycare Dilemma*, Lexington, Mass: Heath, 1983, p. 25.

3   Belsky, J. and Steinberg, L.D., 'The Effects of Daycare: A Critical Review', *Child Development*, Vol. 49, 1978: pp. 929-49; see commentary in Christensen, B.J., *op. cit.*, pp. 67-82.

4   Schwarz, J.C., Strickland, R. and Krolick, G., 'Infant Daycare: Behavioural Effects at Pre-school Age', *Developmental Psychology*, Vol. 10, 1974, p. 105.

5   Field, T. *et al.*, 'Infant Daycare Facilitates Pre-school Social Behaviour', *Early Childhood Research Quarterly*, Vol. 3, 1988, pp. 341-59.

6   Haskins, R., 'Public School Aggression among Children with Varying Daycare Experience', *Child Development*, Vol. 56, 1985, pp. 689-703.

7   Robertson, A., 'Daycare and Children's Responsiveness to Adults' in Zigler E.F. and Gordon E.W. (eds.), *Daycare: Scientific and Social Policy Issues*, Boston: Auburn House Publishing Company, 1982.

8   See Schwarz, J., 'Infant Daycare: Effects at Two, Four and Eight Years', paper presented to Society for Research in Child Development, Detroit, 1983 (Abstract: Resources in Education, January 1984, ERIC Clearinghouse on Elementary and Early Education; Barton, M., and Schwarz, J., *Daycare in the Middle-Class: Effects in Elementary*

School, paper presented at the American Psychological Association's annual convention, Los Angeles, August 1981.

9 McCartney, K., Scarr, S., Phillips, D., Grajek, S. and Schwarz, J.C., 'Environmental Differences among Daycare Centers and Their Effects on Children's Development' in Zigler, E.F. and Gordon, E. (eds.), *Daycare: Scientific and Social Policy Issues,* Boston: Auburn House Publishing Company, 1982.

10 Golden, M. *et al., The New York Infant Daycare Study*, New York: Medical and Health Research Associates of New York, 1978.

11 Rubenstein, J., and Howes, C., 'Adaptation to Toddler Care', in Kilmer, S. (ed.), *Advances in Early Education and Daycare,* Greenwich, Conn: JAI Press, 1983, p. 34.

12 Burchinal, M.R., Landesman Ramey, S., Reid, M.K. and Jaccard, J., 'Early Childcare Experiences and their Association with Family and Child Characteristics during Middle Childhood', *Early Childhood Research Quarterly,* Vol. 10,1995, pp. 33-61.

13 Belsky, J. and Eggebeen, D., 'Early and Extensive Maternal Employment and Young Children's Socio-emotional Development: Children of the National Longitudinal Survey of Youth', *Journal of Marriage and the Family,* Vol. 53, 1991, pp. 1083-110.

14 Egeland, B. and Hiester, M., 'The Long-Term Consequences of Infant Daycare and Mother-Infant Attachments', *Child Development*, Vol. 66, 1995, pp. 474-85.

15 Vandell, D.L. and Corasaniti, M.A., 'Childcare and the Family: Complex Contributors to Child Development' in McCartney, K., *Childcare and Maternal Employment: A Social Ecology Approach*, San Francisco: Jossey-Bass Inc. 1990, pp. 23-37.

16 Robertson, A., 'Daycare and Children's Responsiveness to Adults' in Zigler E.F. and Gordon E.W., (eds.), *Daycare: Scientific and Social Issue*, Boston: Auburn House Publishing Company, 1982.

17 Barton, M. and Schwarz, J., *Daycare in the Middle-Class: Effects in Elementary School,* paper presented at the annual meeting of the American Psychological Association, Los Angeles, August 1981, p. 7.

18 Osborn, A.F. and Millbank, J.E., *The Effects of Early Education,* Oxford: Clarendon Press, 1987; see also Osborn, A.F., Butler, N.R. and Morris, A.C., *The Social Life of Britain's Five-Year-Olds*, London: Routledge and Kegan Paul, 1984.

19 Douglas, J.W.B. and Ross, J.M., 'The Later Educational Progress and Emotional Adjustment of Children who went to Nursery Schools or Classes', *Educational Research*, Vol. 7 No. 2, 1965, pp. 73-80.

20 Evans, B. and Saia, G.E., *Daycare for Infants*, Boston: Beacon Press, 1972, p. 6.

21 Clarke Stewart, A.K., 'Maligned or Malignant?', *American Psychologist*, February 1989, p. 269.

22 See Leach, P., *Children First*, Harmondsworth: Penguin Books, 1994, p. 92.

23 Harper, C. and Huie, F., 'Relations Among Pre-school Children's Adult and Peer Contacts and Later Academic Achievements', *Child Development*, Vol. 58, 1987, pp. 1051-65.

24 Rabinovich, B.A., Zaslow, M.J., Berman, P.W. and Heyman, R. 'Employed and Homemaker Mothers' Perceptions of Their Toddlers' Compliance Behaviour in the Home', paper presented at the biennial meeting of the Society for Research in Child Development, Baltimore, 1987; Hoffman, L.W., 'Maternal Employment and the Young Child' in Perlmutter, M. (ed.), *Parent/child Interaction and Parent/child relations in Child Development*, The Minnesota Symposia on Child Psychology, Vol. 17, Hillsdale, NJ: Erlbaum, 1984, pp. 101-28.

25 Howes, C., Phillips, D. and Whitebook, M., 'Thresholds of Quality: Implications for the Social Development of Children in Center-based Childcare', *Child Development*, Vol. 63, 1992, pp. 449-60.

26 Haskins, *op. cit.*, 1985.

27 Phillips, D.A. and Howes, C., 'Indicators of Quality in Childcare: Review of the Research' in Phillips, D.A. (ed.), *Quality in Childcare: What Does Research Tell Us?*, Research Monograph of the National Association for the Education of Young Children, 1987, pp. 1-20; Belsky J, 'Two Waves of Daycare Research: Developmental Effects and Conditions of Quality', in Ainslie, R. (ed.), *The Child and the Daycare Setting*, New York: Praeger, 1984, pp. 1-34.

28 Phillips, D.A., McCartney, K. and Scarr S., 'Childcare Quality and Children's Social Development', *Development Psychology*, Vol. 25, 1987, pp. 413-20; Howes, C. and Olenick, M., 'Childcare and Family Influences on Toddlers' Compliance',*Child Development*, Vol. 57, 1986, pp. 202-16.

29 Heinicke, C., Friedman, D., Prescot, E., Puncel, C. and Sale, J., 'The Organisation of Daycare: Considerations Relating to the Mental Health of Child and Family', *American Journal of Orthopsychiatry*, Vol. 43, 1973, pp. 8-22; see also references in Belsky, Steinberg and Walker.

30 Howes, C. and Olenick, M., 'Family and Childcare Influences on Toddler's Compliance', *Child Development*, Vol. 57, 1986, pp. 101-10.

31 Howes, C., Phillips, D.A. and Whitebook, M., 'Thresholds of Quality: Implications for the Social Development of Children in Center-based Childcare', *Child Development*, Vol. 63, 1992, pp. 449-60.

32 McCartney, K., Scarr, S., Phillips, D., Grajek, S. and Schwarz, J.C., 'Environmental Differences Among Daycare Centres and their Effects on Children's Development' in Zigler, E.F. and Gordon, E.W. (eds.), *Daycare: Scientific and Social Policy Issues,* Boston: Auburn House Publishing Company, 1982.

33 Field, T. *et al.*, *op. cit.*, 1988.

34 Brookhart, T. and Hock, E., 'The Effects of Experimental Contest and Experiential Background on Infants' Behaviour Toward Their Mothers and a Stranger', *Child Development*, Vol. 47, 1976, pp. 333-40.

35 Robertson, A., *op. cit.*

36 Howes, C. and Olenick, M., 'Family and Childcare Influences on Toddler's Compliance', *op. cit.*

37 Martin, J., *A Longitudinal Study of the Consequences of Early Mother/Infant Interaction: A Microanalytic Study*, Monographs of the Society for Research on Child Development, 1981.

38 Wallerstein, J.S. and Blakeslee, S., *Second Chances*, New York: Ticknor & Fields, 1989.

39 Robertson, A., 'Daycare and Children's Responsiveness to Adults' in Zigler, E.F. and Gordon E.W., (eds.), *Daycare: Scientific and Social Issues*, Boston: Auburn House Publishing Company, 1982, p. 169.

Chapter 4: 'Quality Control'

1 *Mind the Children*, London: Adam Smith Institute, 1989, p. 25.

2 Phillips, D., McCartney, K, and Scarr, S., 'Child-Care Quality and Children's Development', *Developmental Psychology*, Vol. 23, No. 4, 1987, pp. 537-43.

3 Howes, C., 'Caregiving Environments and Their Consequences for Children: The Experience in the United States' in Melhuish, E.C. and Moss, P., *Daycare for Young Children: International Perspectives, op. cit.*, 1991; Clarke Stewart, A., 'Predicting Child Development from Childcare Forms and Features: the Chicago Study' in Phillips, (ed.), *Quality in Childcare: What Does Research Tell Us?*, Washington DC: National Association for the Education of Young Children, 1987.

4 McCartney, K., Scarr, S., Phillips, D., Grajek S. and Schwarz, J.C., 'Environmental Differences among Daycare Centers on Children's Development' in Zigler E.F. and Gordon, E.W. (eds.), *Daycare: Scientific and Social Policy Issues*, Boston: Auburn House Publishing Company, 1982.

5 Howes, C., 'Social Competency with Peers: Contributions from Childcare', *Early Childhood Research Quarterly*, Vol. 2, 1987, pp. 155-167.

6 Roupp, R., Travers, F., Glantz, F. and Coelen, C., *Children at the Center: Final Results of the National Daycare Study*, Cambridge, MA: Abt Associates, 1979.

7 McCartney, K., Scarr, S., Phillips, D., Grajek S., and Schwarz, J.C., 'Environmental Differences among Daycare Centers on Children's Development' in Zigler E.F. and Gordon, E.W. (eds.), *Daycare: Scientific and Social Policy Issues*, Boston: Auburn House Publishing Company, 1982.

8 Fein, G.G., 'Infants in Group Care: Patterns of Despair and Detachment', *Early Childhood Research Quarterly*, Vol. 10, 1995, pp. 261-75.

9 Vandell, D.L., Henderson, V.K., Wilson, K.S., 'A Longitudinal Study of Children with Daycare Experiences of Varying Quality', *Child Development*, Vol. 59, 1988, pp. 1286-92.

10 Provence, S., Nayler, A. and Paterson, J., *The Challenge of Daycare*, New Haven: Yale University Press, 1977, p. 227.

11 Leach, P., *Children First*, Harmondsworth: Penguin Books, 1994, p. 83.

12 Whitebrook, M., Howes, C., and Philips, D., *Who Cares?: Childcare Teachers and the Quality of Childcare in America*, Oakland CA: Childcare Employee Project, 1989.

13 Melhuish, E. and Moss, P., *The Daycare Project*, Thomas Coram Research Institute, Institute of Education, University of London, (undated summary of research findings), p. 3; see also Melhuish, E.C. 'Research on Daycare for Young Children in the United Kingdom' in Melhuish, E.C. and Moss, P., *Daycare for Young Children: International Perspectives*, London: Tavistock/Routledge, 1991; Moss, P. and Melhuish, E., *Current Issues in Daycare for Young Children*, London: HMSO, 1991; Moss, P. and Melhuish, E., 'The Daycare Project' in Robbins, D. and Walters, A. (eds.), *Department of Health Yearbook of Research and Development*, London: HMSO, 1990.

14 Hennessy, E., Martin, S., Moss, P., Melhuish, E., *Children and Daycare: Lessons from Research*, London: Paul Chapman Publishing Company, 1992.

15 Raikes, H., 'Relationship Duration in Infant Care: Time with a High-Ability Teacher and Infant-Teacher Attachment', *Early Childhood Research Quarterly*, Vol. 8, 1993 pp. 322-23.

16 Hennessy, E., *Children and Daycare: Lessons from Research*, London: Paul Chapman Publishing Ltd, 1992, pp. 27-28.

17 Leach, P., *op. cit.*, p. 89.

18 Young, K. and Zigler, E., 'Infant and Toddler Daycare: Regulations and Policy Implications' in Zigler, E.F and Frank, M., *The Parental Leave Crisis*, Yale University Press, 1987, p. 130.

19 Moss, P., 'Daycare for Young Children in the United Kingdom', Melhuish, E.C. and Moss, P., *Daycare for Young Children: International Perspectives*, London: Tavistock/Routledge, 1991, p. 136.

20 *The New Review*, November/December 1994.

21 Bonnar, D., 'The Place of Caregiving Work in Contemporary Societies' in Hyde, J.S. and Essex, M. (eds.), *Parental Leave and Childcare*, Philadelphia: Temple University Press, 1991.

22 Blum, M., *The Daycare Dilemma*, Lexington, Mass: Heath, 1983.

23 Suransky, V. P., *The Erosion of Childhood*, University of Chicago Press, 1982, p. 186.

24 *Ibid.*, pp. 109-10.

25 *Ibid.*, p. 121.

26 *Ibid.*, p. 111.

27 *Ibid.*, p. 123.

28 *Ibid.*, p. 181.

29 *Ibid.*, pp. 131 and 187.

30 See, typically, Dex, S. and Puttick, E., 'Women's Working Lives: A Comparison of Women in the United States and Great Britain' in Hunt, A. (ed.), *Women and Paid Work*, London: Macmillan, 1988: pp. 194-95.

31 Broberg, A. and Hwang, C.P., 'Daycare for Young Children in Sweden' in Melhuish, E.C. and Moss, P., *Daycare for Young Children: International Perspectives*, London and New York: Tavistock/Routledge, 1991; and Morgan, P., *Families in Dreamland*, London: Social Affairs Unit, 1991.

32 Grice, E., 'Mind Your Toys, the Inspectors are Here', *The Daily Telegraph*, 29 October 1992.

33 *Ibid.*

34 Report by Kathy Marks 'When Nursery is No Place for Men', *The Times*, 4 October 1993; see also Finkelhor, D., *Nursery Crimes,* 1989, which claims that in the 1980s, out of seven million children moving through daycare in America, at least 2,500 had been abused over three years.

35 Hughes, M. *et al.*, *Nurseries Now,* Harmondsworth: Penguin Books, 1980, p. 171.

36 *Ibid.*, p. 173.

37 Jackson, B., 'The Childminders', *New Society*, 29 November 1973, p. 524.

38 *Op. cit.,* p. 175.

Chapter 5: 'Time Go Home?'

1 Kirkbride, J., 'MPs are told about childcare benefits by an expert, aged seven', *The Daily Telegraph*, 1 July 1994.

2 Leach, P., *Children First*, Harmondsworth: Penguin Books, 1994, p. 248.

3 Galambos, N.L. and Maggs, J.L., 'Out of School Care of Young Adolescents and Self-Reported Behaviour', *Developmental Psychology,* Vol. 27, 1991, p. 654.

4   Richardson, J.L. *et al.*, 'Substance Use Among Eight-grade Students
    Who Take Care of Themselves After School.' *Paediatrics*, Vol. 84,
    1989, pp. 556-566.

5   Steinberg, L., 'Latchkey Children and Susceptibility to Peer Pressure:
    An Ecological Analysis', *Developmental Psychology*, Vol. 22, No. 4,
    1986, pp. 433-39.

6   'Lisa', 14, in *Shout Magazine*, No. 79, 1-14 March 1996.

7   Vandell, D.L. and Ramanan, J., 'Children of the National
    Longitudinal Survey of Youth: Choices in After-School Care and Child
    Development,' *Developmental Psychology*, Vol. 27, No. 4, 1991, pp.
    637-43.

8   Vandell, D.L. and Corasaniti, M.A., 'The Relations Between Third
    Graders' After-School Care, and Social, Academic and Emotional
    Functioning', *Child Development*, 59, 1988, pp.868-75.

9   Vandell, D.L. and Corasaniti, M.A., 'Childcare and the Family:
    Complex Contributors to Child Development' in McCartney, K.,
    Childcare and Maternal Employment, San Francisco: Jossey-Bass,
    1990.

10 The Children Act 1989, Guidance and Regulations, Vol. 2, Family
    Support, Daycare and Educational Provision for Young Children,
    London: HMSO, 1991.

11 *Ibid.*, p. 48.

12 *Ibid.*

13 *Ibid.*

14 School-Age Childcare Project, 'School-Age Childcare' in Zigler, E.F.
    and Gordon, E.W. (eds.), *Daycare: Scientific and Social Policy Issues*,
    Boston: Auburn House Publishing Company, 1982, p. 471.

Chapter 6: 'A Head Start?'

1   Hodge, M., 'Invest Now, Save Later', *The Daily Telegraph*, 4 January
    1995.

2   Haskins, R., 'Beyond Metaphor: the Efficacy of Early Childhood
    Education' *American Psychologist*, February 1989, pp. 274-81.

3   Hodge, M., Labour MP for Barking, letter to *The Times*, 30 April 1996.

4   Equal Opportunities Commission, *The Key to Real Choice*, Man-
    chester, 1990.

5   *Educational Provision for the Under-Fives*, Education, Science and
    Arts Committee, House of Commons paper 30-1, London: HMSO,
    1989.

6   See extract from The National Commission on Education report
    'Learning to Succeed', Chapter 6, 'A Good Start in Education', Vol. 2,
    Minutes of Evidence to the Employment Committee, *Mothers in
    Employment*, London: HMSO, 1995.

7   'I visited three European countries for this report and all of them
    regard childcare provision as a right of working mothers and their
    children. That right is underlined by public funding which gives
    families access to quality childcare regardless of their income—not
    just as a carrot to get women back to work, but because it is beneficial
    to the development of pre-school children.' (Drummond, M., 'Who's
    Holding the Baby?',*Telegraph Weekend Magazine*, August 1990.)

8   Bryant, B., Harris, M. and Martin, D., *Children and Minders*, 1980,
    London: Grant McIntyre; Mayall, B. and Petrie, P., *Minder, Mother
    and Child*, University of London Institute of Education, 1977.

9   Frailberg, S., *Every Child's Birthright*, 1977, pp. 81-82.

10 Osborn, A.F. and Milbank, J.E., *The Effects of Early Education*,
    Oxford: Clarendon Press, 1987.

11 Woodhead, M., 'School Starts at Five ... or Four Years Old? The
    Rationale for Changing Admission Policies in England and Wales',
    Journal of Education Policy, Vol. 4, No. 1, 1989, pp. 1-21; and Her
    Majesty's Inspectorate, Aspects of Primary Education, *The Education
    of Children Under Five*, London: HMSO, 1989.

12 Leach, P., *Children First*, Harmondsworth: Penguin Books, 1995, p.
    91.

13 Blum, M., *The Daycare Dilemma*, Lexington, Mass: Heath, 1983, p. 23.

14 Frailberg, S., *op. cit.*, p. 86.

15 Coles, R., 'Talk with Selma Fraiberg', *Empathic Parenting*, Vol. 6, No.
    3, 1983, p. 14.

16 Clarke-Stewart, K.A., 'A Home is not a School: Effects of Childcare on
    Children's Development', *Journal of Social Issues*, Vol. 47, No. 2,
    1991, pp. 105-23.

17 Tizard, B., *Early Childhood Education: A Review and Discussion of
    Current Research in Britain,* Slough: NFER, 1975.

18 Hennessy, E., *Children and Daycare: Lessons from Research*, London:
    Paul Chapman, 1992, pp. 27-28.

19 Mott, F.L., 'Developmental Effects of Infant Care: The Mediating Role
    of Gender and Health', *Journal of Social Issues*, Vol. 47, No. 2, 1991,
    pp. 139-58.

20 Burchinal, M.R., Landesman Ramey, S., Reid, M.K. and Jaccard, J.,
    'Early Childcare Experiences and their Association with Family and
    Child Characteristics during Middle Childhood', *Early Childhood
    Research Quarterly*, Vol. 10, 1995, pp. 33-61.

21 Burchinal, M., Lee, M. and Ramey, C.T., 'Type of Daycare and Pre-
    school Intellectual Development in Disadvantaged Children', *Child
    Development*, Vol. 60, 1989, pp. 128-37.

22 Wasik, B.H., Ramey, C.T., Bryant, D.M. and Sparling, J.J., 'A Longitudinal Study of Two Early Intervention Strategies: Project CARE', *Child Development*, Vol. 61, 1990, pp. 1682-96.

23 *Ibid.,* p. 1686.

24 Gordon, A.M., 'Adequacy of Responses Given by Low-Income and Middle-Income Kindergarten Children in Structured Adult/Child Conversations', *Developmental Psychology*, Vol. 20, No. 5, 1984, pp. 881-91.

25 Gamble, T., and Zigler, E., 'Effects of Infant Daycare' in Zigler, E.F. and Frank, M., (eds.), *The Parental Leave Crisis*, New Haven and London: Yale University Press, 1988.

26 Lazar, I., Darlington, R., Murray, H., Royce, J., and Snipper, A. 'Lasting Effects of Early Education: A Report from the Consortium for Longitudinal Studies, *Monographs of the Society for Research into Child Development*, (2-3, Serial No. 195), 1982; see also Haskins, R., 'Beyond Metaphor: The Efficacy of Early Childhood Education', *American Psychologist*, February 1989, pp. 274-82.

27 Haskins, R., *op. cit.*, p. 276.

28 McKey, R.H., Condelli, L., Ganson, H., Barrett, B.J., McConkey, C. and Platz, M.C., *The Impact of Head Start on Children, Families and Communities*, Final Report of the Head Start Evaluation, Synthesis, and Utilization Project, Washington DC: CSR, 1985.

29 Osborn, A.F., Butler, N.R. and Morris, A.C., *The Social Life of Britain's Five-Year-Olds*, London: Routledge and Kegan Paul, 1984; and Osborn, A.F. and Millbank, J.E., *The Effects of Early Education*, Oxford: The Clarendon Press, 1987.

30 Osborn, A.F. and Millbank, J.E., *op. cit.*, p. 217.

31 Daniels, S., 'Can Pre-school Education Affect Children's Achievement at Key Stage 1?', *Oxford Review of Education*, Vol. 21, No. 2, June 1995.

32 With the voucher scheme imminent, the Audit Commission rapidly carried out 51 inspections. A few LEA provisions got the highest grades, while most fell in the middle range and none fell at the poor or unsatisfactory level. Private provisions and playgroups spanned the middle to poor range. *Counting to Five*, Audit Commission, London. HMSO, 1996.

33 'Newcastle University Performance Indicators in Primary Schools' in *Counting to Five*, Audit Commission, London: HMSO, 1996.

34 Jowett, S. and Sylva, K., 'Does Kind of Pre-school Matter?', *Educational Research*, Vol. 28, No. 1, 1986 pp. 21-31.

35 Douglas, J.W.B. and Ross, J.M., 'The Later Educational Progress and Emotional Adjustment of Children who went to Nursery Schools or Classes', *Educational Research*, Vol. 7, No. 2, 1965, pp. 73-80.

36 Bynner, J. and Steedman, J., *Difficulties with Basic Skills*, London: The Basic Skills Agency, 1995, pp. 63 and 35.

37 Gorman, T. and Fernandes, C., *Reading in Recession*, Slough: NFER, 1992.

38 *The SHA Survey of Intake Tests in Secondary Schools*, The Secondary Heads Association, November 1995.

39 See, for example Davie, R., Butler, N. and Goldstein, H., *Birth to Seven*, London: Longman, 1972; and Osborn, A.F. and Millbank, J.E., *The Effects of Early Education*, Oxford: The Clarendon Press, 1987.

40 Bynner, J. and Steedman, J., *op. cit.*, p. 65.

41 *Ibid.*

42 *Ibid.* p. 46.

43 Lewis, C., Newson, E. and Newson, J., 'Father Participation Throughout Childhood and its Relationship with Career Aspirations and Delinquency' in Beail, N. and McGuire, J. (eds.), *Fathers: Psychological Perspectives*, London: Junction Books, 1982, p. 104.

44 Keyes, W., *Aspects of Science in English Schools*, Slough: NFER-Nelson, 1987.

45 Haskins, R., *op. cit.*, p. 280.

46 Osborn, A.F. and Millbank, J.E., *The Effects of Early Education*, Oxford: The Clarendon Press, 1987 p. 200.

47 Reynolds, A. J., 'One Year of Pre-school Intervention or Two: Does It Matter?', *Early Childhood Research Quarterly*, Vol. 10, 1995 pp. 1-31.

48 'Childcare and Nursery Education: a TUC Charter', *Mothers in Employment,* Vol. 2, Minutes of Evidence Employment Committee, House of Commons, London: HMSO, 1995, p. 332.

Chapter 7: 'The Perry Pre-school Project'

1 National Commission on Education, *Learning to Succeed*, Chapter 6, 'A Good Start in Education', quoted in Minutes of Evidence, Vol. 2, *Mothers in Employment*, London: HMSO, 1995, p. 107.

2 Schweinhart, L.J. and Weikart, D., *Significant Benefits: the High/Scope Perry Pre-school Study through Age 27,* Michigan: High/Scope Ypsilanti, 1993.

3 Rowan, P., Editor of *The Times Educational Supplement,* reports from the British Association Conference in 1995. *The Times,* 1 September 1995.

4 Roberts, I., and Pless, B., 'Social Policy as a Cause of Childhood Accidents: the Children of Lone Mothers', *British Medical Journal*, Vol. 311, 7 October 1995, p. 927.

5 *Ibid.,* p. 232.

6 *Ibid.,* p. 231.

7   Schweinhart, L.J., Weikart, D. P. and Larner, M.B., 'Consequences of Three Preschool Curriculum Models through Age 15', *Early Childhood Research Quarterly*, Vol. 1, 1986, pp. 15-45.

8   Haskins, R., 'Beyond Metaphor: the Efficacy of Early Childhood Education', *American Psychologist*, February 1989, p. 279.

9   Bynner, J. and Steedman, J., *Difficulties with Basic Skills*, London: The Basic Skills Agency, 1995.

Chapter 8: 'Semi-attached?'

1   Scarr, S. and Dunn, J., *Mother Care: Other Care*, second edition, Harmondsworth: Penguin Books, 1987 pp. 23-24.

2   Belsky, J., 'Parental and Non-Parental Childcare and Children's Socio-emotional Development: A Decade in Review', *Journal of Marriage and the Family*, Vol. 52, 1990, pp.885-903.

3   Vaughn, B., Gove, F.L. and Egeland, B., 'The Relationship between Out-of-Home-care and the Quality of Infant-Mother Attachment in an Economically Disadvantaged Population', *Child Development*, Vol. 51, 1980, pp.1203-14.

4   Farber, E. and Egeland, B., 'Developmental Consequences of Out-of-Home-care for Infants in a Low-income Population' in Zigler, E.F. and Gordon, E.W. (eds.), *Daycare: Scientific and Social Policy Issues*, Boston: Auburn House, 1982.

5   Egeland, B. and Hiester, M., 'The Long-Term Consequences of Infant Daycare and Mother/Infant Attachments', *Child Development*, Vol. 66, 1995, pp. 474-85.

6   *Ibid.*, p. 481.

7   Schwartz, P., 'Length of Daycare Attendance and Attachment Behaviour in Eighteen-Month-Old Infants', *Child Development*, Vol. 54, 1983, pp. 1073-78.

8   Jacobson, J. and Wille, D.E., 'Attachment and Separation Experience on Separation Distress at 18 months', *Developmental Psychology*, Vol. 20, No. 3,1984, pp. 477-84.

9   Phillips, D.A., McCartney, K., Scarr, S. and Howes, C., 'Selective Review of Infant Daycare Research: A Cause for Concern', *Zero to Three*, February 1987, p. 18.

10 Howes, C. *et al.*, 'Attachment and Childcare: Relationships with Mother and Caregiver', *Early Childhood Research Quarterly*, Vol. 3, 1988, pp. 403-16.

11 See Belsky, J., 'The "Effects" of Infant Daycare Reconsidered', *Early Childhood Research Quarterly*, Vol. 3, 1988, pp. 235-72.

12 These include:
    a) Barglow, P., Vaughan, B. and Molitor, N., 1987 'Effects of Maternal Absence due to Employment on the Quality of Infant-Mother Attachment in a Low-risk Sample', *Child Development*,

152   WHO NEEDS PARENTS?
Vol. 58, pp. 945-54.

This contrasted middle- and upper middle-class families that used in-home help, nannies, *au pairs* etc., for more than 20 hours per week with those which relied exclusively on maternal care. Infants who had been in alternative care for at least four months at a 12 month assessment were significantly more likely to be anxious/avoidant in their attachment, as well as generally showing insecure patterns.

b) Owen, M.T. and Cox, M.J., 'The Transition to Parenthood' in Gottfried, A.E., Gottfried, A.W. and Bathurst, K., *Maternal Employment, Family Environment and Children's Development: Infancy Through the School Years*, Plenum Press, 1988.

These results from a longitudinal study of young families showed that twice as many infants were securely attached (67 per cent) as insecurely attached when their mothers were not employed, while twice as many infants were insecurely attached as securely attached (33 per cent) when their mothers were employed full-time. Here it was resistant behaviours like temper tantrums, refusing comfort and contact and throwing objects that were significantly associated with maternal employment at any time in the first year of life and grew with the number of hours the mother worked.

c) Weinraub, M. and Jaeger E, 'Timing the Return to the Workplace: Effects on the Mother/Infant Relationship' in Hyde J.S. and Essex, M. (eds.), *Parental Leave and Childcare,* Philadelphia: Temple University Press, 1991.

In this report on 65 middle-class mother/infant pairs the employed mothers worked for at least 25 hours a week. When mothers returned to work before their babies were eight months of age, 45 per cent of the children were classified as insecure/avoidant; 49 per cent as securely attached and seven per cent as insecure/resistant. This compares with 81 per cent securely attached in the non-employed group, with similar higher security levels for mothers employed at later stages of their children's development. The more favourable results for the non- and late-employed groups are despite the fact that the employed had more years of education, and early employed mothers had bigger family incomes.

13 Belsky, J. and Rovine, M.J., 'Non-maternal Care in the First Year of Life and the Security of Infant/Parent Attachment', *Child Development*, Vol. 59, 1988, pp. 157-67.

14 Chase Lansdale, P.L. and Owen, M.T., 'Maternal Employment in a Family Context: Effects on Infant/Mother and Infant/Father Attachments', *Child Development*, Vol. 58, 1987, pp. 1505-12. Initially there did not seem to be a significant relation specifically between infant/mother attachment and non-maternal care experience initiated in the first six months of life. It may have been because this study enrolled some families at a time when mothers had already returned to work and knew how their relationships were working out. The rate of insecure mother/infant relationships was much higher, or more

then treble, in the sub-sample of infants with extensive non-parental care whose families were recruited before birth.

15 Belsky, J., 'The "Effects" of Infant Daycare Reconsidered', *Early Childhood Research Quarterly*, Vol. 3, 1988, pp. 235-72.

16 Roggman, L.A., Langlois, J.H., Hubbs-Tait, L. and Rieser-Danner, L.A., 'Infant Daycare, Attachment, and the "File-Drawer" Problem', *Child Development*, Vol. 65, 1994, pp. 1429-43.

17 Clarke-Stewart, K.A., '"The 'Effects' of Infant Daycare Reconsidered" Reconsidered', *Early Childhood Research Quarterly*, Vol. 3, 1988, p. 293.

18 Lamb, M.E., Sternberg, K.J. and Prodromidis, M., 'Non-maternal Care and the Security of Infant-Mother Attachment: A Reanalysis of the Data', *Infant Behaviour and Development*, Vol. 15, 1992, pp. 71-83.

19 In this particular meta-analysis, insecure attachments were significantly more common among infants who entered care between seven and twelve months of age rather than before, particularly when this was centre-care. The rates of insecurity were not consistently highest for those in care for more than 20 hours per week, but as the sample size was so small for part-time care, the study was inconclusive on this point. *Ibid*.

20 Belsky, J., 'A Reassessment of Daycare' in Zigler, E.F. and Frank, M. (eds.), *Parental Leave Crisis*, New Haven and London: Yale University Press, 1988. p. 105.

21 Belsky, J., 'The "Effects" of Infant Daycare Reconsidered', *op. cit.*, p. 256.

22 Violata, C. and Russell, C., 'Effects of Non-maternal Care on Child Development: A Meta-analysis of Published Research', Paper presented at the 55th Annual Convention of the Canadian Psychological Association, Penticton, British Columbia, Canada, 1994.

23 Benn, R., 'Factors Promoting Secure Attachment Relationships Between Employed Mothers and their Sons', *Developmental Psychology*, Vol. 10, 1987, pp. 601-10; and Howes, C., Rodning, C., Galluzzo, D.C. and Myers, L., 'Attachment and Childcare; Relationships with Mother and Caregiver', *Early Childhood Research Quarterly*, Vol. 3, 1988, pp. 403-16.

24 Raikes H., 'Relationship Duration in Infant Care: Time with a High-Ability Teacher and Infant/Teacher Attachment', *Early Childhood Research Quarterly*, Vol. 8, 1993, pp. 309-25.

25 Everson, M.D., Sarnat, L. and Ambron, S.R., 'Daycare and Early Socialisation: The Role of Maternal Attitudes' in Ainslie, R.C. (ed.), *The Child and the Daycare Setting: Qualitative Variations and Development*, New York: Praeger, 1984.

26 Howes. C., Rodning, C., Galluzzo, D. and Myers, L., 'Attachment and Childcare: Relationships with Mother and Caregiver', *Early Childhood Research Quarterly*, Vol. 3, 1988.

27 Cochlan, M.M. and Gunnarson, L., 'A Follow-up Study of Group Daycare and Family-based Childrearing Patterns', *Journal of Marriage and the Family,* Vol. 47, 1985, pp. 297-309; and Melhuish, E.C. *et al.,* 'How Similar are Daycare Groups Before the Start of Daycare?', *Journal of Applied Developmental Psychology*, Vol. 12, 1991 pp. 331-45.

28 Volling, B. and Belsky, J., *Demographic, Maternal and Infant Factors Associated with Maternal Employment in the Infant's First Year of Life,* Unpublished, mentioned in Belsky, J., 'The "Effects" of Infant Daycare Reconsidered', *op. cit.;* and Burchinal, M.R., Landesman Ramey, S., Reid, M.K. and Jaccard, J., 'Early Childcare Experiences and their Association with Family and Child Characteristics during Middle Childhood', *Early Childhood Research Quarterly*, Vol. 10, 1995, pp. 33-61.

29 Sharp, D. *et al.,* 'The Impact of Postnatal Depression on Boys' Intellectual Development', *Journal of Child Psychology and Psychiatry,* Vol. 36, No. 8, pp. 1315-36.

30 Melhuish, E.C. *et al., op. cit.*

31 Mott, F.L., 'Developmental Effects of Infant Care: the Mediating Role of Gender and Health', *Journal of Social Issues*, Vol. 47, No. 2, 1991 pp. 139-58.

32 Belsky, J. and Rovine, M.J., *op. cit.*

33 Crockenberg, S., 'Infant Irritability, Mother Responsiveness, and Social Support Influences on the Security of Mother/Infant Attachment', *Child Development*, Vol. 52, 1981, pp. 857-65.

34 Vaughn, B., Gove, F.L. and Egeland, B., *op. cit.*

35 Burchinal, M.R., Bryant, D.M., Lee, M.W. and Ramey, C.T., 'Early Daycare, Infant/Mother Attachment, and Maternal Responsiveness in the Infant's First Year', *Early Childhood Research Quarterly*, Vol. 7, 1992, pp. 383-96.

36 Belsky, J. and Rovine, M.J., *op. cit.,* p. 165.

37 Egeland, Bryon and Hiester, *op. cit.*

38 Hoffman, L.W., 'Effects of Maternal Employment in the Two-Parent Family', *American Psychologist*, February 1989, p. 288.

39 Stewart, K.A.C., 'Infant Daycare: Maligned or Malignant?', *American Psychologist*, February 1989, pp. 266-73.

40 Clarke-Stewart, K.A., and Fein, G., 'Early Childhood Programs' in Maith, M.M. and Campos, J.J. (eds.), *Handbook of Child Psychology: Vol. 2, Infancy and Developmental Psychobiology*, New York: John Wiley & Sons, p. 949.

41 For example, the Q-Sort, which involves scoring 100 behaviour descriptions, for observations of children under naturalistic conditions. While this does not depend upon reactions to separations engineered in tests, it is hard to know what is random, and so it

carries the risk of reading meanings into chance findings and is best employed with other measures. See Belsky, J. and Rovine, M., 'Q-Sort Security and First Year Non-maternal Care' in McCartney, K., *Childcare and Maternal Employment· A Social Ecology Approach*, Jossey-Bass, 1990.

42 Belsky, J. and Braungart, J.M., 'Are Insecure-Avoidant Infants with Extensive Daycare Experience Less Stressed by and More Independent in the Strange Situation?', *Child Development*, Vol. 62, 1991, pp. 567-71.

43 Jacobson, J. and Wille, D.E., 'Attachment and Separation Experience on Separation Distress at 18 months', *Developmental Psychology*, Vol. 20, No. 3, 1984, pp. 477-84.

44 Martin, S., 'Is Daycare Good for Young Children?', *Nursery World*, 17 January 1991.

45 *Ibid.*, p. 268.

46 Howes. C., Rodning, C., Galluzzo, D. and Myers, L., 'Attachment and Childcare: Relationships with Mother and Caregiver', *Early Childhood Research Quarterly*, Vol. 3, 1988, pp. 403-16.

47 Egeland, B. and Hiester, M., *op. cit.*

48 Belsky, J., 'A Reassessment of Daycare' in Zigler, E.F. and Frank, M. (eds.), *op. cit.*, p. 106.

49 See Howes, C., 'Social Competency with Peers: Contributions from Childcare', *Early Childhood Research Quarterly*, Vol. 34, No. 2, 1987, pp. 155-67; and Rutter, M., 'Clinical Implications of Attachment Concepts: Retrospect and Prospect', *Journal of Child Psychology and Psychiatry*, 1995, pp. 549-68.

50 Cassidy, J. and Berlin, L.J., 'The Insecure/Ambivalent Pattern of Attachment: Theory and Research.' *Child Development,* Vol. 65, 1994, pp. 971-91.

51 See Lutkenhaus, P., Grossman, K.E. and Grossman, K., 'Infant/ Mother Attachment at Twelve Months and Style of Interaction with a Stranger at the age of Three Years', *Child Development,* Vol. 56, 1985, pp. 1538-42; Matas, L., Arend, R.A. and Sroufe, A., 'Continuity of Adaptation in the Second Year the Relationship between Quality of Attachment and Later Competence', *Child Development*, Vol. 49, 1978, pp. 547-56; and Stroupe, A.L., Fox, N.E. and Pancake, V.R., 'Attachment and Dependency in Developmental Perspective', *Child Development*, Vol. 54, 1983, pp. 1615-27.

52 Main, M. and Weston, D.R., 'The Quality of the Toddler's Relationship to Mother and to Father: Related to Conflict Behaviour and the Readiness to Establish New Relationships', *Child Development*, Vol. 52, 1981, pp. 932-40.

53 Belsky, J., *op. cit.*, 1990, pp. 890-91.

54 Erickson, M.F., Sroufe, A. and Egeland, B., 'The Relationship between Quality of Attachment and Behaviour Problems in Pre-school in a High-risk Sample' in Bretherton, I. and Waters, E. (eds.), *Growing Points of Attachment Theory and Research: Monographs of the Society for Research in Child Development*, Serial No. 209, 1985; and Lewis, M., Fiering, C., McGuffog, C. and Jaskir, J., 'Infant/Mother Attachment at Twelve Months and Style of Interaction at Twelve Months and Style of Interaction with a Stranger at the Age of Three Years', *Child Development*, Vol. 56, 1985, pp. 1538-42.

55 Pettit, G.S. and Bates, J.E., 'Family Interaction Patterns and Children's Behaviour Problems from Infancy to Four Years', *Developmental Psychology*, Vol. 23, 1989, pp. 413-20; and Bradley, R.H., Caldwell, B.M. and Rock, S.L., 'Home Environment and School Performance: A Ten-year Follow-up and Examination of Three Models of Environmental Action', *Child Development*, Vol. 59, 1988, pp. 852-67.

56 Estrada, P., Arsenio, W.F., Hess, R.D. and Holloway, S.D., 'Affective Quality of the Mother/Child Relationship: Longitudinal Consequences for Children's School relevant Cognitive Functioning', *Developmental Psychology*, Vol. 23, No. 2, 1987, pp. 210-15.

57 Gamble, T. and Zigler, E.F., 'Effects of Infant Daycare: Another Look at the Evidence', in Zigler, E.F. and Frank, M. (eds.), *Parental Leave Crisis*, New Haven and London: Yale University Press, 1988.

58 Werner, E. and Smith, R., *Vulnerable But Invincible*, New York: McGraw-Hill, 1982.

59 Lewis, M. *et al.*, 'Predicting Psychopathology in Six-year-olds from Early Social Relations', *Child Development*, Vol. 55, 1984, pp. 123-36.

Chapter 9: 'Stressed-out Parents'

1 Scarr, S. and Dunn, J., *Mother Care: Other Care*, Harmondsworth: Penguin Books, second edition, 1987, p. 20.

2 Fuchs, V.R., *Women's Quest for Equality*, Mass: Harvard University Press, 1988; and Mattox W.R., 'Running on Empty: America's Time-Starved Families with Children', Working Paper, No. 6, Council on Families in America, 1991.

3 Burns, S., *Time, Work and the Family*, Parents at Work, London, 1995.

4 Koester, L.S., 'Supporting Optimal Parenting Behaviours During Infancy' in Hyde and Essex, *op. cit.*

5 Bronfenbrenner, U., *The Ecology of Human Development*, Harvard University Press, 1979.

6 Mckee, V., 'High Flyers with Secret Families', *The Times*, 10 June 1991.

7   Brazelton, T.B., 'Issues for Working Parents' in Zigler, E.F. and
    Frank, M. (eds.), *Parental Leave Crisis*, New Haven and London: Yale
    University Press, 1988. p. 38.

8   Cox, M.J., Margand, N.A., Owen, M.T. and Henderson, V.K.,
    'Prediction of Infant/Father and Infant/Mother Attachment',
    Developmental Psychology, Vol. 28, No.3, 1992, pp. 474-83.

9   Belsky J., 'A Reassessment of Infant Daycare' in Zigler E.F. and
    Frank, M. (eds.), *The Parental Leave Crisis*, London: Yale University
    Press, 1988, pp. 100-19.

10 Leach, P., *Children First,* Harmondsworth: Penguin Books, 1994. p.
    79.

11 Belsky, J., 'Infant Daycare and Socio-emotional Development: The
    United States', *Journal of Child Psychology*, Vol. 29 1988, pp. 398-408.

12 Blum, M., *The Daycare Dilemma,* Lexington, Mass: Heath, 1983, p.
    28.

13 Clarke Stewart, A.K., 'Infant Daycare: Maligned or Malignant', *op.
    cit.,* p. 270.

14 Burns, S., *op. cit.*

15 Daniels, P. and Weingarten, K., *Sooner or Later*, W. Norton & Co.
    1982.

16 Lewis, S.N.C. and Cooper, C.L., 'Stress in Two-earner Couples and
    Stage in the Life Cycle', *Journal of Occupational Psychology*, Vol. 60,
    1987, pp. 289-303.

17 Vaughn, B., Gove, F.L. and Egeland, B., 'The Relationship between
    Out-of-Home-care and the Quality of Infant-Mother Attachment in an
    Economically Disadvantaged Population', *Child Development*, Vol. 51,
    1980, pp.1203-14; and Egeland, B. and Hiester, M., 'The Long-Term
    Consequences of Infant Daycare and Mother/Infant Attachments',
    Child Development, Vol. 66, 1995, pp. 474-85.

18 Lewis, S.N.C. and Cooper, C.L., *op. cit.*

19 Garner, L., 'The Price of Taking Home a Pay Packet' in *The Daily
    Telegraph*, 6 July 1988.

20 Hughes, D. and Galinsky, E., 'Balancing Work and Family Lives:
    Research and Corporate Applications' in Gottfried, A.E., Gottfried,
    A.W. and Bathurst, K. (eds.), *Maternal Employment, Family
    Environment and Children's Development: Infancy Through the School
    Years*, Plenum Press, 1988.

21 Owen, M.T. and Cox, M.J., 'The Transition to Parenthood', in
    Gottfried, A.E., Gottfried, A.W. and Bathurst, K. (eds.), *Maternal
    Employment, Family Environment and Children's Development:
    Infancy Through the School Years*, Plenum Press, 1988.

22 Owen M.T. and Cox, M.J., 'The Transition to Parenthood' in Gottfried,
    A.E., Gottfried, A.W. and Bathurst, K. (eds.), *op. cit.*

23 O'Neil, R. and Berger, E.G., 'Patterns of Commitment to Work and Parenting: Implications for Role Strain', *Journal of Marriage and the Family*, Vol. 56, February 1994, pp. 101-18.

24 Hoffman, L.W., 'Effects of Maternal Employment in the Two-Parent Family', *American Psychologist*, February 1989, p. 284.

25 Stith, S.M. and Davis, A.J., 'Employed Mothers and Family Daycare Substitute Caregivers: A Comparative Analysis of Infant Care', *Child Development*, Vol. 55, 1984, pp. 1340-48.

26 Zaslow, M.J., Pedersen, F.A., Suwalsky, J.T.D., Cain, R.L. and Fivel, M., 'The Early Resumption of Employment by Mothers: Implications for Parent-Infant Interaction', *Journal of Applied Developmental Psychology*, Vol. 6, 1985, pp. 1-16.

27 Everson, M.D., Sarnat, L. and Ambron, S.R., 'Daycare and Early Socialisation: The Role of Maternal Attitudes' in Ainslie, R.C. (ed.), *The Child and the Daycare Setting: Qualitative Variations and Development*, New York: Praeger, 1984.

Chapter 10: 'Mothers Go Mad'

1   Equal Opportunities Commission, *The Key to Real Choice; An action plan for childcare*, 1990.

2   Clouston, E., 'Housewives "endure slow torture"', *The Guardian*, 28 November 1994.

3   Kahn, H. and Cuthbertson, J., 'Mothers at Work and Mothers at Home', summary from Heriot Watt Business School, Edinburgh, forthcoming.

4   Pet, M.A., Vaughan-Cole, E. and Wampold, B.E., 'Maternal Employment and Perceived Stress: Their Impact on Children's Adjustment and Mother/Child Interaction in Young Divorced and Married Families', *Family Relations*, Vol. 43, 1994 pp. 151-58.

5   Prichard, C.W., 'Depression and Smoking in Pregnancy in Scotland', *Journal of Endocrinology and Community Health*, Vol. 48, 1994 pp. 377-82.

6   Murray, L., 'The Impact of Postnatal Depression on Infant Development', *Journal of Child Psychology and Psychiatry*, Vol. 33, 1992 pp. 543-61; Murray, L. *et al.*, 'Depressed mothers' speech to their infants and its relation to infant gender and cognitive development', *Journal of Child Psychology and Psychiatry*, Vol. 34, 1993 pp.1083-101.

7   Hay, D.F and Kumar, R., 'Interpreting the Effects of Mother's Postnatal Depression on Intelligence: A Critique and Reanalysis', *Child Psychiatry and Human Development*, Vol. 25, Part 3, 1995, pp. 165-81.

8   Sharp, D. *et al.*, 'The Impact of Postnatal depression on Boys Intellectual Development', *Journal of Child Psychology and Psychiatry*, Vol. 36, No. 8, pp. 1315-36.

9 Osborn, A.F., Butler, N.R. and Morris, A.C., *The Social Life of Britain's Five-Year-Olds*, London: Routledge and Kegan Paul, 1984.

10 Drago Piechowski, L., 'Mental Health and Women's Multiple Roles in Families in Society', *The Journal of Contemporary Human Sciences*, March 1992, Family Service America, pp. 131-38.

11 Owen, M.T. and Cox, M.J., 'The Transition to Parenthood', in Gottfried, A.E., Gottfried, A.W. and Bathurst, K. (eds.), *Maternal Employment, Family Environment and Children's Development: Infancy Through the School Years*, Plenum Press, 1988.

12 *Ibid.*, p. 112.

13 Bonnar, D., 'The Place of Caregiving Work in Contemporary Societies', in Hyde, J.S. and Essex, M.J. (eds.), *Parental Leave and Childcare*, Philadelphia: Temple University Press, 1991, p. 203.

14 Ross, C.E. and Huber, J., 'Hardship and Depression', *Journal of Health and Social Behaviour*, Vol. 26, 1985, pp. 312-27.

15 See Morgan, P., *Farewell to the Family?*, London: IEA Health and Welfare Unit, 1995, Chapter 3: 'Money and Marriage'.

16 McLanahan, S. and Adams, J., 'Parenthood and Psychological Well-Being', *Annual Review of Sociology*, Vol. 5, 1987, pp. 243-54.

Chapter 11: 'What Use Is A Father?'

1 'Dad's Still a Dud About the House', *The Daily Telegraph*, 21 March 1992.

2 McLanahan, S. and Adams, J., 'Parenthood and Psychological Well-Being', *Annual Review of Sociology*, Vol. 5, 1987, p. 254.

3 Goldberg, W.A. and Easterbrooks, M.A., 'Maternal Employment when Children are Toddlers and Kindergartners' in Gottfried, A.E., Gottfried, A.W. and Bathurst, K. (eds.), *Maternal Employment, Family Environment and Children's Development: Infancy Through the School Years*, Plenum Press, 1988; Goldberg, W.A. and Easterbrooks, M.A., 'Toddler Development in the Family: Impact of Father Involvement and Parenting Characteristics', *Child Development*, Vol. 55, 1984, pp. 740-52.

4 Chase-Lansdale, P.L., 'Maternal Employment in a Family Context: Effects on Infant-Mother and Infant-Father Attachments', *Child Development*, Vol. 58, 1987, pp. 1505-12.

5 Werner, E. and Smith, R., *Vulnerable but Invincible*, New York: McGraw-Hill, 1982.

6 Anderson, C.P., *Father: The Figure and the Force*, New York: Warner, 1983.

7 Coote A., Harman. H. and Hewitt. P., *The Family Way*, London: Institute for Public Policy Research, 1990, p. 36.

8   Brannen, J. and Moss, P., *Managing Mothers: Dual Earner House-holds After Maternity Leave,* London: Macmillan, 1991, p. 168.

9   Blankenhorn, D., *Fatherless America: Confronting Our Most Urgent Social Problem,* New York: Basic Books, 1995, p. 112.

10 Bronstein, P., 'Differences in Mothers' and Fathers' Behaviour Towards Children: A Cross-cultural Comparison', *Developmental Psychology,* Vol. 20, No. 6, 1984, pp. 995-1003.

11 Goldberg, W.A. and Easterbrooks, M.A., *op. cit.,* p. 750.

12 Crouter, A.C., Perry-Jenkins, M., Huston, T.L. and McHale, S.M., 'Processes Underlying Father Involvement in Dual-earner and Single-earner Families', *Developmental Psychology,* Vol. 23, pp. 431-40; also Peterson, R.R. and Gerson, K., 'Determinants of Responsibility for Childcare Arrangements among Dual-Earner Couples', *Journal of Marriage and the Family,* Vol. 54, 1992, pp. 527-36.

13 Bayler, N. and Brooks-Gunn, J., 'Effects of Maternal Employment and Child-Care Arrangements on Preschoolers' Cognitive and Behavioural Outcomes: Evidence From the Children of the National Longitudinal Survey of Youth', *Developmental Psychology,* Vol. 27, No. 6, 1991, pp. 932-45.

14 Ferri, E. and Smith, K., *Parenting in the 1990s,* in press, Family Policy Studies Centre.

15 Crouter, A.C., Perry-Jenkins, M., Huston, T.L. and McHale, S.M. 'Processes Underlying Father Involvement in Dual-earner and Single-earner Families', *op. cit.,* p. 439.

16 *Ibid.*

17 Jump, T.L. and Haas, L. in Kimmel, M.S. (ed.), *Changing Men: New Directions in Research on Men and Masculinity,* London: Sage, 1987.

Chapter 12: 'Working Mothers and Their Children'

1   Eberstadt, M., 'Putting Children Last', *The Wall Street Journal,* 2 May 1995.

2   *The Key to Real Choice: An Action Plan for Childcare,* Equal Opportunities Commission, 1990.

3   Gold, D. and Andres, D., 'Relations Between Maternal Employment and the Development of Nursery School Children', *Canadian Journal of Behavioural Science,* Vol. 10, No. 2, 1978; Gold, D. and Andres, D., 'Developmental Comparisons Between 10-year-old Children with Employed and Non-employed Mothers', *Child Development,* Vol. 49, 1978, pp. 75-84; and Hoffman, L.W., 'Maternal Employment', *American Psychologist,* Vol. 34, 1979, pp. 859-65.

4   Desai, S., Chase-Lonsdale, P.L. and Micheal, R.T., 'Mother or Market? Effects of Maternal Employment on the Intellectual Ability of Four-year-old Children', *Demography,* Vol. 24, 1989, pp. 545-61.

5   Scarr, S. and Dunn, J., *Mother Care: Other Care,* Harmondsworth: Penguin Books, second edition, 1987, p. 27.

6   Milne, A.M., Myers, D.E., Rosenthal, A.S. and Ginsburg, A., 'Single Parents, Working Mothers and the Educational Achievement of School Children', *Sociology of Education,* Vol. 59, 1986, pp. 125-39.

7   Bayler, N. and Brooks-Gunn, J., 'Effects of Maternal Employment and Childcare Arrangements on Preschoolers' Cognitive and Behavioural Outcomes: Evidence from the Children of the National Longitudinal Survey of Youth', *Developmental Psychology,* Vol. 27, No. 6, 1991, pp. 932-45.

8   Belsky, J. and Eggebeen, D., 'Early and Extensive Maternal Employment and Young Children's Socio-emotional Development: Children of the National Longitudinal Survey of Youth', *Journal of Marriage and the Family,* Vol. 53, 1991, pp. 1083-110.

9   Osborn, A.F., Butler, N.R. and Morris, A.C., *The Social Life of Britain's Five-Year-Olds,* London: Routledge and Kegan Paul, 1984.

10 Gottfried, A.E., Gottfried, A.W and Bathurst, K. (eds.), *Maternal Employment, Family Environment and Children's Development: Infancy Through the School Years,* Plenum Press, 1988.

Chapter 13: 'Chasing a Chimaera'

1   Sroufe, L.A., 'A Developmental Perspective on Daycare', *Early Childhood Research Quarterly,* Vol. 3, 1988, pp. 283-91.

2   Gamble, T. and Zigler, E.F., 'Effects of Infant Daycare: Another Look at the Evidence' in Zigler, E.F. and Frank, M. (eds.), *The Parental Leave Crisis,* New Haven and London: Yale University Press, 1988, p. 94.

3   Maynard, F., *The Childcare Crisis,* Penguin Books, Canada, 1985, p. xvi.

4   Rutter, M., 'Social-Emotional Consequences of Daycare for Pre-school Children' in Zigler, E.F. and Gordon, E.W., *Daycare: Scientific and Social Policy Issues,* Boston: Auburn House Publishing Company, 1982; see also Zigler, E.F., Frank, M. and Emmel B., Introduction, *ibid.*

5   'Joshi, H. and Davies, H., 'Mothers' Human Capital and Childcare in Britain', *National Institute Economic Review,* November 1993, pp. 50-63.

6   Cohen, B. and Fraser, N., *Childcare in a Modern Welfare System,* London: Institute for Public Policy Research, 1991, p. 81.

7   Holtermann, S., *Investing in Young Children: Costing an Education and Daycare Service,* London: National Children's Bureau, 1992.

8   Holtermann, S. and Clarke, K., *Parents' Employment Rights and Childcare,* Manchester: Equal Opportunities Commission, 1992, p. 54.

9   *Ibid.,* p. 66.

10 The Equal Opportunities Commission to the Employment Committee, *Mothers in Employment*, Minutes of Evidence, House of Commons Session 1994-5, 15 February 1994, p. 64.

11 Bradshaw, J. and Millar, J., *Lone Parents in the UK*, London: HMSO, 1991.

12 Employment Committee, *Mothers in Employment*, First Report, Vol. 3, Appendices to the Minutes of Evidence House of Commons, London: HMSO, 15 February 1995 p. 399; see also Memo from University of Manchester, *ibid.*

13 See Morgan, P., *Families in Dreamland*, London: Social Affairs Unit, 1992.

14 Duncan, A., Giles, C. and Webb, S., *The Impact of Subsidising Childcare*, Research Discussion Series No. 13, Manchester: Equal Opportunities Commission, 1995.

15 *Ibid.*, p. 38.

16 Leach, P., *Children First*, Harmondsworth: Penguin Books, 1994, p. 69.

17 Firestone, S., *The Dialectic of Sex*, London: The Women's Press, 1979, p. 194, first published, New York: William Morrow, 1970.

18 Dench, G., *The Frog, the Prince and the Problem of Men*, London: Neanderthal Books, 1994, revised as *Transforming Men.*, Transaction Publications, 1996, p. 200.

19 Memo from the Daycare Trust Employment Committee, *Mothers in Employment*, Vol. 3, Appendices to the Minutes of Evidence, p. 574.

20 See Elkind, D., *The Hurried Child*, Addison-Wesley, 1982; also Blum, M., *op. cit.*

21 Blankenhorn, D., *Fatherless America*, New York: Basic Books, 1995, p. 115.

Chapter 14: 'What Parents Really Want'

1 Gyngell, K., 'To Work or Not To?', Letter, *The Evening Standard*, 17 January 1992.

2 Oppenheim Mason, K. and Kuhlthau, K., 'Determinants of Childcare Ideals among Mothers of Preschool-Aged Children', *Journal of Marriage and the Family*, Vol. 51, August 1989, pp. 593-603.

3 White, L.J., Leibowitz, A. and Witsberger, C., 'What Parents Pay For: Childcare Characteristics, Quality, and Costs', *Journal of Social Issues*, Vol. 47, No. 2, 1991, pp. 33-48.

4 Ashford, S., 'Family Matters' in Jowell, R. *et al.*, (eds.), *British Social Attitudes*, Gower, 1988; also *Social Focus on Women*, Central Statistical Office, HMSO, 1995; see also Scott, J., Braun, M. and Alwin, D., 'The Family Way' in Jowell, R. *et al.*, (eds.), *International Social Attitudes: the 10th BSA Report*, SCPR, Dartmouth Publishing, 1993.

5   *Social Focus on Women,* Central Statistical Office, London: HMSO, 1995.

6   'Parents, Employment Rights and Childcare', *News Release,* Equal Opportunities Commission, 3 December 1992.

7   *The Farley Report,* Farley Health Products Ltd., Nottingham, 1991.

8   Also for Canada, see, *The State of the Family in Canada,* Angus Reid Group, 1994.

9   Porokhnuik, E.V. and Shepeleva, M.S., 'Combining Work and Household Duties', and Kuleshava, I.M. and Mamontava, T.I., 'Part-time Employment of Women', both in Warshofsky, L.G. (ed.), *Women, Work and Family in the Soviet Union,* New York: 1982.

10 Vedel-Petersen, J., 'Children in Denmark: Daycare Issues', *Child Welfare,* Vol. LXVII, No. 2, March-April 1989.

11 Moss, P., *Childcare and Equality of Opportunity: Consolidated Report to the European Commission,* 1988, p. 26.

12 Bonnar, D., 'The Place of Caregiving Work in Contemporary Societies', in Hyde, J.S. and Essex, M.J., (eds.), *Parental Leave and Childcare,* Philadelphia: Temple University Press, 1991, p. 200.

13 Klein, U., 'Returning to Work: A Challenge for Women', *World of Work,* International Labour Office, No. 12, May/June 1995.

14 Benenson, H., 'Women's Occupational and Family Achievement in the US Class System: A Critique of the Dual-career Family Analysis', *British Journal of Sociology,* Vol. 35, No. 1, pp. 19-36.

15 Thomas, M., ex-deputy editor of *Marie Claire* quoted in Cantecuzino, M., 'When Motherhood is the Best Career', *The Independent,* 13 January 1991.

16 Lewis, H., *Sweden's Right to be Human,* Allison and Busby Ltd, 1982; and see Morgan P., *Families in Dreamland,* Research Report, No. 15, London: Social Affairs Unit, 1992.

17 Quoted in Leach, P., *Children First,* Harmondsworth: Penguin Books, 1994, p.72.

18 Hoem, J.M., 'Social Policy and Recent Fertility Change in Sweden', *Population and Development Review,* December 1990.

19 Kamerman, S.B., 'Childcare Policies and Programs: An International Overview', *Journal of Social Issues,* Vol. 47, No. 2, 1991, p. 193.

20 McKay, S., 'Diversity of Family Policy and Childcare Arrangements', Report of a conference held at Gozdd Martuljek, Slovenia in May 1995, *Changing Britain,* Economic and Social Research Council, October 1995.

Chapter 15: 'Putting A Price on Love'

1   Scarr, S. and Dunn, J., *Mother Care: Other Care,* Harmondsworth: Penguin Books, 1987 p. 31.

2   Carlson, A.C., 'The Family and the Welfare State', *The St. Croix Review*, Vol. XXVIII, No. 4, 1995, pp. 21-30.

3   *Ibid.,* Carlson, A.C., referring to Francis Fox Piven and Carole Pateman.

4   Fitch, A., reported by Jardine, C. in 'If It's All Right For Mother and Father ...', *The Daily Telegraph*, 5 July 1995.

5   Bonnar, D., 'The Place of Caregiving Work in Contemporary Societies', in Hyde, J.S. and Essex, M.J., (eds.), *Parental Leave and Childcare*, Philadelphia: Temple University Press, 1991; and Bourke, J., *Working-class Cultures in Britain 1890-1960: Gender, Class and Ethnicity*, London: Routledge, 1994.

6   Todd, E., *The Causes of Progress*, Oxford: Blackwell, 1987.

7   O'Neill, J., *The Missing Child in Liberal Theory*, Toronto University Press, 1994, pp. 69-70.

8   Carlson, A.C., 'The Family and the Welfare State', *The St. Croix Review*, Vol. XXVIII, No. 4, pp. 30-31; also, Carlson, A.C., *From Cottage to Work Station*, San Francisco: Ignatius Press, 1993.

9   Morgan, P., *Are Families Affordable? Tax, Benefits and the Family*, London: Centre for Policy Studies, 1996.

10 McLanahan, S. and Adams, J., 'Parenthood and Psychological Well-being', *Annual Review of Sociology*, Vol. 5, 1987, pp. 243-54.

11 For a detailed account of this process see Morgan, P., *Farewell to the Family*, London: IEA Health and Welfare Unit, 1995.

Conclusion: 'The Daycare Juggernaut'

1   Blum, M., *The Daycare Dilemma*, Lexington, Mass: Heath, 1983.

2   Hodge, M., letter to *The Times,* 30 April 1996.

3   Report by Dobson, R., 'Our Gulag', *Independent on Sunday*, 9 June 1996.

4   Cohen, B., 'Caring for Children: Services and Policies for Childcare and Equal Opportunities in the UK', Report for the European Commission's Childcare Network, Commission of the European Communities, 1988, p. 138.

5   Bush, J., 'The Child is the Father of the Man', *The Times*, 24 December 1993.

6   Christensen, B., *Utopia Against the Family*, San Francisco: Ignatius Press, 1990.

7   Skinner, B.F., *Walden Two*, (1948), reprint, New York: Macmillan, 1976, pp. 132-34, quoted in Christensen, B.J., *Utopia Against the Family* , San Francisco: Ignatius Press, 1990, p. 8.

8 Glass, B.L. and Stolee, M.K., 'Family Law in Soviet Russia 1917-
   1945', *Journal of Marriage and the Family*, Vol. 49, 1987, pp. 893-901.

Appendix: 'Working Through Parents'

1 Trickett, P.K., Apfel, N.H., Rosenbaum, L.K. and Zigler, E.F., 'A Five
   Year Follow Up of Participants in the Yale Child Welfare Research
   Program' in Zigler, E.F. and Gordon, E.W., (eds.), *Daycare: Scientific
   and Social Policy Issues*, Boston: Auburn House Publishing Co., 1982.

2 Reynolds, A.J., 'One Year of Pre-school Intervention or Two: Does it
   Matter?', *Early Childhood Research Quarterly*, Vol. 10, 1994, pp. 1-31.

3 Campbell, F.A. and Ramey, C.T., 'Effects of Early Intervention on
   Intellectual and Academic Achievement: A Follow-up Study of
   Children from Low-Income Families', *Child Development*, Vol. 65, pp.
   684-98.

4 Bynner, J. and Steedman, J., *Difficulties with Basic Skills*, London:
   The Basic Skills Agency, 1995.